Water

Drawing on some recent developments in the blue humanities, this book addresses water as a material, political and cultural phenomenon across a variety of spatial and temporal contexts.

Moving beyond the somewhat hackneyed concepts of fluidity and flows, this volume gathers critical perspectives that balance between the scientific, the social, the (bio-)political and the cultural. The contributors to this book draw on a wide and rapidly growing body of scholarship that includes (but is not limited to) maritime, climate change and Anthropocene studies as well as the 'blue humanities.' Three major, broadly conceived currents of thought run through these essays: the protean relationalities that water enables; appropriations of water in modernist logics of regulation and management; and the problematic figurations of water in scientific, philosophical, cultural, political and legal discourses. Thematically, the chapters address a wide range of phenomena, events and concepts, including Mediterranean migrant deaths, water as a medium of not-only-human intimacy and queer potentiality, swimming pools, the 2000 Cochabamba water war, the legacy of Grotius's legal philosophy, imperialist and capitalist notions of property and ownership, notions of purity and contamination, hydroelectricity's impact on the perception of time, the inadequacy of disciplinary knowledge and pedagogy, and 'maternal' figurations of water in some contemporary feminist theorizations.

This book will be of interest to scholars working at the intersection of, broadly conceived, cultural and water studies. It can also be used as a coursebook for teachers offering courses on the politics and aesthetics of water. It was originally published as a special issue of *Angelaki*.

Ewa Macura-Nnamdi is Assistant Professor at the Institute of Literary Studies, University of Silesia, Poland. Her main research interests revolve around the aesthetics and politics of two issues: refugeehood (and migration more generally) and environmental degradation in the Global South. She examines both phenomena across a cultural archive encompassing literature, film and philosophy. She is currently working on a book titled *Law, Refugees and the Sea: Interim Lives* (under contract with Routledge) and leading a research grant project titled 'Weathers of the Future: Climate Change and Displacement'.

Tomasz Sikora teaches literature, culture and theory at UKEN University, Krakow, Poland. His varied research interests include queer theory, literature and cultural studies, gothic and grotesque, biopolitics, environmental humanities and more. He has published two books: *Virtually Wild: Wilderness, Technology and the Ecology of Mediation* (2003) and *Bodies Out of Rule: Transversal Readings in Canadian Literature and Film* (2014). He is one of the founders and editors of *InterAlia: A Journal of Queer Studies* (interalia.queerstudies.pl).

Angelaki: New Work in the Theoretical Humanities

Series Editors:
Charlie Blake, *University of Brighton, UK*
Pelagia Goulimari, *University of Oxford, UK*
Salah el Moncef, *University of Nantes, France*
Gerard Greenway (Managing Editor), *Oxford, UK*

New Work in the Theoretical Humanities is associated with *Angelaki: Journal of the Theoretical Humanities*, a leading international interdisciplinary journal that has done much to consolidate the field of research designated by its subtitle and which has been at the forefront of publication for three decades. This book series publishes generous edited collections across the humanities as informed by European philosophy and literary and cultural theory. It has a strong interest in aesthetics and art theory and also features work in those areas of the social sciences, such as social theory and political theory, that are informed by *Angelaki's* core disciplinary concentration. This broad latitude is disciplined by a strong sense of identity and the series editors' long experience of research and teaching in the humanities. The *Angelaki* journal is well known for its exceptionally substantial special issues. **New Work in the Theoretical Humanities** publishes vanguard collections on current developments in the energetic and increasingly international field of the theoretical humanities as well as volumes on major living thinkers and writers and those of the recent past. Volumes in this series are conceived as broad but integrated treatments of their themes, with the intention of producing contributions to the literature of lasting value.

Ontogenesis Beyond Complexity
Edited by Cary Wolfe and Adam Nocek

Sloterdijk's Anthropotechnics
Edited by Patrick Roney and Andrea Rossi

The Pulse of Sense
Encounters with Jean-Luc Nancy
Edited by Marie Chabbert and Nikolaas Deketelaere

After Life
Recent Philosophy and Death
Edited by Rona Cohen and Ruth Ronen

After Modernism
Women, Gender, Race
Edited by Pelagia Goulimari

Philosophy with Clarice Lispector
Edited by Fernanda Negrete

Water
Crises, Critiques, Imaginaries
Edited by Ewa Macura-Nnamdi and Tomasz Sikora

For more information about this series, please visit:
www.routledge.com/New-Work-in-the-Theoretical-Humanities/book-series/ANG

Water

Crises, Critiques, Imaginaries

Edited by
Ewa Macura-Nnamdi and Tomasz Sikora

LONDON AND NEW YORK

First published 2025
by Routledge
4 Park Square, Milton Park, Abingdon, Oxon OX14 4RN

and by Routledge
605 Third Avenue, New York, NY 10158

Routledge is an imprint of the Taylor & Francis Group, an informa business

Foreword, Introduction, Chapters 1–3, 5–8 and 10 © 2025 Taylor & Francis.
Chapter 4 © 2023 Mikki Stelder. Originally published as Open Access.
Chapter 9 © 2023 Eszter Timár. Originally published as Open Access.

With the exception of Chapters 4 and 9, no part of this book may be reprinted or reproduced or utilised in any form or by any electronic, mechanical, or other means, now known or hereafter invented, including photocopying and recording, or in any information storage or retrieval system, without permission in writing from the publishers. For details on the rights for Chapters 4 and 9, please see the chapters' Open Access footnotes.

Trademark notice: Product or corporate names may be trademarks or registered trademarks, and are used only for identification and explanation without intent to infringe.

British Library Cataloguing in Publication Data
A catalogue record for this book is available from the British Library

ISBN13: 978-1-032-72966-4 (hbk)
ISBN13: 978-1-032-72967-1 (pbk)
ISBN13: 978-1-003-42326-3 (ebk)

DOI: 10.4324/9781003423263

Typeset in Minion Pro
by Newgen Publishing UK

Publisher's Note
The publisher accepts responsibility for any inconsistencies that may have arisen during the conversion of this book from journal articles to book chapters, namely the inclusion of journal terminology.

Disclaimer
Every effort has been made to contact copyright holders for their permission to reprint material in this book. The publishers would be grateful to hear from any copyright holder who is not here acknowledged and will undertake to rectify any errors or omissions in future editions of this book.

Contents

	Citation Information	vii
	Notes on Contributors	ix
	Foreword *Ewa Macura-Nnamdi and Tomasz Sikora*	xii
	Introduction: Water *Ewa Macura-Nnamdi and Tomasz Sikora*	1
1	Hydropower: Residual Dwelling between Life and Nonlife *Edwige Tamalet Talbayev*	7
2	Intercorporeity of Animated Water: Contesting Anthropocentric Settler Sovereignty *Joseph Pugliese*	20
3	Just Keep Swimming? Queer Pooling and Hydropoetics *Jeremy Chow and Maite Urcaregui*	34
4	A Sinking Empire *Mikki Stelder*	51
5	Social Property in The Cochabamba Water War, Bolivia 2000 *Massimiliano Tomba*	71
6	A Timeful Theory of Knowledge: Thunderstorms, Dams, and the Disclosure of Planetary History *Kieran M. Murphy*	85
7	Learning Waters *Gil Anidjar*	97
8	Figurations of Water: On Pathogens, Purity, and Contamination *Agnieszka Pantuchowicz*	109

CONTENTS

9 *Mère Métaphore*: The Maternal Materiality of Water in Astrida Neimanis's *Bodies of Water*   126
Eszter Timár

10 The Other Water   137
Andreas Philippopoulos-Mihalopoulos

Index   142

Citation Information

The following chapters in this book were originally published in *Angelaki*, Volume 28, issue 1 (2023). When citing this material, please use the original page numbering for each article, as follows:

Foreword

Foreword
Ewa Macura-Nnamdi and Tomasz Sikora
Angelaki, Volume 28, issue 1 (2023), pp. 1–2

Introduction

Water
Ewa Macura-Nnamdi and Tomasz Sikora
Angelaki, Volume 28, issue 1 (2023), pp. 3–8

Chapter 1

Hydropower: residual dwelling between life and nonlife
Edwige Tamalet Talbayev
Angelaki, Volume 28, issue 1 (2023), pp. 9–21

Chapter 2

Intercorporeity of Animated Water: contesting anthropocentric settler sovereignty
Joseph Pugliese
Angelaki, Volume 28, issue 1 (2023), pp. 22–35

Chapter 3

Just Keep Swimming? queer pooling and hydropoetics
Jeremy Chow and Maite Urcaregui
Angelaki, Volume 28, issue 1 (2023), pp. 36–52

Chapter 4

A Sinking Empire
Mikki Stelder
Angelaki, Volume 28, issue 1 (2023), pp. 53–72

viii CITATION INFORMATION

Chapter 5

Social Property in The Cochabamba Water War, Bolivia 2000
Massimiliano Tomba
Angelaki, Volume 28, issue 1 (2023), pp. 73–86

Chapter 6

A Timeful Theory of Knowledge: thunderstorms, dams, and the disclosure of planetary history
Kieran M. Murphy
Angelaki, Volume 28, issue 1 (2023), pp. 87–98

Chapter 7

Learning Waters
Gil Anidjar
Angelaki, Volume 28, issue 1 (2023), pp. 99–110

Chapter 8

Figurations of Water: on pathogens, purity, and contamination
Agnieszka Pantuchowicz
Angelaki, Volume 28, issue 1 (2023), pp. 111–127

Chapter 9

Mère Métaphore: *the maternal materiality of water in astrida neimanis's bodies of water*
Eszter Timár
Angelaki, Volume 28, issue 1 (2023), pp. 128–138

Chapter 10

The Other Water
Andreas Philippopoulos-Mihalopoulos
Angelaki, Volume 28, issue 1 (2023), pp. 139–143

For any permission-related enquiries please visit:
www.tandfonline.com/page/help/permissions

Notes on Contributors

Gil Anidjar teaches in the Department of Religion and the Department of Middle Eastern, South Asian, and African Studies at Columbia University, New York, United States. He has been learning for some time about Jews and Arabs, political theology, race and religion, Semites, blood and Christianity, survival, and more recently about destruction. His most recent book is *On the Sovereignty of Mothers: The Political as Maternal* (2024).

Jeremy Chow is an assistant professor of English at Bucknell University, Lewisburg, United States, which occupies the unceded homelands of the Susquehannock peoples. Chow is the author of *The Queerness of Water: Troubled Ecologies in the Eighteenth Century* (2023) as well as the editor of three essay collections: *Eighteenth-Century Environmental Humanities* (2023), *Unsettling Sexuality: Queer Horizons in the Eighteenth Century* (2025) with Shelby Johnson, and *The Edinburgh Companion to Queer Reading* (2025) with Declan Kavanagh.

Ewa Macura-Nnamdi is Assistant Professor at the Institute of Literary Studies, University of Silesia, Poland. Her main research interests revolve around the aesthetics and politics of two issues: refugeehood (and migration more generally) and environmental degradation in the Global South. She examines both phenomena across a cultural archive encompassing literature, film and philosophy. She is currently working on a book titled *Law, Refugees and the Sea: Interim Lives* (under contract with Routledge) and leading a research grant project titled 'Weathers of the Future: Climate Change and Displacement'.

Kieran M. Murphy is Associate Professor of French and Humanities at the University of Colorado, Boulder, United States. His work explores the intersections of culture, science and technology through various angles that include transatlantic studies, continental philosophy and the history of knowledge. He recently published *Electromagnetism and the Metonymic Imagination* in the AnthropoScene book series.

Agnieszka Pantuchowicz, Ph.D., is Associate Professor at the SWPS University in Warsaw, Poland, where she teaches translation and literary studies. Her research interests are translation theory and cultural studies, comparative literature and feminist criticism. She has published numerous articles and edited volumes on literary criticism, theoretical aspects of translation as well as on cultural and ideological dimensions of translation in the Polish context.

Andreas Philippopoulos-Mihalopoulos is an academic, artist and fiction author. His practice includes legal theory, performance, ecological pedagogy, lawscaping, performance lecture, video art, spatial justice, moving-poems, critical autopoiesis, online performance, radical ontologies, installation art, picpoetry, performance machines, fiction writing, sculpture, wavewriting, political geography, clay-making, gender and queer studies, painting, continental philosophy, posthumanism and anthropocenes. He is Professor of Law & Theory at the University of Westminster, London, United Kingdom, and Director of The Westminster Law & Theory Lab. His academic books include the monographs *Absent Environments* (2007), *Niklas Luhmann: Law, Justice, Society* (2009) and *Spatial Justice: Body Lawscape Atmosphere* (2014). His fiction *The Book of Water* is published in Greek and English. His work has been presented at Palais de Tokyo, the 58th Venice Art Biennale 2019, the 16th Venice Architecture Biennale 2016, the Tate Modern, Inhotim Instituto de Arte Contemporânea Brazil, Arebyte Gallery, The Onassis Cultural Centre Athens, Ca' Pisani Venice, Danielle Arnaud Gallery, etc.

Joseph Pugliese is Professor of Cultural Studies, Macquarie University, Sydney, Australia. Selected publications include *Biometrics: Bodies, Technologies, Biopolitics* (Routledge, 2010) and *State Violence and the Execution of Law: Biopolitical Caesurae of Torture, Black Sites, Drones* (Routledge, 2013). With Suvendrini Perera and a team of international collaborators, he established Deathscapes: Mapping Race and Violence in Settler States (www.deathscapes.org/). With Suvendrini Perera, he is co-editor of *Mapping Deathscapes: Digital Geographies of Racial and Border Violence* (Routledge, 2022). His monograph, *Biopolitics of the More-Than-Human: Forensic Ecologies of Violence* (2020), was awarded the 2022 Transdisciplinary Humanities Book Award, presented by the Institute for Humanities Research at Arizona State University, Arizona. His latest monograph is *More-Than-Human Diasporas: Topologies of Empire, Settler Colonialism, Slavery* (Routledge, 2025).

Tomasz Sikora teaches literature, culture and theory at UKEN University, Krakow, Poland. His varied research interests include queer theory, literature and cultural studies, gothic and grotesque, biopolitics, environmental humanities and more. He has published two books: *Virtually Wild: Wilderness, Technology and the Ecology of Mediation* (2003) and *Bodies Out of Rule: Transversal Readings in Canadian Literature and Film* (2014). He is one of the founders and editors of *InterAlia: A Journal of Queer Studies* (interalia.queerstudies.pl).

Mikki Stelder is Assistant Professor of Global Arts and Politics at the University of Amsterdam, Netherlands, affiliated with the Amsterdam School for Cultural Analysis, and works at the intersection of critical ocean studies and postcolonial and anticolonial thought with a focus on Dutch imperialism and the cultural-legal imaginary of Hugo Grotius. They were a recipient of a three-year Marie Skłodowska Curie Global Fellowship and their work has appeared in journals such as *Postcolonial Colonial Studies, Journal of Palestine Studies, Settler Colonial Studies,* and *Angelaki*. They are a recipient of the ASCA Article of the Year Award for "The colonial difference in Hugo Grotius: rational man, slavery, and Indigenous dispossesion" (*Postcolonial Studies*, 2022) and also work as an occasional artist. Their video essay *Attending to the Leusden* was presented at the exhibition *Unimaginable: Clarion Calls from Rising Seas* (Bradwolff Gallery, Amsterdam).

Edwige Tamalet Talbayev is Associate Professor of French and an affiliate of the Environmental Studies Program at Tulane University in New Orleans, United States, where she founded the Middle East and North Africa Studies Program. She is currently at work on several projects that delve into the materiality of water as a site of alternative epistemologies and experiences of being. Among them, her book-in-progress, *The Residual Migrant*, draws on biotheory, new materialism, and ecocriticism to theorize the dissolutive ontologies specific to drowned migrants whose submerged bodies are amalgamated into their ecologically ravaged, deep-sea environment. A second project, a co-edited volume entitled *Water Logics* (2025), proposes new epistemological models focused on seawater as an analytical category. Talbayev is also Professor Extraordinarius at the University of South Africa.

Eszter Timár is Associate Professor at the Department of Gender Studies at Central European University, Austria, where she started teaching after getting her Ph.D. in comparative literature at Emory University, Atlanta, United States. Her research interests include the history of sexuality and the discourses of fraternity in the philosophy of democracy, queer theory, deconstruction and feminist theory. Her articles on deconstruction, queer theory and new materialism have appeared in

InterAlia: A Journal of Queer Studies, Oxford Literary Review, Paragraph, Parallax, and *Postmodern Culture.* She is currently working on queer Eastern European affect.

Massimiliano Tomba (Ph.D. in political philosophy at the University of Pisa, Italy) is Professor in the Department of History of Consciousness, University of California, Santa Cruz, United States. He has published several texts on political theory and philosophy. Among them *Marx's Temporalities* (2013) and the 2021 David and Elaine Spitz Prize-winning *Insurgent Universality: An Alternative Legacy of Modernity* (2019). His forthcoming book, *Revolution and Restoration: The Politics of Anachronism,* is currently in press with Fordham University Press.

Maite Urcaregui is Assistant Professor of English and Comparative Literature at San José State University, California, United States, which occupies the ancestral lands and unceded territory of the Muwekma Ohlone Tribe of the San Francisco Bay Area. Her research and teaching explore multiethnic US literatures and visual cultures through feminist, queer and critical race theories. Her current project, *Seeing Citizenship: Visual Poetics & Racial Politics in Multiethnic U.S. Literatures,* examines multimedia literature that collages word and image to critique citizenship's inconsistencies and inequalities to envision alternative formations of political belonging and community.

Foreword

Ewa Macura-Nnamdi
and Tomasz Sikora

Water does rather than is. It wets, humidifies, evaporates, crystallizes, permeates, fills, leaks, drips, trickles, softens, hardens, congeals, dilutes, shapes, drills, erodes, corrodes, bonds, dissolves, buoys, transports, conducts, reflects, hides, reveals, refracts, diffracts, circulates, depletes, repletes, facilitates, blocks, disrupts, cools, heats, and more. In its protean capacity it forms into flows, tides, waves, currents, whirlpools, pools, drops, streams, oceans, and more. Its properties are often referred to as mysterious, unusual, weird, strange, counterintuitive, inexplicable, and queer. In what we have come to call the "Anthropocene," water is likely to soon become both the destroyer of whole cities and countries, and a scarce resource around which bitter wars will be fought.

This issue aims to expand the existing research on the material, political, and affective life of water as well as to enable novel waves and ways of thinking with and through water. Moving beyond the somewhat hackneyed concepts of fluidity and flows, we have gathered critical perspectives that balance between the scientific, the social, the (bio-)political, and the cultural. The contributors to this issue draw on a wide and rapidly growing body of scholarship that includes (but is not limited to) maritime, climate change, and Anthropocene studies as well as the "blue humanities." Three major, broadly conceived currents of thought run through these essays: the protean relationalities that water enables; appropriations of water in modernist logics of regulation and management; and the problematic figurations of water in scientific, philosophical, cultural, political, and legal discourses. Thematically, the articles address a wide range of phenomena, events, and concepts, including Mediterranean migrant deaths, water as a medium of not-only-human intimacy and queer potentiality, swimming pools, the 2000 Cochabamba water war, the legacy of Grotius's legal philosophy, imperialist and capitalist notions of property and ownership, notions of purity and contamination, hydroelectricity's impact on the perception of time, the inadequacy of disciplinary knowledge and pedagogy, water's potential to resist aquapolitical governmentality, and "maternal" figurations of water in some contemporary feminist theorizations.

Variously theorized, studied, legislated, managed, and exploited, water – or whatever we decide to understand as water – remains an inescapable concern. In a time of widespread droughts and floods, rising sea levels, omnipresent industrial pollution, rampant privatization of vital resources, and tightening of water borders against migrants, thinking about / with / through water offers one of the ways we can rethink identities, embodiments, politics, naturecultures, and planetary engagements. As many of the authors included in this issue point out, or at least imply, thinking about / with / through water is an invitation to search for new ways of knowing, being, and relating.

There are not enough mouths to utter
All your fleeting names, O water.
— Wisława Szymborska, "Water"

Wisława Szymborska's poetic take on water is driven by a paradox. On the one hand, the poem speaks to, and celebrates, water's material heterogeneity and the multiplicity of its forms and hence meanings. On the other, however, it points to the impossibility to grasp the abundant materiality of water and to the inadequacy of language to keep up with its fugitive realities and shapes. The "names" are provisional and potentially countless, the lines suggest, turning the poem, it might seem, into a dubious exercise in poetic creation. Indeed, Szymborska's piece does what it declares impossible: it offers beautifully crafted names in an explicit recognition of their insufficiency and futility. And yet the lines also, and perhaps by this very reason, suggest that there are no other ways to access water except through the endless acts of naming (as Jamie Linton provocatively puts it: "Water is what we make of it" (3)). What is at stake, however, is much more than water's "symbolic potency" or its discursive life (MacLeod 40). These acts posit us as always in a relation to water – as observers, (ab)users, thinkers, admirers, and survivors, to name only the few the poem references. This is why in Szymborska's poem, water is at once elusive though palpably material; offering itself but also withholding; historical and yet to come; life-giving and life-taking; scarce and excessive; violent and benign; an object of our deeds, needs, and thoughts and an agent constantly chiselling the limits of what we do, need, and think.

Introduction: Water

Ewa Macura-Nnamdi
and Tomasz Sikora

Szymborska's 1962 poem beautifully encapsulates some of the major currents of thought coalescing around what Cecilia Chen et al. have named a "hydrological turn" (3). More specifically, they have offered "thinking with water" in place of "thinking about water" as an approach most sensitive and attentive to the materialities of water and their political and poetic significance. To think with water, they argue, is to place water alongside our intellectual endeavours recognizing it is meaning-creating matter. It is also to acknowledge that water is a creative subject in its own right, generating our worlds, communities, and ways of knowing, frequently redefining our knowledges and theories about the world and ourselves. Szymborska's endless "fleeting names" is a poetic recognition that "water does not exist in the abstract. It must take up a body or place (a hedgehog, a weather front, a turn of phrase) somewhere, sometime, somehow" (Chen et al. 8). These names also serve as a reminder that "water has a remarkable capacity to resist containments of all kinds" (12), including semantic containers (poetic or not). They intimate "water's relationality" (5), bringing to the foreground the idea that, as Cecilia Chen succinctly and elegantly puts it, "waters are situated, lively, and shared" (275).

The methodological call to go beyond the understandings of water as a mere resource and an inert object of our inquiries is, of course, not unprecedented, although it may not always have been given a specific name it receives in *Thinking with Water*. Jamie Linton's work *What is Water? The History of a Modern Abstraction* aims precisely to trace the history of how water came to be abstracted from its material environment and the relations in which it has occurred. Turned into a homogenized object of (scientific) inquiry, water as H_2O has not only lost its materiality but also distanced waters from the myriad relations by which they are constituted and which they in turn constitute as well. For Linton, "water is not a thing, but, rather, is a process of engagement" (30). Ivan Illich's much earlier *H_2O and the Waters of Forgetfulness* offers a powerful narrative of how water as H_2O became "a resource" in need of "technical management" (Illich and Nandy 76) but also of how water has been "a fluid that drenches the inner and outer spaces of the imagination" (24). In his 2004 book *Social Power and the Urbanization of Water*, Erik Swyngedouw examines the urban circulation of water, its physical and symbolic metabolizations which can reveal how power is not only wielded but also thought of in city space. What interests Swyngedouw, among others, is the various ways water's urban life erodes the boundaries between categories such as nature/culture which we have traditionally used to structure and imagine the world.

The recent upsurge in research on the political, social, and aesthetic life of water no doubt owes its impetus to maritime, climate change, Anthropocene, and feminist studies (Steinberg and Peters, Neimanis, Blum, Mel Chen, and others). Critics have looked into the environmental, (post)colonial, geographic, political, and cultural significance and use of water across some very specific contexts (e.g., the Arctic, the Indian Ocean, film, literature, capitalism, water management, urban spaces, maritime crossings), engaging with both its realities and representations. The former has been addressed by, among others, Hawkins et al., Anand, Neimanis, and Helmreich. The latter has drawn critics such as Yates, Anidjar, Mentz, Neimanis, and Protevi, to name just a few. Philosophical discourses, on the other hand, have drawn on what water resists, enables, and connotes and the values thus generated: its mobile and liquid and life-giving nature. Gaston Bachelard probes into the imaginary textures of matter via literary representations of water. Gilles Deleuze and Felix Guattari have resorted to the physical properties of water to theorize what they call the smooth space. Michel Serres focuses on the acoustic life of the sea to talk about noise as the other of order and regulation. For (Freud's) psychoanalysis, the oceanic is "the unconscious of the unconscious" (Rooney). A 2013 special issue of *feminist review* has focused on "gender–water geographies" (1), aiming to examine how water constitutes "subjectivities, bodies and communities" (2). One recent special issue of *English Language Notes* edited by Laura Winkiel inaugurates *hydro-criticism*, a term which marks novel interventions in the field of maritime studies and beyond. Kim De Wolff et al.'s 2021 collection titled *Hydrohumanities: Water Discourse and Environmental Futures* offers the term *hydrohumanities* to refer to the "emerging discourse surrounding water-human-power" which remains especially attentive to "the active role of water" in the creation of the variety of forms it assumes across disparate contexts (1). In the field of literary studies, Hannah Boast has recently deployed the concept of *hydrofictions* to speak of Israeli and Palestinian literature where water is not merely a motif but a substance affecting and constituting political and economic realities.

The wealth and breadth of this scholarship is impossible to recount here. At the same time, to think with water in an exhaustive way and to give it definitive names once and for all is an ambition that would reproduce the fantasy of containment Szymborska's poem cheekily attempts yet also deconstructs. The contributors to this issue draw on this expansive body of scholarship but also chart some novel terrains. They address a variety of contexts, geographical, historical, political, and aesthetic, and they examine diverse watery loci. As we see it, three major, broadly conceived, currents of thought run through their essays: the protean relationalities that water enables; appropriations of water in modernist logics of regulation and management; and the problematic figurations of water in scientific, philosophical, cultural, and political discourses.

A number of researchers have already addressed water's relationality, among them Cecilia Chen et al., Irene J. Klaver, Stacy Alaimo, and Astrida Neimanis. Challenging the idea of modern water as an objectified abstraction (Linton), these scholars have variously emphasized water's connective potential, its capacity to bring together or sever other watery bodies and to perpetually institute a "lively relationality" based on mutual and ongoing permeations (C. Chen 275). Astrida Neimanis's seminal work on bodies of water proposes the idea of the "hydrocommons of wet relations" (4) or "embodied hydrocommons" (95), an idea which goes beyond our anthropocentric horizons, redefining our notions of embodiment and of what it means to be a human body. In this special issue, Edwige Tamalet Talbayev, Joseph Pugliese, Andreas Philippopoulos-Mihalopoulos, and Jeremy Chow and Maite Urcaregui push the parameters of these inquiries to further probe the material, political, conceptual, and aesthetic effects of water's relationality. Talbayev's essay

"Hydropower: Residual Dwelling Between Life and Nonlife" offers a radical reading of human residuality. Looking at the context of Mediterranean migrant deaths, Talbayev examines the power of seawater to corrode and dissolve human remains into the geological forms of aquatic worlds. Here, the wet relations transcend biopolitical classifications, unsettling the division between life and nonlife. Talbayev's *residual dwelling* is a site of decomposition, amalgamation, and bonding where the need to rethink the political and its constitutive categories becomes more than urgent. For Pugliese, water is not merely a substance able to form and sustain relations with other entities, but constitutive of "the very conditions of possibility of relationality for all life." Drawing on Indigenous cosmo-epistemologies and the phenomenology of Maurice Merleau-Ponty, Pugliese uses the concept of *intercorporeity* to convey the ways in which water is both enfleshed and enfleshing other bodies. This phenomenology of water at times fails to resist what Pugliese calls "aquapolitical regimes of governmentality"; at others, it propels "an insurgent aquapolitical agency" that consistently undoes such regimes. Andreas Philippopoulos-Mihalopoulos's piece is a creative meditation on intimacy, relationality, and water. The text celebrates water's permeability and its material recalcitrance whereby water is always an agent bringing bodies into proximity, a connective material perennially sabotaging the boundaries we draw between bodies of water, human, and other-than-human. For Philippopoulos-Mihalopoulos water comes to embody intimacy, becoming the quintessential form/material of relationality. The point is not that it lubricates relations, but that it materializes and signifies togetherness: we are all (in) water together. Using the framework of hydropoetics and ecosexuality, Jeremy Chow and Maite Urcaregui propose a similar idea in reference to specifically *queer* relationality and intimacy by looking at the much more domesticated instance of water use: pools. In pools, they say, "bodies come together in fluid ways" enabling queer affirmation, intimacy, and attachments. While the authors recognize the problematic role pools play in the exploitative economy that depletes natural water resources in an age of climate change, they believe the emphasis on large bodies of water – seas and oceans – in the blue humanities should be corrected by more attention to contained, domesticated, intimate water spaces as sites of queer potentiality.

Much work has been done to date on the commodification of water by such scholars as Karen Bakker, Jamie Linton, Erik Swyngedouw, and others. Mikki Stelder's and Massimiliano Tomba's contributions to the current issue offer a complementary perspective by focusing on the imperial and capitalist economies water has been made to enable but also incessantly unsettle. More specifically, they explore the economies of water in order to investigate how water has come to inform the economic ideas about ownership and property. Stelder probes the depths of Hugo Grotius's ocean to examine what she terms the "conquest of maritime imagination" – the ways his notions of the ocean as *perpetual res nullius* not only did not escape "the logic of property," but in fact enabled this logic in the first place. Yet while Stelder traces the ways in which Grotius's idea of the ocean as common property has rendered "the globe capturable," she also looks to how the materiality of water undoes the economic and legal regimes Grotius helped to institute. Tomba turns to the context of the Cochabamba water war in 2000 – a case that has drawn much critical attention in political and social water studies – with the aim of investigating how it inaugurated the notion of social property. Interested in extracting theory from practice, Tomba analyses the social and legal entanglements that accompanied the war and argues that social property is a practice of democracy beyond "the colonial appropriative parable." Ultimately, then, the war was not only about access to water but also about an "alternative political and legal framework" based to a large extent on indigenous opposition to modernist logics of water

management. Modernization, and particularly the capture of water's energy through the momentous project of hydroelectricity, is also Kieran Murphy's point of departure in his attempt to reimagine our temporal and spatial relationship with water through the concept of deep time. Drawing on Gaston Bachelard's elaborations on imagination as driven by the waters of deep time, Martin Heidegger's emphasis on an elemental wonder that "taps into an upstream reservoir of forgotten knowledge," and Dipesh Chakrabarty's notion of planetary history, Murphy postulates a "deep time theory of knowledge" grounded in a geological consciousness that extends far beyond current scientific-technological epistemologies and practices. Together with natural electricity (thunderstorms), water seems to carry in it some planetary memory, especially life's planetary memory. As such, it is in a privileged position to teach us "timefulness" (a term Murphy borrows from Bjornerud), or a sense of our physical and mental participation in the planet's deep temporality.

The inadequacy of received epistemologies also animates Gil Anidjar's meditation on the practice of teaching and learning with water. Taking the simple (yet infinitely complex) object of a plastic bottle of water as a point of departure, Anidjar meanders through questions of plastic production, water marketing and consumption, water's affinity to – or continuity with – speech and memory (Bachelard), to finally arrive at the ultimate lesson that water can teach us: that "there are more things in heaven and earth, more things *than* heaven and earth, and more waters too, than in any science or philosophy." The text's conclusion harks back, again, to Wisława Szymborska's insight briefly discussed above, in that water resists the disciplinarian compartmentalization of distinct sciences and practices of knowledge. One might further conclude that water, just as knowledge about water, always overflows distinctions and resists the state of absolute purity. For Pantuchowicz, who follows Jacques Derrida in this respect, water – including the spring water in Anidjar's plastic bottle – always figures both purity and threats of contamination. She draws on a wide philosophical literature (including Plato, Nietzsche, Derrida, Esposito) in order to delineate the ways in which the figure of water management works to control the "purity of cultural exchanges and transmissions." To overcome that logic, Pantuchowicz invokes "a politics of affirmation" which she recognizes in the posthumanist perspectives of Donna Haraway, Rosi Braidotti, and Astrida Neimanis. Agnieszka Pantuchowicz's focus on figurations of water is methodologically echoed in Eszter Timár's article in the present issue. But where Pantuchowicz offers a broad picture that spans from Plato to posthumanism, Timár performs a rigorous deconstructive critique of what she posits as Astrida Neimanis's construction of (bodies of) water through "maternal materiality." If, for Pantuchowicz, water's purity is inevitably haunted by contamination and contagion, for Timár the ontologization of water as life-affirming, gestational, nurturing, and maternal is necessarily haunted by figures of separation, loss, anxiety, and death. Timár's analysis points to what Benjamin Noys termed "the persistence of the negative" which continues to haunt (to remain in the realm of haunting) the "politics and metaphysics of affirmationism" prevalent in contemporary philosophies of resistance (x). Matter's "negativity" – inextricable from its affirmative figurations – has important implications for, among others, the way we relate to our (posthumanist) watery embodiment. Indeed, the central concern of the current issue – water's materiality – may be refreshingly revisited through the lens of what Timár calls, after Geoffrey Bennington, the desire for ontology.

Variously theorized, studied, legislated, managed, and exploited, water – or whatever we decide to understand as water – remains an inescapable concern. In a time of widespread droughts and floods, rising sea levels, omnipresent industrial pollution, rampant privatization of vital resources, and tightening of water borders against migrants, thinking about / with / through water offers one of the ways we can rethink identities, embodiments, politics, naturecultures, and planetary engagements. As many of the authors included in this issue point out, or at least imply, thinking about / with / through water is an invitation to search for new ways of knowing, being, and relating.

acknowledgements

We owe thanks to Charlie Blake and Gerard Greenway for their assistance and support throughout the process, from the issue's conceptualization to its final materialization. We would also like to thank all the peer reviewers who generously shared their expertise to make the issue more focused, original, and enjoyable. Ewa Macura-Nnamdi's research for this special issue was supported by the National Science Centre, Poland, under research project *Fictions of Water: Refugees and the Sea*, grant number 2019/33/B/HS2/02051.

bibliography

Alaimo, S. "States of Suspension: Trans-Corporeality at Sea." *Interdisciplinary Studies in Literature and Environment*, vol. 19, no. 3, 2012, pp. 476–93, https://doi.org/10.1093/isle/iss068.

Anand, Nikhil. *Hydraulic City: Water and the Infrastructures of Citizenship in Mumbai*. Duke UP, 2017.

Anidjar, Gil. *Blood: A Critique of Christianity*. Columbia UP, 2014.

Bachelard, Gaston. *Water and Dreams: An Essay on the Imagination of Matter*. The Dallas Institute of Humanities and Culture, 1983.

Bakker, Karen. *An Uncooperative Commodity: Privatizing Water in England and Wales*. Oxford UP, 2004.

Blum, Hester. "Introduction: Oceanic Studies." *Atlantic Studies: Global Currents*, vol. 10, no. 2, 2013, pp. 151–55, https://doi.org/10.1080/14788810.2013.785186.

Boast, Hannah. *Hydrofictions: Water, Power and Politics in Israeli and Palestinian Literature*. Edinburgh UP, 2022.

Chen, Cecilia. "Mapping Waters: Thinking with Water Places." *Thinking with Water*, edited by Cecilia Chen et al., McGill-Queen's UP, 2013, pp. 274–98.

Chen, Cecilia, et al., editors. *Thinking with Water*. McGill-Queen's UP, 2013.

Chen, Mel Y. *Animacies: Biopolitics, Racial Mattering, and Queer Affect*. Duke UP, 2012.

Deleuze, Gilles, and Felix Guattari. *A Thousand Plateaus: Capitalism and Schizophrenia*. U of Minnesota P, 2005.

De Wolff, Kim, et al., editors. *Hydrohumanities: Water Discourse and Environmental Futures*. U of California P, 2021.

Hawkins, Gay, et al. *Plastic Water: The Social and Material Life of Bottled Water*. MIT Press, 2015.

Helmreich, Stefan. *Alien Ocean: Anthropological Voyages in Microbial Seas*. U of California P, 2009.

Illich, Ivan, and Ashis Nandy. *H_2O and the Waters of Forgetfulness*. 1985. Maryon Boyars, 2012.

Klaver, Irene J. "Radical Water." *Hydrohumanities: Water Discourse and Environmental Futures*, edited by Kim De Wolff et al., U of California P, 2022, pp. 64–88.

Linton, Jamie. *What is Water? The History of a Modern Abstraction*. UBC Press, 2010.

MacLeod, Janine. "Water and the Material Imagination: Reading the Sea of Memory against the Flows of Capital." *Thinking with Water*, edited by Cecilia Chen et al., McGill-Queen's UP, 2013, pp. 40–60.

Mentz, Steve. "Seep." *Veer Ecology: A Companion for Environmental Thinking*, edited by Jeffrey Jerome Cohen and Lowell Duckert, U of Minnesota P, 2017, pp. 282–96.

Neimanis, Astrida. *Bodies of Water: Posthuman Feminist Phenomenology*. Bloomsbury, 2017.

Noys, Benjamin. *Persistence of the Negative: A Critique of Contemporary Continental Theory*. Edinburgh UP, 2010.

Protevi, John. "Water." *Rhizomes: Cultural Studies in Emerging Knowledges*, issue 15, Winter 2007, www.rhizomes.net/issue15/protevi.html.

Pugliese, Joseph. "Bodies of Water." *Heat: Literary International*, vol. 12, 2006, pp. 12–20.

Rooney, Caroline. "What Is the Oceanic?" *Angelaki*, vol. 12, no. 2, 2007, pp. 19–32, https://doi.org/10.1080/09697250701754921.

Serres, Michel. *Genesis*. U of Michigan P, 1995.

Steinberg, Philip, and Kimberley Peters. "Wet Ontologies, Fluid Spaces: Giving Depth to Volume through Oceanic Thinking." *Environment and Planning D: Society and Space*, vol. 33, no. 2, 2015, pp. 247–64, https://doi.org/10.1068/d14148p.

Swyngedouw, Erik. *Social Power and the Urbanization of Water*. Oxford UP, 2004.

Szymborska, Wisława. "Water." *View with a Grain of Sand: Selected Poems*, translated by Stanisław Barańczak and Clare Cavanagh, Harcourt Brace, 1995.

Winkiel, Laura, editor. *Hydro-criticism*. Spec. issue of *English Language Notes*, vol. 57, no. 1, 2019.

Yates, Julian. "Wet?" *Elemental Ecocriticism: Thinking with Earth, Air, Water, and Fire*, edited by Jeffrey Jerome Cohen and Lowell Duckert, U of Minnesota P, 2015.

Ewa Macura-Nnamdi
Tomasz Sikora

Matter in all its expressions and formations is not a fixed object, it is not substance, it is process.

– Papadopoulos 72

Recent theorizations of water have emphasized its characteristics as a material substance (Steinberg and Peters; Alaimo); as a symbolic entity both embedded in *and* producing social processes (Swyngedouw); and as an agential body generative of singular forms of sentient epistemology (Bennett; Ingersoll). Working at the intersection of these three strands of criticism, this argument takes the conceptualization of water further by spotlighting its physical, molecular properties – more specifically its chemical power to alter and decompose biological matter submerged in it. This essay ponders the drownings punctuating the clandestine trans-Mediterranean crossings to Europe brought to the world's attention during the so-called "migrant crisis" of the mid-2010s. It reflects on the concept of "hydropower" – the corrosive power of seawater to amalgamate Life and Nonlife, reshuffling naturalized narratives around humans' place in nature, competing forms of materiality, and the shifting prerogative of agency in human/more-than-human encounters.

This reflection takes as its theoretical starting point the distressing reality of clandestine migrants crossing the sea from Africa to Europe in an oft-frustrated attempt to lay claim to the privileges of citizenship enshrined in European liberal democracies (Brugère and Le Blanc).[1] In this reading, the Mediterranean functions as an aqueous border, a liquid "wall" (Bensaâd) figuring the unbridgeable fracture between the northern shore of the

Hydropower: Residual Dwelling between Life and Nonlife

Edwige Tamalet Talbayev

sea, the purported domain of democratic norms and law – in sharp distinction to the exclusive logic for which the wall metaphorically stands for – , and an underclass of migrating humanity – abjected subjects relegated to the edge of Europe's regime of lawfulness and deprived of the protections that they afford. Through a focus on the submersion process intrinsic to the failed maritime crossing, my approach interrelates the order of biopolitical violence enacted by Europe's restrictive migration policies, based on exclusive understandings of political subjectivity (left-to-die migrants abandoned off the shores of Europe and drowning in the depths of the Mediterranean Sea), and the thick time of the geophysical – planetary temporalities where "the nonhuman environment is present not merely as a framing device but as a presence that begins to suggest that human history is implicated in natural history" (Buell 7).

In what has been dubbed the "materialist turn" in the humanities, a renewed focus on the sciences has sought to undo a "perceived neglect or diminishment of matter in the dominant Euro-Western tradition as a passive substance intrinsically devoid of meaning" (Gamble et al. 111). This privileging of Life over Nonlife, Anthropocentric in its deployment, rests on the belief that humans operate from a position of remove from matter, from a vantage point which alone allows for the kind of objective insight pertaining to a human-observer positionality – and to its power to determine all other forms of planetary existence. In contrast, I here train my lens closer to the intimate, embodied vulnerability of submerged bodies at the mercy of elemental violence as a tactic to rethink the supposed human advantage. I shine a light on the *residual* ontologies that these macabre encounters with the maritime environment afford. Rejected at the edges of Europe, drowned at sea, these dehumanized bodies fall prey to dissolution and dispersal under the combined power of corrosive seawater, marine sea life, tides, and currents. They are ensnared in the violent, ultimate exposure[2] that the drowning and the subsequent baring of the body by hydropower constitute. The degradation process perpetrated on these derogated corpses calls into question the ideals of subjective individualism, autonomy, and sovereignty underpinning the regime of rights and privileges derived from the Enlightenment. Reduced to their most immediate, molecular materiality, these infrahuman bodies only take on meaning within the endless cycle of decomposition and reformation they undergo under the influence of organic and non-organic forces. Disintegrated and displaced around the hydrosphere, the molecules that compose them enter the food chain. They become absorbed and re-embodied in different biological structures. They disperse and settle on the seabed awaiting stratification into lithic time. Poised between "the biological validity of bone and the dead matter of the fossil," the process of sedimentation they undergo brings them to the territory of "geologic corporeality," one "at once geologic, biologic and social in its composition" (Yusoff, "Geologic Life" 5). Their dissipative existence morphs in the continuum between human subject positions and inhuman forces; it conjures a mixed ontological model that puts significant pressure on the putatively watertight divide between "the autonomy of Life and its opposition to and difference from Nonlife" (Povinelli 14).

Through hydropower's obliteration of the migrants, an alternative understanding of Anthropos emerges, one marked by objectification and materiality through assimilation into the water element in a material continuum revealing human/more-than-human solidarities in the "sacrifice zone" (Klein).[3] If we hold true Elizabeth Povinelli's contention that "biopower (the governance through life and death) has long depended on a subtending geontopower (the difference between the lively and the inert)" (5), then the decomposition of migrants into molecularity (and their subsequent sedimentation into forms of both Life and Nonlife) accomplishes two things: (1) it spells the completion of Europe's necropolitical[4] project of eradication of unlawful life at the maritime borders; (2) it concurrently marks out the very limits of such necropolitical management projects[5] as the multiple, Life/Nonlife ontological assemblages issuing forth from aqueous dissolution shatter biopolitical orders of subjectivity knotted around exiguous definitions of the human – or the inhuman, which is here rethought not simply in terms of incommensurability with subjecthood and autonomy, but also as a reflection of the ontological porousness between embodied forms of Life and their geophysical environments.

Adapting Elizabeth Grosz's concept of "geopower" to the forces of water, hydropower capitalizes on the elemental polyvalence of water to incrementally displace the devastating tactics of biopolitics by rending asunder the unbridgeable divide between Life and Nonlife on which they rely. In this argument, hydropower is momentously reclaimed from its techno-scientific legacy as a method of hydroelectric power production perpetrating environmental violence through interventionist engineering models based on the interruption and harnessing of natural flows.[6] At an angle to this anthropogenic model, I seek to lay bare the multiple resonances of hydropower as a critical fulcrum through which to reveal the properties of water as a natural force exceeding its attempted biopolitical harnessing – a force elaborating alternative modes of recognition of the human world as co-constituted by non-human forms of existence. Hydropower works right at the site of one of the most dramatic fault lines of our contemporary era – the divide between Europe and the Global South. But it also reveals a second fault line between disparate categories of humanity, which are defined through their varying degrees of mastery over resources and nature, or lack thereof. Intervening in the organic cohesion of the human body, interfering with its integrity, acting as a solvent, seawater here functions as a biopolitical agent turning enclosed bodies into dissipating matter, biological matter into molecular residue. Hydropower thus reveals the limitations of embodiment as a marker of Life – the skin acting as a membrane insulating the incarnated self from its most immediate, pervasive, inert environment. Beyond the putative protection of this biological "en-skinning" (Povinelli et al. 181) of subjecthood (epidermis as an ontological boundary), this essay investigates this specific becoming residue of bodies under the influence of hydropower in what it divulges of identity's ever dynamic nature. Through the dissolutive ontologies it enables, hydropower proffers new definitions of the Anthropological category at the core of the concept of the Anthropocene. It concurrently highlights new forms of dwelling – and, potentially, a common extinction horizon – across the fault line dividing the human from the inhuman in Western ontology.

borderscapes

Setting the working parameters for a concept of hydropower implies determining the very nature of its elemental core – seawater, here taken in the context of the Mediterranean deadly crossings. Capitalizing on recent research in ocean studies (Helmreich; Steinberg; Steinberg and Peters; Talbayev, "Seawater"), hydropower enacts a move away from surface-level representations of maritime bodies as a dematerialized abstraction. By so doing, it deprioritizes geopolitical readings of the sea as an arena for social agon. Hydropower's deployment rests on the integrated world of geophysical forces, where elements are co-constituted through their large-scale, longue durée interactions. In the Mediterranean "borderscape" (Perera),[7] hydropower spotlights water's elemental texture, its ability to transform itself from a purveyor of surface-level, static ontologies to a physical force capable of interrupting and re-ordering the structure of embodied life through corrosion and decomposition.

Enveloped within the logic of empire, water materializes as both a surface sustaining the arrow-like deployment of colonialism and a subordinated agent curtailing undesirable lives at its periphery. Conceiving of the borderscape in terms of surface yields an understanding of the sea as a planar space where struggles over territoriality, resources, securitization, and containment unfold (Steinberg and Peters 252). It reactivates empire and its interlocking orders of exclusion. Blended into social constructions of identity and transnational historical narratives, European seafaring narratives depicted the ocean as an empty buffer zone concurrently separating and extending the land-rooted logics of organized polities. These colonialist thought experiments indexed Europe's self-definition to its negation of various forms of otherness encountered in the wake of imperial expansion. For Cesare Casarino the modernist sea narrative figured a "representation-producing machine for the turbulent transitions from mercantile capitalism to industrial capitalism, into a laboratory for the conceptualizations of a [...] multiple, interconnected, and global [world system]" (9) – a world system constituted through trading routes and networks, common epistemologies, but also drowned bodies roiled in the dark waters of empire, extending this dichotomous logic below the surface.

Drawing our attention to the shipwreck modernity[8] incarnated in the drowning of racialized migrant bodies capsized on the edges of Europe, Paul Gilroy sheds unremitting light on the space lying beneath the oceanic surface of trade routes and economic nomos – a space of submersion and obliteration that pinpoints seawater's complicity in furthering vertical power constructions: "Slavery's pelagic theatre of power reveals its hidden character in a grey, watery confrontation between the properly human and the supposedly infrahuman" (5–6). Gilroy's argument overlays the fluidity of water with the pervasiveness of capitalist expansion and its biopolitical, racialized logic. It also points out the unbridgeable divide between the two subcategories of humans that the "pelagic theatre" of Atlantic modernity has pitted against each other, a chasm predicated on remanent, dichotomous narratives of universal progress based on supposedly irreconcilable civilizational models: "The belligerent, oceanic operations [of Western modernity] were possible only because those vulnerable people were, and often still are, judged to belong to nature rather than to history, society or culture" (5). Colonial hierarchies have marked out the autotelic, sovereign subjects of Western modernity – those putatively insusceptible to the concatenated orders of biopolitical and geophysical violence – as incommensurable with their subaltern others. By so doing, they have rescripted derogated biological Life as Nonlife. Undoing the privileges ascribed to the Western, colonial, political subject over this objectified "infrahumanity" requires dislodging the prominence of models of thought that restrict the human to mastery over nature – and over other forms of life that have been assimilated to it, as Gilroy's ascription makes clear. It implies destabilizing bifurcated orderings of life. It is to extend conceptions of the sea to include fractal encounters, deviations from dichotomies, and incompatibilities, to shatter the very regimentation of human and social worlds that territoriality seeks to effect. In short, it is to attend to the critical potential of *water as substance* that hydropower sets in motion.

In excess of territorializing logics and static locations, Philip Steinberg and Kimberley Peters have argued that water functions as an "ungraspable space that is continually being reproduced by mobile molecules; water has a taken-for-granted materiality (liquidity, or wetness)" (252). The geographers' reading emphasizes the rhythmic mobility of water, its malleability, its enfolding viscosity. By emphasizing the "wetness" of water as substance, Steinberg and Peters rethink the ocean "not as a space of discrete points between which objects move but rather as a dynamic environment of flows and continual recomposition where, because there is no static background, 'place' can be understood only in the context of mobility" (257). Drawing on Lagrangian fluid dynamics, the geographers' notion of movement is tributary to the spatial displacement of material elements rather than disincarnated forces. Oceanic space is formed from this perpetual mobility, reformed through each enfolding. Whereas land gives rise to fixed terrestrial ontologies, water in the liquid form favored by hydropower emphasizes flow, circulation, mobility.[9] Its state of flux belies political attempts at delimiting territory, complicating surveillance and control through its pervasiveness, its indomitable volume. Water's three-dimensional materiality thus blurs the very dichotomy between surface and depth, entwining attempted control with enduring resistance in the perpetual churning of the sea. Thinking water elementally spotlights its shape-shifting quality that exceeds the strict coordinates of geographic emplacement and the political uses to which they are put. It opens the door to a rethinking of the restrictive territoriality of ocean space, to an opening up of the oceanic to its geophysical might. In Kathryn Yusoff's words, it performs the shift from a "geography of power to geophysics of power" ("Geophysics After Life"), or to a geopower, a concept which has long underpinned biopower, as Povinelli pointedly notes about her own coinage "geontopower" ("the governance through life and death" (5)).

from *bios* to *geos*

A recent theoretical turn to the geological has attempted to supplant understandings of biopower knotted around biological life (Yusoff, "Geophysics After Life"). Kathryn Yusoff's work undercuts the many exclusive propositions based on racial, gendered, and other forms of discrimination that have come to color the deployment of life in biopolitical paradigms. Yusoff resituates biopolitics in the broader order of the universe, whose very scale belies the supposed exhaustivity of Western models of subjectivity: "the social plane and the formation of subjectivity are constituted by more than social forces, and constrained (as much as enabled) by the geologic formations that underpin them" ("Geophysics After Life"). Elizabeth Grosz's own concept of geopower showcases the power of the earth to implement a fundamental order of organization between multiple, conflicting forces ranging from the geophysical to biotic life forms. Grosz reads this original "encounter between forms of life and forms of the earth" as a foundational, necessary stage allowing for social hierarchies categorizing the human to subsequently develop (975).[10] In this perspective, any form of power relations structuring life stems from an original, agonistic struggle between geological and human bodies, from their relations of force and, though Grosz doesn't quite bring this in focus in her conceptual overview, from the relation of dominance that is triggered in their wake. Grosz's reflections on geopower – the forces of the earth that both underpin and overrun embodied forms of life and the political power relations that organize them – highlight the primordial, "preindividual" encounter between life forces and the forces of the earth. They anticipate the primordial geophysical origin of all hierarchical orderings of the human into incommensurable categories. Contrapuntally to the dominant claim that humans have morphed into fully fledged, nefarious geological agents

in the Anthropocene (Zalasiewicz et al.; Chakrabarty), Grosz's geological reading establishes that human life also bears the imprint of earth's influence. Through a reflection on the multiple ways in which bodies are shaped, reshaped, and acted upon by the forces of nature, her provocation ultimately entices us to reconsider terrestrial forces as the point of inception of biopolitical dynamics aiming to regiment and control bodies, a move that reveals geophysics and biopolitics to be entangled through human dependency on – and mimicry of – terrestrial processes.

The concept of hydropower animating this argument proposes to probe the intersection of geopower, here recalibrated to the forces of the hydrosphere, and biopower, as it has been defined by Michel Foucault, a term which as Nigel Clark states in his gloss of Grosz's position "refer[s] not simply to the practices by which objects or bodies come to be regulated by modern governing agencies but to the elemental forcefulness of the earth itself" (Clark 223) – or rather, in our context, the elemental forcefulness of water. Starting from the assumption that geography is the by-product of power relations, Grosz's reflection finds grounding in the tension between Michel Foucault's own two concepts of biopolitics and geopower. Whereas Foucauldian biopower disciplines bodies from without, Grosz teases out the potential of Foucault's notion of geopower, which crystallizes the multiple forms of agency (human and more-than-human) that collide on the surface of the earth:

> Biopower is, for Foucault, the power over life that regulates it from outside; but geopower has no outside, no "place" or "time" before or beyond it: it is the force, the forces, of the earth itself [...] the earth remains the literal ground and condition for every human, and non-human, action. (Grosz et al. 135)

Grosz calls these indomitable forces of nature the "inhuman," a notion to be parsed not so much in opposition to the order of Anthropos, as the privative prefix might suggest, but rather as a life force immanent in both organic and inorganic bodies. Grosz's emphasis on the inhuman relegates the human to a non-dominant place in the order of the universe. It also puts pressure on Foucault's own understanding of biopower by exposing the ability of geopowers to exceed the social and political forces structuring life. As Nigel Clark and Kathryn Yusoff point out in their 2017 interview with Grosz, "while these geopowers might subtend political potentials, they are never reducible to them – and so always remain radically open to transformation. Geopowers might well be channelled in capitalism, but the organization of power belongs to the earth" (Grosz et al. 131). This fundamental overcoming of regulating social forces endows geopowers, including hydropower, with the ability to resist human and social control. Geopowers are not always subordinated to organizing processes; they are not always contained by biopolitical forces. In fact, they both precede them and overrun them, flagging the intrinsic fallibility and limitations of rational forms of management.

Drawing on Gilbert Simondon, Grosz's delineation of the inhuman situates it at the intersection of the "pre-individual" and the "trans-individual" (Grosz et al. 136). What she means by this is that planetary forces both pre-date the constitution of the human as a force *and* unite all humans in a common form of belonging. In the context of water, a "pre-/transindividual" framework reveals the fundamental wateriness of our being – the omnipresence of water in us, through us, and beyond us, from our aquatic evolutionary origins to the kinds of hydrocommunities that contemporary forms of activist, ecological consciousness has devised. Rachel Carson's identification of seawater as the origin of all life ascribes the chemical makeup of human bodies to their permeability to the maritime environment from which they evolved:

our lime-hardened skeletons are a heritage from the calcium-rich ocean of Cambrian time [...] each cell of our bodies has the chemical structure impressed upon all living matter when the first simple creatures

were brought forth in the ancient sea [...] each of us begins his individual life as a miniature ocean within his mother's womb. (14)

Encapsulating the longue durée of evolutionary time, water molecules connect humans to other terrestrial animals and forms of inorganic life, making human bodies a living archive of planetary history (Shubin). A shared ontological principle, water enacts continuity and kinship across categories of life. Further destabilizing the putative self-contained quality of human bodies, Astrida Neimanis's work on bodies of water impugns the notion of sovereignty and undercuts human exceptionalism, restoring the human to its relational place in a planetary system saturated by water. By foregrounding the hydro-commonality connecting irruptive bodies and non-organic forms of life, Neimanis's reading concatenates the inhuman kernel within humans to pervasive geopowers without. Weakening human heft for the benefit of ecological epistemologies, hydropower subtends an aqueous redefinition of the human. It concurrently nurtures the dissolutive process through which water-sustained networks of planetary affiliation emerge – agential currents incommensurable to the regimenting forces of biopower.

In the context of migratory necropolitics under scrutiny here, hydropower marks the site where human *and* water's resistance to biopower coalesce, the site where a discarded class of infrahumanity blends into a geophysical force, breaking into the elemental cycle of life, enduring through its multiple reformations. Geopowers stretch and extend life forces beyond the impermanent boundaries of embodiment. In the interface between necropolitical forces and the human bodies on which they exert their power, human and hydrological agencies come to meet to defy the necrotic order of the biopolitical. For, in Yusoff's trenchant prose,

geosocial understanding of bodies in the Anthropocene cannot be limited by biopolitical concerns and their focus on biology in the ordering of political power, because geology extends the body beyond itself into material forms and modes of expression that continue beyond the frame of "life" and the imperative of its privileged perseverance. ("The Anthropocene" 214)

resistant residuality

The moving divide between water and flesh, between geology and living beings is corroded through hydropower's decomposition/recomposition of bodies. Neimanis has argued that "all [...] bodies are necessarily brought into being by another body of water that dissolves, partially or completely, to water the bodies that will follow" (87). From one body surges another body, through dissolution, transmutation, and reformation, in a poignant reminder that being-in-water requires a morphology of becoming.

In the context of enslaved Black bodies thrown overboard during the trans-Atlantic crossing, Christina Sharpe identifies what she calls "residence time," or "the time of the wake," the persistent endurance of (bodily) matter in the afterlife of drowning. In Sharpe's resonant prose, these jettisoned bodies "like us, are alive in hydrogen, in oxygen; in carbon, on phosphorous, and iron; in sodium and chlorine [...] they are with us still" (19). Henriette Gunkel identifies in Sharpe's concept an acknowledgement of water's memorial heft, of its elemental ability to sustain the undulations of remembrance (Gunkel 61). It is not this sentient quality of water that I wish to illuminate here but rather the cyclical endurance of matter that happens on the molecular level when bodies decompose and are re-incorporated. Sharpe unpacks the multilayered resonance of her wake paradigm throughout various histories of biopolitical containment and eradication – the various incarnations of the slave ship trope. How to read the unstable dinghies propelling migrants' perilous journeys across the sea in search of dignity and rights but in the shadow of the slave ship? How to cipher the disaggregating bodies of the dead but through the specter of its wake?

Sharpe's argument rehearses Anne Garduski's insights into the chemical process of bodily degradation at sea: a drowned body would be picked clean before reaching the seabed, turning nutrient to other organisms that will in turn become nutrients themselves. Through this nutrition cycle the molecules forming the body are released in the ocean column, consumed and dispersed through each consumption to the extent that more than 90–95 percent of submerged tissue enter this cycle (Sharpe 40–41). Physical matter is thus offered a long-reaching afterlife, its energy endlessly recycled, its matter forming part of new bodies and organisms, ultimately penetrating the texture of all life forms. This uniting feature of submerged matter points to a connectivity of the shared experience of Blackness, giving new resonance to Kamau Brathwaite's pronouncement that in the Black diaspora "the unity is submarine." The unity is indeed submarine, in the concatenation of the fallen bodies forever merged in biological, material assimilation, but also, and equally important, in the cross-ocean interface between human and more-than-human matter.

It is the remaining 5–10 percent of unabsorbed matter – the human/inhuman *residue* that eludes interspecies consumption to linger, to *dwell* in the water – that I wish to bring into focus here; its process, its itinerary, the entanglements it forms. Drawing on Frantz Fanon, Sharpe calls being in the wake "*inhabiting* [a] 'zone of non-Being,'" insisting that "[i]nhabiting here is the state of being inhabited/occupied and also being or dwelling in" (20). The choice of "dwelling" is a reverberating one. Dwelling in the wake denotes existence in an ontological black hole against any attempt at erasure. It implies crafting modes of being that defy the very logic of biopolitical refusal imposed on the irrefutable reality of Black life. Beyond any kind of memorial aftermath, of lingering forms of dwelling, decomposed matter points to the cross-contamination of water and body tissue, to their joining in death and through endless cycles of material afterlife, through animal consumption[11] or, here, eventual geological sedimentation of the remains. For dwelling also invites remanence, "staying with the trouble" in Donna Haraway's memorable phrase, rescripting new relationships to place, matter, sovereignty, and time. It requires training our lens on our vibrant, embroiled present where "making oddkin," be it with animal or mineral life forms, guards against the threat of extinction in times of crisis: "we require each other in unexpected collaborations and combinations, in hot compost piles. We become-with each other or not at all" (Haraway 4). Here oddkin connections surge from the depths of death, as one last act of (geo)-physical endurance for precarious, dispossessed bodies. This permeability of the self to its inhuman other is bereft of any humanistic pretension. This thick co-presence leads to a reappreciation of bounded subjectivity, enlarging thinking categories beyond the inherited paradigms of anthropological exceptionalism. Through her category of "humus" Haraway intimates another order of being exceeding the confines of one's bodies, an ontology transcending the friction between human and more-than-human (140).

In a reflection on the time of oceanic mutability, Ayesha Hameed likens Sharpe's residence time to mineralization: "solids turning to salinity as bones turn to calcium, and vice versa. This is the temporalization of organic matter becoming inorganic and flipping back again" (Hameed 49). This circulatory movement illuminates the ontological thickness of water, its assimilation of material residue scrambling the line between living and inorganic beings. It highlights "mutability and kinship with the more-than-human world" (DeLoughrey 358). By marking out bodies and the earth as co-inscribed across time, residuality reveals the porousness of the two, and their reciprocity, with bodies converting into geologic dust which itself becomes actualized through its re-embodiment in new forms of life. In residue, deep and shallow time coincide in a temporal loop where the afterhuman is concomitantly also the prehuman. Just as hydropower overflows the necropolitical functions ascribed to it by the disciplining forces of Western modernity, so the residual migrant eludes total

annihilation to shapeshift, transmute, and merge with geophysical matter to the point of indistinguishability.

In the bifurcation between biopower and hydropower, residuality becomes a space of resistance, a space of excess defying attempts at biopolitical capture. Susan Leigh Star and Geoffrey C. Bowker's work on residuality poses the question of the political valence of dwelling in the margins. In the information systems context they explore, the residual surges at the intersection of repressed experiences and silencing categories as

> the active choice not to allow yourself to be put into the available category set – the inevitable silencing (because your story can't be heard, even if told) is also politically powerful (because it lives out the faultlines of the system). (Star and Bowker 276)

What constitutes the residual becomes a matter of perspective, either the domain of epistemic obliteration and invisibility, if seen from the standpoint of the system, or an opportunity for resistance, dissent, and praxis. This portrayal of residuality as a "choice," which resonates with Alaimo's injunction to willfully expose oneself, rests on the same presupposition of agency on the part of the silenced subjects, recasting their deliberate self-relegation to the margins as a gesture of challenge to thought systems and their purported all-encompassing logic. Undoubtedly, as the result of a coercive process, hydropower-induced residue is quite different. The dissolutive ontologies it unleashes envision no abstract, hedonic forms of interspecies kinship, no salvational refiguration of the human/nature relationship. The new vistas traced in these pages all unambiguously point to a forced dispossession of sovereignty, to the loss of physical integrity, of human form and its associated privileges. Yet Star and Bowker's intuition productively identifies potential sites of dissent in the spaces "left aside in the rational and economic management of 'things,'" which for Grosz contain "something left over that remains resistant, that wants what it wants, before and beyond biopower" (Grosz et al. 137).

Kathryn Yusoff has argued that geopower "is a plane of social reproduction that both constrains and is expressive of possible modes of expression and thus of political freedom" ("The Anthropocene" 206). Geophysical volatility redraws the boundaries of political terrains; it excavates spaces of resistance. The recognition of nonhuman powers' endurance on the prehuman (and posthuman) plane beyond their capture in political forces shifts the prerogative of agency toward geophysical remanence.

conclusion

In Povinelli's portentous words, "the *Anthropos* remains an element in the set of life only insofar as Life can maintain its distinction from Death/Extinction *and* Nonlife" (9). If, as Grosz proposes, the difference between Life and Nonlife is one "in degree" and not "in kind" (Grosz et al. 136), then the remanence of aqueous, residual forms of existence shatters the dividing line separating Anthropos from disincarnated matter, revealing the vacuity of all hierarchical paradigms erected in its name. Through residue, a discarded humanity endures, forming new discrepant modes of being across the human/more-than-human divide. These ontologies, to borrow Dimitris Papadopoulos's words, are not "a description of a final state of things, but of processes that includes alternative possibilities of world-making" (71), possibilities that rest on a politics of matter whereby agency is recast in terms of "the possibility of co-acting with living and abiotic matter. Matter is hope" (76). Matter itself, Karen Barad reminds us, is

> neither fixed and given nor the mere end result of different processes. Matter is produced and productive, generated and generative. Matter is agentive, not a fixed essence or property of things. Mattering is differentiating, and which differences come to matter, matter in the iterative production of different difference. (137)

Against the attempted biopolitical suppression of a certain form of humanity, the residual dwelling enacted by hydropower reaffirms the irrepressibility of existence across duration spans exceeding that of a human life while championing the inclusion of new constellations of matter in our political thought processes.

By highlighting the convergence between an abjected, residual infrahumanity and geological matter, hydropower disrupts exclusive, deterministic conceptions of antagonism between humans and their environment. Through the dissolutive ontologies it sets forth derogated humans and depredated maritime environments collide in the formation of "sacrifice zones" as the expendable waste of modernity. Through hydropower, antagonism is rethought as tension between competing "forms of human life-worlds and their different effects on the given-world" (Povinelli 12). Calling attention to the networks of complicity that concatenate human extractive practices to the environmental harm that they incite, hydropower ultimately points out the need for an ethics of sustainability to animate the interactions between consuming subjects and depleted resource environments. For as recent catastrophic floods, eroding coastlines, and ever more powerful and frequent "once in a hundred year" hurricanes amply demonstrate (Klein), water remains unmanageably labile as a hydropower which "we summon up rather than control" (Grosz et al. 135). The figure of the residual migrant comes to embody, or rather disembody, humankind's position of utter vulnerability in the face of uncontrollable hydropower – and other geopowers – in our era of ecological catastrophe. It heralds the potential fate of *all* humans at a juncture of "surplus death of both individuals and of kinds," which has become the trademark of disaster capitalism (Haraway 134).

Reorganizing the repartition of Life and Nonlife is a means through which to destabilize the necropolitical claims staked on a biological order of conceptuality. It is breaking apart the arrangements of power sutured to a conception of subjectivity centered on Life and its production of difference. Marking out a distinction between Anthropos – the subset of humanity responsible for causing environmental destruction and resource depletion – and the infrahumanity sacrificed to the relentless pursuit of accumulation is to open the category of the human to political contestation and critique. Parsed from the lens of residuality, hydropower reveals all at once humans' full ontological coincidence with matter writ large, their endurance and solubility in geological life forces, but also the necessity to think agency in terms of human/inhuman continuity. The process of obliteration this form of Life undergoes begs "awareness of our dependence on and relationships with those countless others being driven over the edge of extinction" (van Dooren). For it is only through a rigorous deconstruction of *bios*-centered, differential conceptions of Life and the devising of other geosocial formations rooted in collaborative tactics between the human and the inhuman that anything amounting to long-term survival on earth can be imagined.

disclosure statement

No potential conflict of interest was reported by the author.

notes

1 It would require more attention than I am able to dedicate here to fully parse the multiple considerations attached to the process of migrant decomposition as a matter of ethical and theoretical concern. I will direct the reader to my forthcoming essay "The Residual Migrant" for a more thorough discussion of these points.

2 My use of the concept of exposure shares some semantic territory with Stacy Alaimo's notion in *Exposed*. However, as the rest of this essay will ascertain, it also complicates it in significant ways as Alaimo's injunction to willfully expose oneself to the power of the elements rests on deliberate self-abandonment as a gesture of challenge to dichotomous logics of being. To rehearse Yusoff's paradigm, Alaimo's exposure indulges in "*freedom from*" rather than "*coercion to*," at an angle to the devastating intrusion of necropolitical forces that hydropower reveals (Yusoff, "The Anthropocene" 207).

3 In Klein's writing, "sacrifice zone" designates geographic areas permanently damaged by the extractive logic of the fossil fuel industry, though her critical horizon can unquestionably be extended to other exploitative paradigms. Deliberately laid to waste, these sacrificed areas also include their disenfranchised and indigenous residents. The casualties of extreme depredation, the environment and its inhabitants are united in a common position of abjection and deliberate destruction. They constitute the occulted and neglected underbelly of liberalism's predatory nature. See also Iovino and Verdicchio; Oppermann.

4 I am referring to Achille Mbembe's concept of "necropolitics" here defined in relation to sovereignty:

> The ultimate expression of sovereignty largely resides in the power and capacity to dictate who is able to live and who must die. To kill or to let live thus constitutes sovereignty's limits, its principal attributes. To be sovereign is to exert one's control over mortality and to define life as the deployment and manifestation of power [necropower]. (66)

5 A similar weaponization of the river Evros on the Greek border has been the object of recent scholarship (Duncan and Levidis). Likewise, Jason De León has shed light on the instrumentalization of the inhospitable environment of the Sonoran Desert to curtail clandestine crossings into the United States. See also Heller et al.

6 These instances of violence, at times overlapping with Rob Nixon's "slow violence" paradigm, include topographical changes enacted through the redirection of the water bodies being exploited, as well as interruptions of wildlife migration patterns, environmental degradation, and loss of livelihood for struggling neighboring communities. This infrastructural approach to hydropower pits Western notions of sustainability (which here still abide by and reinforce the logic of economic gain and overconsumption, in this case of electricity) against ancestral socio-ecological concepts of land and water use. Such approach therefore articulates "structural forms of injustice and dispossession (both material and cultural)" that reaffirm a

"vision of nature as commodity" (Blake and Barney 810).

7 Suvendrini Perera speaks of a "borderscape" uniting under its fractal concept "[a] geo-politico-cultural space, shaped by embedded colonial and neo-colonial histories and continuing conflicts over sovereignty, ownership, and identity" (206).

8 *Shipwreck Modernity* is also the title of Steve Mentz's 2015 book on early modern ecological narratives.

9 Later work by Peters and Steinberg points out the limits of thinking water as wetness, calling instead for a consideration of "more-than-wet" water ontologies, i.e., ontologies taking into account the mutability of oceanic water, whose physical form spans the spectrum from ice to liquid to vaporized mist. In this new configuration the opposition between landed and aqueous logics loses some of its impact.

10 Grosz adopts a teleological approach here, insisting that

> *before* there can be relations of oppression, that is relations between humans categorised according to the criteria that privilege particular groups, *there must be* relations of force that exist in an impersonal, preindividual form that are sometimes transformed into modes of ordering the human. (975; my emphasis)

We can laminate the human dissymmetry evoked by Grosz onto the kind of biopolitical ordering hinging on racialized, antagonistic imaginaries of Life. In a recent interview, Grosz also ascribes a spatial dimension to the process (Grosz et al. 133).

11 See Pugliese; Nair.

bibliography

Alaimo, Stacy. *Exposed: Environmental Politics: Pleasures in Posthuman Times*. U of Minnesota P, 2016.

Barad, Karen. *Meeting the Universe Halfway: Quantum Physics and the Entanglement of Matter and Meaning*. Duke UP, 2006.

Bennett, Jane. *Vibrant Matter: A Political Ecology of Things*. Duke UP, 2010.

Bensaâd, Ali. "La Méditerranée, un mur en devenir?" *Rencontres d'Averroès # 12: De la richesse et de la pauvreté entre Europe et Méditerranée*, edited by Thierry Fabre, Editions Parenthèses, 2006, pp. 99–112.

Blake, David J.H., and Keith Barney. "Structural Injustice, Slow Violence? The Political Ecology of a 'Best Practice' Hydropower Dam in Lao PDR." *Journal of Contemporary Asia*, vol. 48, no. 5, 2018, pp. 808–34.

Brugère, Fabienne, and Guillaume Le Blanc. *La Fin de l'hospitalité. L'Europe, terre d'asile?* Flammarion, 2017.

Buell, Lawrence. *The Environmental Imagination: Thoreau, Nature Writing, and the Formation of American Culture*. Harvard UP, 1995.

Carson, Rachel L. *The Sea Around Us*. Oxford UP, 1951.

Casarino, Cesare. *Modernity at Sea: Melville, Marx, Conrad in Crisis*. U of Minnesota P, 2002.

Chakrabarty, Dipesh. *The Climate of History in a Planetary Age*. U of Chicago P, 2021.

Clark, Nigel. "Politics of Strata." *Theory, Culture, & Society*, vol. 34, nos. 2–3, 2017, pp. 211–31.

De León, Jason. *The Land of Open Graves: Living and Dying on the Migrant Trail*. U of California P, 2015.

DeLoughrey, Elizabeth. "Ordinary Futures: Interspecies Worldings in the Anthropocene." *Global Ecologies and the Environmental Humanities: Postcolonial Approaches*, edited by Elizabeth DeLoughrey et al., Routledge, 2015, pp. 352–72.

Duncan, Ifor, and Stefanos Levidis. "Weaponizing a River." *e-flux*, Apr. 2020, www.e-flux.com/architecture/at-the-border/325751/weaponizing-a-river/.

Gamble, Christopher N., et al. "What is New Materialism?" *Angelaki*, vol. 24, no. 6, 2019, pp. 111–34.

Gilroy, Paul. "'Where Every Breeze Speaks of Courage and Liberty': Offshore Humanism and Marine Xenology, or, Racism and the Problem of Critique at Sea Level." *Antipode: A Radical Journal of Geography*, vol. 50, no. 1, 2017, pp. 3–22.

Grosz, Elizabeth. "Geopower." "Geopower: A Panel on Elizabeth Grosz's *Chaos, Territory, Art: Deleuze and the Flaming of the Earth*." By Kathryn

Yusoff et al. *Environment and Planning D: Society & Space*, vol. 30, no. 6, 2012, pp. 971–88.

Grosz, Elizabeth, et al. "An Interview with Elizabeth Grosz: Geopower, Inhumanism and the Biopolitical." *Theory, Culture, & Society*, vol. 34, nos. 2–3, 2017, pp. 129–46.

Gunkel, Henriette. "Alien Time: Being in Vertigo." *Visual Cultures as Time Travel*, edited by Henriette Gunkel and Ayesha Hameed, Sternberg Press, 2021, pp. 59–80.

Hameed, Ayesha. "Sea Changes and Other Futurisms." *Visual Cultures as Time Travel*, edited by Henriette Gunkel and Ayesha Hameed, Sternberg Press, 2021, pp. 25–55.

Haraway, Donna. *Staying with the Trouble: Making Kin in the Chthulucene*. Duke UP, 2016.

Heller, Charles, et al. *Report on the Left-to-Die Boat*. Forensic Architecture, 2012, www.forensic-architecture.org/wp-content/uploads/2014/05/FO-report.pdf.

Helmreich, Stefan. "Nature/Culture/Seawater." *American Anthropologist*, vol. 113, 2011, pp. 132–44.

Ingersoll, Karin Amimoto. *Waves of Knowing: A Seascape Epistemology*. Duke UP, 2016.

Iovino, Serenella, and Pascuale Verdicchio. "Naming the Unknown, Witnessing the Unseen: Mediterranean Ecocriticism and Modes of Representing Migrant Others." *Ecozon@*, vol. 11, no. 2, 2020, pp. 82–91.

Klein, Naomi. "Let Them Drown: The Violence of Othering in a Warming World." *London Review of Books*, vol. 38, no. 11, 2 June 2016, pp. 11–14.

Mbembe, Achille. *Necropolitics*. Duke UP, 2019.

Mentz, Steve. *Shipwreck Modernity: Ecologies of Globalization, 1550–1719*. Minnesota UP, 2015.

Nair, Supriya. "Mo[u]rning in the Mediterranean: Liquid Mortuaries and the Arts of Re-Membering." *Water Logics*, edited by yasser elhariry and Edwige Tamalet Talbayev, forthcoming.

Neimanis, Astrida. "Hydrofeminism: Or, On Becoming a Body of Water." *Undutiful Daughters: New Directions in Feminist Thought and Practice*, edited by Henriette Gunkel et al., Palgrave, 2012, pp. 85–100.

Nixon, Rob. *Slow Violence and the Environmentalism of the Poor*. Harvard UP, 2013.

Oppermann, Serpil. "Introducing Migrant Ecologies in an (Un)Bordered World." *ISLE*, vol. 24, no. 2, 2017, pp. 1–14.

Papadopoulos, Dimitris. "Politics of Matter: Justice and Organisation in Technoscience." *Social Epistemology*, vol. 18, no. 1, 2014, pp. 70–85.

Perera, Suvendrini. "A Pacific Zone? (In) Security, Sovereignty, and Stories of the Pacific Borderscape." *Borderscapes: Hidden Geographies and Politics at Territory's Edge*, edited by Prem Kumar Rajaram and Carl Grundy-Warr, U of Minnesota P, 2007.

Peters, Kimberley, and Philip Steinberg. "The Ocean in Excess: Toward a More-than-Wet Ontology." *Dialogues in Human Geography*, vol. 9, no. 3, 2019, pp. 293–307.

Povinelli, Elizabeth A. *Geontologies: A Requiem to Late Liberalism*. Duke UP, 2016.

Povinelli, Elizabeth A., et al. "An Interview with Elizabeth Povinelli: Geontopower, Biopolitics, and the Anthropocene." *Theory, Culture, & Society*, vol. 34, nos. 2–3, 2017, pp. 169–85.

Pugliese, Joseph. "Bodies of Water." *Heat*, vol. 10, 2006, pp. 13–20.

Sharpe, Christina. *In the Wake: On Blackness and Being*. Duke UP, 2016.

Shubin, Neil. *Your Inner Fish: A Journey into the 3.5 Billion-Year History of the Human Body*. Vintage, 2008.

Star, Susan Leigh, and Geoffrey C. Bowker. "Enacting Silence: Residual Categories as a Challenge for Ethics, Information Systems, and Communication." *Ethics and Communication Technology*, vol. 9, 2007, pp. 273–80.

Steinberg, Philip. "Of Other Seas: Metaphors and Materialities in Maritime Regions." *Atlantic Studies*, vol. 10, 2013, pp. 156–69.

Steinberg, Philip, and Kimberley Peters. "Wet Ontologies, Fluid Spaces: Giving Depth to Volume through Oceanic Thinking." *Environment and Planning D: Society and Space*, vol. 33, 2015, pp. 247–64.

Swyngedouw, Erik. *Social Power and the Urbanization of Water: Flows of Power*. Oxford UP, 2004.

Talbayev, Edwige Tamalet. "The Residual Migrant: Water Necropolitics and Borderization." *Thanatic Ethics*. Spec. issue of *Interventions: A Journal of Postcolonial Studies*, forthcoming.

Talbayev, Edwige Tamalet. "Seawater." *Contemporary French and Francophone Studies*, vol. 25, no. 2, 2021, pp. 207–17.

Van Dooren, Thom. "Keeping Faith with Death: Mourning and De-Extinction." 2 Nov. 2013, www.thomvandooren.org/2013/11/02/keeping-faith-with-death-mourning-and-de-extinction/.

Yusoff, Kathryn. "The Anthropocene and Geographies of Geopower." *Handbook on the Geographies of Power*, edited by Mat Coleman and John A. Agnew, Edward Elgar, 2018, pp. 203–16.

Yusoff, Kathryn. "Geologic Life: Prehistory, Climate, Futures, *or do Fossils Dream of Geologic Life*." eprints.lancs.ac.uk/id/eprint/73620/1/GeologicLife_April2012_yusoff.pdf.

Yusoff, Kathryn. "Geophysics After Life: On the Way to a Political Geology of the Anthropocene." *Post-Anthropozän*. Spec. issue of *Springerin*, vol. 3, 2020, www.springerin.at/en/2020/3/geophysik-nach-dem-leben/.

Zalasiewicz, Jan, et al. "Are We Now Living in the Anthropocene?" *GSA Today*, vol. 18, 2008, pp. 4–8.

Edwige Tamalet Talbayev

In his meditation on the ineluctable relationality between life and water, Dorian Sagan writes: "But life does not only use water in its self-organization. Instead, life straddles the line between liquid and solid" (24). In its topological enfolding of liquid and solid, life mobilises water in the constitution of its multiplicity of entities. The "autopoiesis" of life forms is foundationally predicated on the animating life force of water (Varela et al. 187). Life "itself," as what both philosophically and scientifically continues to elude watertight categorisation, is, as such, always already intercorporeal – an intextuation of water and flesh bound by permeable and breathing membranes, an autopoietic morphology that is always already bound in an aqueous topology. "In the biosphere," Sagan underscores, "water cannot be separated from life, and life cannot be separated from water. It is difficult to determine where the influence of water ends, and the influence of heterogeneous living matter begins" (146).

In this essay, I examine the relationality between life and water in the context of its intercorporeal manifestations. Drawing on key aspects of Merleau-Pontian phenomenology, my concern is to reflect on water's enfleshment of life and its complex ecologies of intercorporeity. These Merleau-Pontian key aspects, I note, are in close dialogue with a number of Indigenous cosmo-epistemologies that envisage the world as constituted by profound ecologies of relationality. More-than-human entities such as water are, across a number of Indigenous cosmo-epistemologies, living beings that are co-constitutive of the world: "Water," writes Nick Estes, a citizen of the Lower Brule Sioux Tribe, "is animated and has agency" (9). The

Intercorporeity of Animated Water: Contesting Anthropocentric Settler Sovereignty

Joseph Pugliese

loci of my analysis are the Sonoran Desert and the lands of the Tohono O'odham people, all situated within the ongoing violent relations of power unleashed by the forces of settler colonialism, including the partitioning of Indigenous nations by the Mexico–US border, the ecological devastation left in the wake of the construction of the Trump border wall and the increasingly fraught situation of undocumented migrants attempting to cross the US border.

Situated within a desert context within which water is at its scarcest, I trace the contours of animated water in terms of its *relational relation* to life: no tautology here, rather a marking of the a priori nature of water in constituting the very conditions of possibility of relationality for all life: in the words of the Oceti Sakowin, "Mni Wiconi – 'water is life'" (Estes 15). The enfleshed bodies of water that I discuss disclose the cycles of life and death that turn on the presence and absence, on the rhythm and arrythmia, of water. These cycles are increasingly ensnared in what I term *aqua-political* regimes of governmentality that, in settler colonial contexts, unleash lethal effects that kill both bodies of water and the entities that depend on them for life (Pugliese, *Biopolitics* 86–87). In the latter part of the essay, I discuss how both the Tohono O'odham people, as Water Protectors, and more-than-human entities, such as the San Pedro River, are actively contesting the violence of anthropocentric settler sovereignty. I write this essay from the position of a diasporic settler who, from the Australian settler colonial context, is attempting to call to account the transnational operations of settler eco-genocide.

intercorporeity of water as "flesh of the world"

Articulating, as an Indigenous Water Protector, both the power and animating force of water, Wabinoquay Otsoquaykwhan, Anishinaabe Nation, explains that "Water isn't just for drinking or washing. Water has spirit. Water is alive. Water has memory. Water knows how you treat it, water knows you. You should get to know water too" (qtd in Indigenous@AmericanIndian8). In what follows, I attempt to enflesh Otsoquaykwhan's vision of animated water. The itinerary that inscribes this attempt is marked by a dialogic intertwining of both Indigenous and Merleau-Pontian philosophies; both philosophies are scored by resonant homologies, even as they emerge from significantly different loci.

In tracing these resonant homologies, however, I also want to underscore the critical differences that attend the two approaches. The Indigenous cosmo-epistemologies of water that I discuss articulate a holistic understanding of the position of humans in relation to the more-than-human world; they

encapsulate a profoundly ethical lived practice, even as they are constituted by complex philosophical articulations of the web of relations that imbue the practices of everyday life in the context of the more-than-human world. In a Native American context, Gregory Cajete notes, "cosmology" means the "lived story of place, kinship, and environmental knowledge" (95). He foregrounds, in other words, the inextricable connection between lived practice *and* epistemology. Zoe Todd emphasises that Indigenous cosmo-epistemologies are always already "embodied expressions of stories, laws, and songs bound within Indigenous-Place-Thought" (9). In contradistinction, the Western phenomenological tradition is largely characterised by the disavowal of its historical, racial and geopolitical situatedness; this denegatory move, as yet another instantiation of disclaimed whiteness, is crucial in enabling it to stake its claim to "universality." I draw attention to these critical differences precisely not to homogenise these two approaches that emerge from different histories and locations and, furthermore, in order not to reproduce the (colonial) dichotomy of (Indigenous) practice and (Western) theory. Having marked these critical differences, in the course of this essay I also want to examine how there are illuminating points of intersection between Indigenous and Merleau-Pontian phenomenologies that shed light on the complex enfleshment of the world through the vital life force of water.

In one of his meditations on the phenomenology of bodies in/of the world, Maurice Merleau-Ponty proceeds to trace the relations that bind these entities by bringing into focus the constitutive role of enfleshing. He delineates the flesh as an "'element,' in the sense of it was used to speak of water, air, earth, and fire, that is, in the sense of a general thing" (Merleau-Ponty 139). The flesh is bound within that originary series of elements that inscribe a cosmology of Being. It emerges, thus, as "a sort of incarnate principle that brings a style of being wherever there is a fragment of being. The flesh is in this sense an 'element' of Being" (139). My concern is to pursue the elemental nature of flesh as that which is inextricably bound with the element of water in the very constitution of life. Rather than view water as an amorphous elemental entity, this phenomenological schema compels the thinking through of water as always already a *body enfleshed*: its presence or appearance in the world is only ever intelligible precisely through the different bodies of water – drops, mists, rivers, oceans – that constitute its "flesh of the world" modalities (123). The binding of one with the other is enabled by a process of enfleshing through *intercorporeity*, as that which "founds transitivity from one body to another" (141, 143). Intercorporeity, then, at once marks the binding tissue between different bodies – what Merleau-Ponty terms "this thickness of flesh between us" – and the ethical charge of refusing to collapse or homogenise difference by being attentive to the very movement of transitivity that marks difference, while simultaneously binding it to intercorporeal relations: "the two leaves of my body and the leaves of the visible world" (131). These different but bound leaves are, through the transitivity of intercorporeity, always already "intercalated" (131).

Merleau-Ponty's phenomenology of intercorporeity possesses a strong affinity with a number of Indigenous cosmo-epistemologies that are predicated on the understanding that all the entities of the earth are ineluctably bound in ecologies of relationality.[1] Indigenous relational cosmo-epistemologies, with their distributed and heterogeneous sense of agentic entities, closely resonate, as Cajete contends, with "a number of the central premises of phenomenology (the philosophical study of phenomena)" and, in particular, Merleau-Ponty's call to "'return to things themselves' in order to make sense of the world" (Cajete 23). This point of intersection is also clearly evidenced in the resonance between Indigenous and Merleau-Pontian philosophies of embodiment and intercorporeality. In conceptualising our relation to the world, Merleau-Ponty posits the flesh as that which conjoins one to the other: "The presence of the world is precisely the presence of its flesh to my flesh" (127). This intercorporeal understanding of

the world meshes, as Robert Yazzie, Chief Justice of the Navajo Nation, notes, with "Native philosophy," which he describes as "the practice of an epistemology in which the mind embodies itself in a particular relationship with all other aspects of the world" (qtd in Cajete 64).

In accord with Indigenous philosophies, Merleau-Ponty's theorising of flesh disrupts the circumscriptions of the anthropocentric frame. Flesh emerges, for him, as both a general and specific modality of being in the world. It is a general modality as flesh signifies the condition of possibility of being in the world. It is a specific modality because flesh is always already situated in the particularity of its worldly locus. Yazzie's articulation of the embodied relationality of all aspects of the world works to articulate two interleaved ethico-philosophical levels: the intercorporeity of all the earth's entities and, critically, the ethical binding that this intercorporeal flesh of the world instantiates. As Winona LaDuke notes, across a corpus of Indigenous cosmo-epistemologies there is enunciated a compelling ethical obligation to water, rocks, trees, rivers, mountains and so on, which is based on a kincentric vision in which all entities are inscribed in an affective and ethical ecology of what she terms "all our relations" (2).

saguaros in a settler colonial context

In his theorisation of the biosphere and its multitude of living entities, Vladimir Vernadsky identifies the pivotal role that water plays in constituting life: "In the biosphere, life cannot be separated from water. It is difficult to determine where the influence of water ends, and the influence of heterogeneous living matter begins" (146). This topological blurring and enfolding of thresholds between water and living matter can be graphically marked, as discussed above, by the Merleau-Pontian concept of intercorporeity and its transitive movement of intercalation. In what follows, I want to unfold this ecology of "animated water" in the context of a desert landscape, the Sonoran Desert, and the saguaro cactus (Estes 9). The Sonoran Desert is home to the Tohono O'odham people. They have endured centuries of settler colonial incursions on their lands, with consequent devastating effects, including genocidal acts of massacre, displacement and expropriation that have been combined with settler practices of ecocide which have repeatedly destroyed the fragile ecologies of the Sonoran Desert (Erickson 69–75, 141–42).

As I discuss below, the limits of transposing and deploying a purely phenomenological approach to water become clearly evident in the context of the biopolitical violence that inscribes the daily operations of the settler colonial state in the Sonoran Desert. Even as a phenomenological understanding of water can be seen to work in consonance with relevant Indigenous cosmo-epistemologies, it fails to name, identify and address settler bio- and aquapolitical regimes of violence. In the course of this essay, thus, I work to interlace a phenomenological understanding of water with Indigenous theories of settler colonial eco-genocide. In his "Testimony: Ecocide and Genocide" (246–55), Jewell Praying Wolf James ("Se-Sealth") unpacks the intertwined settler operations of eco-genocide as what characterise the modus operandi of the settler state on Indigenous lands.

The state of Arizona, which incorporates a large portion of the Sonoran Desert and the Tohono O'odham Nation, is a site harrowed by layered histories of colonial violence that Edward Spicer terms "cycles of conquest" and that commence with the penetration of the region in the sixteenth century by Spanish colonists and missionaries, encompasses the Mexican–American War (1847–48) and culminates in the US annexation of the territory through the Gadsen Purchase (ratified in 1854) – which effectively divided the Tohono O'odham Nation by the creation of the Mexico–US border (4–8). Underscoring this history is a series of military and paramilitary campaigns against the Tohono O'odham people of the Sonoran Desert, with the ultimate

(yet unsuccessful aim) of "eliminating" and "replacing" them, in keeping with the operational structure of settler colonialism (Wolfe 387). I mark this history of settler violence as, in the latter section of this essay, I unfold its contemporary manifestation in the specific context of the Tohono O'odham Nation and the ecocide of natural springs and saguaros through the building of the Trump Mexico–US border wall.

ṣu:dagī 'o wuḍ doakag – "water is life": inter/intracorporeity of animated water

One of the unique features of saguaros is their capacity to swell or shrink according to the availability of water. In times of abundant rains, the saguaro will grow and expand into a virtual "barrel [...] [a] reservoir enriched with heavy water":

> This ability to expand with water uptake is thanks to the peculiar structure of the stems (trunks). In addition to their cuticle covering, the ribs in the circular column are joined by intervening tissues that with water uptake are forced apart, superficially similar to the expansion of an accordion. (Yetman et al. 28)

The saguaro effectively embodies the intercorporeal ecologies of the cyclical movement of water. In times of abundance, the saguaro enfleshes itself with water; the plant emerges as a body engorged in a time of liquid plenty: "Their highly porous tissues can have a relative water content that exceeds 90 percent by mass, thereby allowing saguaros to store massive amounts of water in their stems" (81). In times of aqueous abundance, the saguaro becomes an enfleshed column of water. A double movement of ascendancy and expansion enables the phenomenon of a columnar reservoir of water in the desert. This process of aqueous enrichment also leads to a chromatic transformation, as the colour of the saguaro "gradually changes from a yellow green to a fresher shade of lime green" (70).

Conversely, with the onset of drought, the saguaro initiates a process of diminution. The dearth of water "forces the saguaro to use up its water reserves stored in the pulpy material of its trunk and arms" (Alcock 23). The saguaro consequently begins a process of withdrawing unto itself, enclosing the accordionlike pleats of its waxy skin and thereby shrinking its size. In times of severe drought, the saguaro sets in motion an even more drastic process of self-contraction: as the body of water contained in its flesh decreases, it literally reduces its body mass by sloughing off "entire arms or major portions of them" (23). In a decisive manner, then, the saguaro exemplifies the constitutive power of water in determining a living entity's growth, decay, life and eventual death. Situated in the desert landscape, the saguaro emerges as a vegetal anatomy of water that embodies cycles of growth, expansion, contraction and even self-amputation.

In the context of this saguaro ecology, water becomes, once cast in Merleau-Pontian terms, "the tissue that lines them," enabling the production of the fleshly morphology that contains and defines the saguaro; water is what "nourishes them, and which for its part is not a thing, but a possibility, a latency, and a flesh of things" (132–33). By casting the element of water in Merleau-Pontian terms, water breaches the anthropocentric circumscriptions that reduces it to a "thing," a mere transparent and amorphous medium. Water becomes charged, precisely as animated element, with latent possibilities that are materially realised through the intercorporeal embodiment of the flesh of the world – in all of its manifold manifestations. Here the "thickness of flesh" between saguaro and water "is their means of communication" while, simultaneously, marking the topological fold that blurs the boundaries of individual entities: "Where are we to put the limit," Merleau-Ponty asks, "between the body and the world, since the world is flesh" (135, 138). Merleau-Ponty's flesh of the world is in significant resonance with both James Lovelock's concept of "Gaia" and Lynn Margulis' "symbiotic planet," whereby "the Earth, in the biological

sense, has a body sustained by its own complex physiological processes" that operate in terms of "a huge set of interconnected ecosystems, the Earth as Gaian regulatory physiology transcends all individual organisms" and "it displays the attributes of a living body composed of the aggregate of Earth's incessantly interactive life" (Margulis 115, 120, 123; Lovelock).

Within this interconnected physiological schema, it is water that animates and creates the very possibility of flesh as such. Water overturns the categorical borders between the body and the world precisely because it constitutes the very conditions of possibility of the flesh of the world. Here water emerges as a dispositional element that conditions the material constitution of bodies as such. Its morphology, as body of water, is always predisposed to assuming the corporeal contours of the body of the other: a plant, the ocean, a cloud formation and so on. Water is at once a dispositional-conditioning element *and* a transitional element that is always *becoming*: it is effectively always in a state of transitional becoming through movements of ingestion, absorption, enfleshing, respiration, transpiration and evaporation.

In his "The Natural History of Waters," Vernadsky emphasises the pivotal role of water for life on earth:

> Water has a special place in the history of our planet. There is no natural body that could be compared with water in its influence on the course of most geologic processes. There is no terrestrial material – mineral, rock, or living body – that does not include it. All terrestrial bodies are penetrated and enclosed by water owing to its intrinsic partial forces, vaporous state, and ubiquity in the upper part of the planet. (Qtd in Chudaev et al. 163)

For Vernadsky, "The biosphere, the zone of life, is a water envelope" (qtd in Chudaev et al. 165). Within this zone of life, which is both enabled and sustained by an aqueous envelope, the flesh of the world emerges as "not contingency, chaos, but a texture that returns to itself and conforms to itself" (Merleau-Ponty 147).

For the Tohono O'odham people of the Sonoran Desert, everything is predicated on presence of "ṣu_:_d_a_g_ī" (water): from its life-giving anticipation, as articulated in their refrain "when the rain comes," to their intimate knowledge of the precious bodies of water that inscribe the topography of the desert (Villegas 9; Devereaux 19). For the Tohono O'odham people, "*Ṣu:dagī 'O Wuḍ Doakag* means 'Water is Life'" (Borderlands Restoration Network). One of the key bodies of water in the lands of the Tohono O'odham are the *tinajas* or natural basins formed by the sculpting force of falling water on the stone surfaces of the desertscape:

> The water fills the basin, overflows, then splashes down the slope to the next drop to create another basin. After the rains cease, these catch basins, or *tinajas*, are full of water, and they serve as natural reservoirs for the animals and some plants of the desert. (Erickson 4)

These catch basins exemplify what I would term the *geocorpormorphology* of animated water: water carves a solid geological body of stone into a concave receptacle that simultaneously captures and holds a body of water; here two bodies, as indissociable incarnations of the flesh of the world, are one. Viewed in Merleau-Pontian terms, these geocorpomorphological catch basins evidence the material figuration of *intracorporeity* and the attendant fluid "transitivity from one body to another" (147, 143). Through its erosive power, water enfleshes stone into a concave cavity – a *tinajas* – which, in turn, becomes a liquid body of water. Water, in this instance, emerges as "the formative medium of the object and the subject" (147).

Through the movement of a chiasmic crossing, the intercorporeal is transmuted into the *intracorporeal*. The intracorporeality of this transitive movement is what Merleau-Ponty terms "the double inscription inside outside" that effectively articulates a chiasmic relation which overturns the very categorical boundaries of subject and object. In other words, the *tinajas* body of water is enfleshed simultaneously as a geocorpomorphology of stone. "The flesh of the world," Merleau-Ponty underlines "is [...] absolutely not an ob-ject" (250). The intracorporeal chiasm embodied by the *tinajas*-catch basins instantiates the "doubling up" of water-stone "into inside and outside" (254). The geocorpomorphology of the *tinajas* is illuminated by this Merleau-Pontian insight: "the hold is held, it is *inscribed* and inscribed in the same being that it takes hold of" (266). The hold, water, is held by the geomorphology of the stone that only came into being via the agency of what is now held, water, the liquid element that carved the geological cavity and that is now inscribed in the same being of stone that it takes hold of.

Through the chiasm of intracorporeity, topological boundaries between one and other become so enfolded as to become blurred: no water, no *tinajas*; no *tinajas*, no water reservoirs. This movement of double inscription, and its chiasmic signature of intracorporeity, traces the liquid-stone contours of the hold that is held. As "the concrete emblem of a general manner of being" (Merleau-Ponty 147), the *tinajas*-catch basin reservoirs enable multiple modalities of life that are dependent on these precious bodies of water in the desert. Here the liquid flesh of the world is "shared by the world" (250), simultaneously as it becomes coextensive with the very flesh of the entities which imbibe its animating qualities. What is evidenced within these liquid-stone configurations is a complication of the concepts of both agency and identity through the binding nexus of relationality. Édouard Glissant captures the animating spirit of this relational nexus: "When we ask the question of what is brought into play by Relation, we arrive at that-there that cannot be split up into original elements" (160). Water-*tinajas*-catch basins, in other words, embody the impossibility of splitting up this animated relational nexus: the held-hold is indissociably the that-there.

indigenous contestations of settler colonial aquapolitics

Following his election as US President in 2020, Joe Biden ordered a pause in the construction of the Trump border wall that straddles the Mexico–US border. The scale of destruction left by the construction of the border wall is massive: mountains have been blasted, Native American sacred sites and burial grounds have been destroyed, groves of saguaros have been decimated and precious springs of desert water, such as the Quitobaquito Springs, have been polluted and drained in the production of concrete for the wall (Pugliese, "More-Than-Human Lifeworlds"). Writing in the context of the battle by Indigenous Water Protectors to block the construction of the Dakota Access Pipeline and the ensuing ecocidal destruction of Standing Rock Sioux lands, Dina Gilio-Whitaker writes:

> colonization was not just a process of invasion and eventual domination of Indigenous populations by European settlers but also that the eliminatory impulse and structure it created in actuality began as environmental injustice. Seen in this light, settler colonialism is itself for Indigenous peoples a structure of environmental injustice. (12; see also Powys Whyte 171)

Gilio-Whitaker here brings into focus the intersectional relations that bind the key categories of settler colonialism, eco-genocidal practices and the attendant destruction of ethical responsibilities to more-than-human entities and their lifeworlds.

In centring her analysis of settler colonialism as structurally bound to the production of environmental injustice and in contextualising this in the Sioux Standing Rock Water Protectors' battle to stop the building of the oil pipeline, Gilio-Whitaker writes:

> As the #NoDAPL movement made clear through the slogan "Water is life," Native resistance is inextricably bound to worldviews that center not only the obvious life-sustaining forces of the natural world but also the respect accorded to the natural world in relationships of reciprocity based on accountability toward those life forms. (13)

Édouard Glissant succinctly articulates the generosity of spirit that imbues these instantiations of relational reciprocity – in which "one gives-on-and-with rather than grasps" (144). Encapsulated in this relational view of all life forms is an anti-capitalist ethics that refuses the unilateral violence of capitalist extraction, commodification and expansion without limits.

As a settler colonial state such as the United States is founded on the double logic of Indigenous land expropriation and the usurpation of Indigenous sovereignty, its foundational illegitimacy is effectively occluded through acts of border-making, control and governance: no control over one's borders, no state sovereignty (Bui et al.). Ned Norris, Tribal Chairman of the Tohono O'odham Nation, speaks to the fact of unceded Indigenous sovereignty in defiance of the imposition of settler borders and apparatuses of colonial governance: "even though the area is controlled by the U.S. government, 'we have inhabited this area since time immemorial [...] It's our duty to do what is necessary to protect that'" (BBC News). Settler border-making, as a material form of power-in-spacing, instantiates and continues to re-assert the settler state's (illegitimate) sovereignty. In the context of the Indigenous nations located on and across the Mexico–US border, the violence of this settler border-making finds one of its most graphic instantiations in the building of the Trump wall.

Seeking to concretise one of his key election promises, President Trump, in January 2017, signed Executive Order 13767 which licensed the funding and construction of a wall that would stretch along the length of the Mexico–US border. In the process, through its invocation of the REAL ID Act (2005), the Department of Homeland Security overrode twenty-eight laws, including: "the National Environment Policy Act, the Endangered Species Act, the Clean Water Act, and the Archaeological Resources Protection Act, the Safe Drinking

Water Act, and the Native American Graves Protection and Repatriation Act" (Whitman). The overriding of this constellation of laws demonstrates the manner in which settler law, and the very apparatus of its juridico-criminal-justice complex, is actually constitutive of the systemic violence that characterises its biopolitical operationality in the context of the settler state. Regardless of its ostensible claims, settler law cannot "protect" or deliver "justice" to Indigenous peoples precisely because it is predicated, in its moment of violent colonial foundation, on the eradication of Indigenous peoples, their livelihoods, ecologies and laws (Watson 253–69). Drawing attention to the violent double logic of colonial law, Irene Watson explains how, in settler contexts, "unlawfulness continues in a space declared lawful" (258).

In the process of the building of the border wall, construction crews have blasted the Indigenous sacred site of Monument Hill, which includes O'odham burial sites. Juan Mancias, Tribal Chairman of the Carrizo Comecrudo Tribe, articulates the historical and contemporary intertwining of the settler logic of Indigenous elimination, consequent land expropriation and the assertion of settler sovereignty through the violent imposition of colonial borders: "The border with Mexico divided our people and now, this new wall shows no regard for our ancestors, beliefs or culture which are tied to these lands. They are trying to erase us, and that's genocide" (Lakhani). In keeping with Indigenous cosmopolitics that challenge anthropocentric understandings of violence, I include more-than-human entities under the rubric of genocidal violence. In his address of settler colonial practices of eco-genocide, Nick Estes foregrounds how "Indigenous elimination, as a practice and formal policy, continues today, entailing wholesale destruction of non-human relations. Today's state violence and surveillance against Water Protectors is a continuation of the Indian Wars of the nineteenth century" (90).

Nellie Jo David, an O'odham activist contesting the destruction of her lands in the Organ Pipe Cactus National Monument, Arizona,

speaks to the violent felling and uprooting of the saguaros in the wake of the wall's construction: "the saguaros are not just sacred, they are people unto themselves [...] In O'odham, the word for saguaro is Ha:sañ. Everywhere, in the space where David spoke, where butchered Ha:sañ remains" (Devereaux). Articulated in this O'odham instantiation of an expansive ethics of considerability is an overturning of the Euro-anthropocentric hierarchisation and partitioning of life along an anthropo-supremacist vertical axis, with the attendant non-criminal violence toward more-than-human entities that this at once licenses and enables. Reflecting on the ethical ramifications of such an Indigenous ethico-ecology, Val Plumwood writes:

> The American Indian view that considerability goes "all the way down" requires a response considerably more sophisticated than those we have seen in the West, which consists in drawing lines of moral considerability in order to create an out-group, or in constructing hierarchies of considerability creating de facto out-groups in particular cases. (60–61)

Bearing witness to the ecological destruction unleashed by the construction of the Trump border wall, Laiken Jordahl writes: "I watch saguaro and organ pipe cactus being plowed over by Caterpillar earth-movers, sawed into chunks of firewood and tossed into trash heaps." Instantiated here are acts of ploughing, sawing and gashing these living bodies of water. As latent reservoirs of water – for both humans and other-than-human animals – their destruction ruptures relational networks that bind the differential entities that constitute the flesh of the world as bound through the element of animating water; specifically, these violent acts work to sever water's *relational relation* to life – as the element that constitutes the very conditions of possibility of relationality for all life. The border wall is amplifying its eco-genocidal effects by thwarting the O'odham and Hia C-ed peoples from exercising their care of country through, for example, Water Protector practices that contest the destruction of rivers and aquifers in the process of the building of the wall (Devereaux). The construction of the Trump border wall has entailed the drying up of desert springs and aquifers "as a result of tens or hundreds of gallons of groundwater being pumped" to mix the concrete essential for stabilising the wall's bollards, thereby placing at risk a number of rare desert fish species (Lakhani).

This settler destruction of Tohono O'odham waters exemplifies the operations of *aquapolitics*, which is a specific modality of biopolitics that targets the control of water within regimes of biopolitical governance. For the Tohono O'odham people, the destructive effects of settler aquapolitics are inscribed across the arc of US settler history in the context of their lands (Erickson 77, 163–64). Settler aquapolitics has seen the expropriation of bodies of water – wells, springs, rivers and aquifers – by the settler state in order to ensure the flourishing of its non-Indigenous citizens and the resultant letting die of the very ecologies crucial to the survival of Tohono O'odham people and their more-than-human relations. Nick Estes places the role of settler aquapolitics in acute perspective: "Water is settler colonialism's lifeblood – blood that has to be continually excised from Indigenous peoples" (149). Here the biopolitical effects of settler aquapolitics are lucidly exposed: the flourishing of the corpus of the settler state is secured through the ongoing expropriation of animated water from Indigenous peoples and their more-than-human relations – and their attendant casting as lesser forms of life that can be left to wither and die. Water, in this settler context, is instrumentalised as one more "resource" to be exploited and exhausted through the operations of racialised-extractive capitalism.

settler colonial aquapolitics on the border

In the context of the Sonoran Desert, yet another lethal modality of settler colonial aquapolitics is unfolding across the Mexico–US borderlands. As undocumented people from the Global South attempt to make border crossings,

precisely because of the thwarting presence of the border wall and Border Patrol agents, they are often compelled to take perilous routes across what has been termed the "trail of death" to avoid detection (No More Deaths 55). Deploying the strategy "described as Prevention Through Deterrence," Border Patrol officials have weaponised the Sonoran Desert and the borderlands so that undocumented migrants are compelled to take the most dangerous routes in their attempts to cross the border (Boyce et al. 24, 29). The Border Patrol has, in effect, "created a crucible of death and disappearance in the Arizona–Sonora borderlands" (32).

Compelled to traverse rugged and isolated nature reserves and national parks, undocumented migrants are, in turn, framed by the border agents of the US settler state as "injuring nature." As Juanita Sundberg and Bonnie Kasserman demonstrate, the settler state deploys a series of "corporeal metaphors" that "allow for threats to nature in protected areas to be understood as threats to the nation," as the undocumented migrants are indicted for "scarring" and "wounding" the natural landscape in the course of their travels (734). Exemplifying the way corporeal terms are, because of their semiotic polysemousness, open to oppositional codings and different discursive mobilisation, the flesh of the world can here be seen to be co-opted by the settler state and consequently mobilised as a corpus that is violated and polluted by the "unnatural" and "alien" figure of the undocumented migrant. "The utilization of the body as a metaphor for nature," Sundberg and Kasserman note (in which "nature is cast as the embodiment of the 'American' nation and its national heritage"), "invites questions about whose body is made vulnerable to threat in these instances" (734, 729).

In the wake of the thousands of undocumented people who have died attempting to cross the Mexico–US borderlands, two humanitarian groups – No More Deaths and Samaritans – have left jugs of water across numerous desert trails in the hope of saving the lives of those who are at risk of dying of thirst in the course of their journeys towards asylum. Both humanitarian groups have documented how Border Patrol agents "routinely vandalise containers of water and other supplies left in the Arizona desert for migrants, condemning people to die of thirst in baking temperatures" (Carroll; No More Deaths 37). These acts of vandalism are, moreover, often attended by race-hate speech acts or the deceitful inscription of "words like 'venemo' (poison) [...] onto the bottles to dissuade its use by desperate border crossers" (Boyce et al. 25).

Transposing Merleau-Ponty's concepts of *intercorporeity* and the *flesh of the world* to the aquapolitical settler weaponisation of the Sonoran Desert, what emerges is a necropolitical instrumentalisation of both water and desert. The Border Patrol agents' slashing of the water jugs left by humanitarian groups for undocumented migrants traversing the desert evidences the violation of the ethos of intercorporeity: through the gashing of the bodies of water contained in the jugs, the transitive movement of animating water from one body to another is ruptured. The violent dispersion of the water traces the contours of a wound in the flesh of the world that cuts in two simultaneous directions: it evidences the sovereign biopolitical power of the settler state to determine who may live or be left to die on the very knife-edge of the border, simultaneously as it enacts the tearing asunder of the ethical link that binds different living entities in relational networks of intercorporeity. Furthermore, the Border Patrol agents' recoding of animating water as "poison" (*venemo*) evidences a biopolitical regime of violent inversion: the most life-giving of properties is resignified in terms of a deadly poison. Instantiated here is an aporia predicated on the nonnegotiable logic of the *pharmakon* (Derrida 98): water as both life saver and poison. Once they have been denied access to water because of the slashed jugs or because they have been precluded from drinking water from jugs duplicitously labelled as "poison," undocumented migrants are set on a necropolitical course where, in the chilling words of an Immigration and Naturalization Service official, "geography would do the rest" (qtd in Sundberg 323).

Operative in these fraught borderlands, then, is what Juanita Sundberg terms a "collective," as an "assemblage of heterogenous actors" (330) – that includes the border wall, inhospitable terrain, border agents and gashed water jugs. Critically, Sundberg underscores that these sorts of assemblages are not "fixed entit[ies] in time and place": rather, they operate as collectives of different actors that are "compelled into action at specific moments" (330). Their dispositions and agencies are, in other words, spatio-temporally contingent and open to different agentic mobilisations and effects: for example, water jugs can differentially and contingently be mobilised as either bodies of potable water or "poison."

mnemonics of animated water: more-than-human contestations of anthropocentric settler sovereignty

In their acts of resistance against the building of the Dakota Access oil pipeline at Standing Rock, which "would spell death for the Oceti Sakowin and its nonhuman relations," the "rallying cry Mni Wiconi – 'water is life'" became "an affirmation that water is alive" (Estes 15). That water is alive and that, in the words of Wabinoquay Otsoquaykwhan, "Water has memory" (qtd in Indigenous@AmericanIndian8), is evidenced in the context of the Mexico–US borderlands, the rivers that straddle nation-state borders and the Trump border wall. The Trump wall, as a delegate of the US settler state situated on the topological fault line of the border, does not stand as a unilateral more-than-human agent that is impervious to other-than-human contestations.

For example, the section of the wall that straddles the San Pedro River has already been battered by flash floods that have clogged and damaged sections of the wall with accumulated debris, downing a portion of the wall (Whitman). The San Pedro River, in such instances, embodies and enacts its own histories inscribed with memories of place and agentic returns to its original courses.

Reflecting on the layered histories of the Mississippi River, Toni Morrison writes:

> You know, they straightened out the Mississippi River in places, to make room for houses and livable acreage. Occasionally the river floods these places. "Floods" is the word they use, but in fact it is not flooding; it is remembering. Remembering where it used to be. All water has a perfect memory and is forever trying to get back to where it was. (99)

Morrison here materialises the mnemonics of the river and its contestation and undermining of different modalities of anthropocentric governance. Remembering where it used to be, the San Pedro River, through recursive returns, retraces the sedimented contours of its locus in the Sonoran Desert. The river, in other words, emerges as an inscriptive entity that renders space as intelligible in terms of a historically configured place. It emerges as a living body of water that has spatialised memory, inscriptive powers and a layered history of place that resonates according to the fluid acoustics generated by its dialogue with the geomorphology of its riverine courses. One can thus speak of the river's dynamic sonority as it interacts with the varied textures of the topographies it travels through and shapes.

The San Pedro, Colorado and Rio Grande rivers all straddle the Mexico–US border and, as bodies of animated water charged with a liquid mnemonics of place, they regularly shift across their floodplains, demolishing and reconstructing their riverine footprints and, in the process, playing havoc with nation-state borders and national jurisdictions. In response to this river dynamics, Mexican and US officials formed the International Border and Water Commission (IBWC): "Over the subsequent 75 years, the IBWC adjudicated more than 247 instances when shifting channels of rivers forced the border to be redrawn – only to redraw the border when a river moved again" (Grant). Anterior to aquapolitical regimes of settler governmentality, these bodies of water override the settler state's jurisdictional apparatuses and its anthropocentric borders, even as they also demolish its array of other-than-human delegates such as the Trump border wall. The US settler state's aspiration toward univocal and arrogative exercises of sovereign anthropocentric power, and its labour to concretise its sovereignty through the construction of a unilinear border wall, is contested and overridden by these riverine bodies of water inscribed by their own animated histories and mnemonic returns that, in this borderlands context, emerge as heterogeneous to the settler state, refractory to its borders, heteronomous to its laws and undermining of its anthropocentric sovereignty.

These riverine bodies of water attest to a geomorphic agency constituted by fluvial flux, mnemonic sedimentations, erosive demolitions and intercorporeal reconfigurations predicated on transitive exchanges between water and various geological entities – rocks, sand and soil. The intercorporeal intermixing of water and geology works to constitute the geocorpomorphology of what will be anthropically named the "San Pedro River" or "Rio Grande River" – even as these rivers will continue to defy anthropocentric statist acts of bordering and circumscription. What I would term, in this context, the insurgent aquapolitical agency of water is lucidly described by Cecilia Chen: "The movements, transformations, and relations of water seasonally overflow neat categorizations and normative discourses. As a responsive and promiscuous solvent [...] [water] materially communicates where it has been, what has occurred elsewhere, and even what is possible" (277).

In the course of this essay, I have traced the contours of various bodies of water – including saguaros, *tinajas*-catch basins, water jugs and rivers – that exemplify the dynamic and transitive movement of both intercorporeity and intracorporeity. Situated across the Sonoran Desert, the Tohono O'odham Nation, the US settler state and the Mexico–US borderlands, I have tracked the complex relations of power that inscribe these bodies of water. They emerge at once as statist delegates *and* as contestatory agents that challenge and overturn the anthropocentric intentionalities of the settler state. In the context of a desertscape where water is at its scarcest, these bodies of water emerge as inscribed by both animating and mnemonic qualities. Incorporated through processes of ingestion and absorption, they animate the beings that are dependent on them, literally enfleshing the world through these processes. Inscribed by their own ecologies of distributed cognition and memory, these bodies of water simultaneously attest to water's agentic making and remaking of place through recursive returns and remembered spatial configurations.

disclosure statement

No potential conflict of interest was reported by the author.

note

1 I want to underscore that I do not envision Indigenous cosmo-epistemologies of relationality as somehow homogeneous and essentialised in terms of their address of the more-than-human and related ecological concerns, thereby constructing, by default, yet another iteration of the trope of the "noble savage" in harmony with the environment. Indigenous nations are, it goes without saying, inscribed by internal differences and contradictory positions on these matters, including positions that advocate such things as the mining of country; see, for example, Birch 2–16 and Vincent and Neale.

bibliography

Alcock, John. *When the Rains Come: A Naturalist's Year in the Sonoran Desert*. U of Arizona P, 2009.

BBC News. "Native Burial Sites Blown Up for U.S. Border Wall." *BBC News*, 10 Feb. 2020, www.bbc.com/news/world-us-canada-51449739.

Birch, Tony. "'On What Terms Can We Speak?' Refusal, Resurgence and Climate Justice." *Coolabah*, vols. 24–25, 2018, pp. 2–16.

Borderlands Restoration Network. "Ṣu:dagĭ 'O Wud Doakag Means 'Water is Life.'" N.d., www.borderlandsrestoration.org/water-is-life.html.

Boyce, Geoffrey Alan, et al. "Bodily Inertia and the Weaponization of the Sonoran Desert in U.S. Boundary Enforcement: A GIS Modelling of Migration Routes Through Arizona's Altar Valley." *Journal on Migration and Human Security*, vol. 7, no. 1, 2019, pp. 23–35.

Bui, M., et al. "Extraterritorial Killings: The Weaponisation of Bodies (Australia)." *Deathscapes: Mapping Race and Violence in Settler States*, 2018, www.deathscapes.org/case-studies/case-study-4-extraterritorial-killings-the-weaponisation-of-bodies/#parallaxcategory0.

Cajete, Gregory. *Native Science: Natural Laws of Interdependence*. Clear Light, 2000.

Carroll, Rory. "Humanitarian Groups Report Agents Routinely Destroy Supplies Left in Arizona Desert, Condemning People to Die of Thirst." *The Guardian*, 18 Jan. 2018, www.theguardian.com/us-news/2018/jan/17/us-border-patrol-sabotage-aid-migrants-mexico-arizona.

Chen, Cecilia. "Mapping Waters: Thinking with Watery Places." *Thinking with Water*, edited by Cecilia Chen et al., McGill-Queen's UP, 2013, pp. 274–98.

Chudaev, O., et al. "V.I. Vernadsky and Main Research Avenues in Modern Hydrogeochemistry." *Procedia Earth and Planetary Sciences*, vol. 7, 2013, pp. 163–66.

Derrida, Jacques. "Pharmakon." *Dissemination*, translated by Barbara Johnson, Chicago UP, 1981, pp. 95–116.

Devereaux, Ryan. "'We are Still Here': Native Activists in Arizona Resist Trump's Border Wall." *The Intercept*, 25 Nov. 2019, theintercept.com/2019/11/24/arizona-border-wall-native-activists/.

Erickson, Winston P. *Sharing the Desert: The Tohono O'odham in History*. U of Arizona P, 1994.

Estes, Nick. *Our History is the Future: Standing Rock Versus the Dakota Access Pipeline and the Long Tradition of Indigenous Resistance*. Verso, 2019.

Gilio-Whitaker, Dina. *As Long as the Grass Grows: The Indigenous Fight for Environmental Justice, from Colonization to Standing Rock*. Beacon Press, 2019.

Glissant, Edouard. *Poetics of Relation*. Translated by Betsy Wing, U of Michigan P, 2010.

Grant, Daniel. "With or Without a Wall, the Border Isn't Where You Think It Is." *Washington Post*, 28 Feb. 2021, www.washingtonpost.com/outlook/2021/02/28/with-or-without-wall-border-isnt-where-you-think-it-is/.

Indigenous@AmericanIndian8. "Water isn't just for drinking." *Twitter*, 3 Mar. 2019.

James, Jewell Praying Wolf ("Se-Sealth"). "Testimony: Ecocide and Genocide." *Ecocide of Native America: Environmental Destruction of Indian Lands and Peoples*, edited by Donald A. Grinde and Bruce E. Johansen, Clear Light, 1995, pp. 246–55.

Jordahl, Laiken. "Trump's Wall is Destroying the Environment Activists are Protecting." *On Spec*, 31 Jan. 2020, medium.com/onspec/trumps-wall-is-destroying-everything-we-worked-to-protect-65bc687518d1.

LaDuke, Winona. *All Our Relations: Native Struggles for Land and Life*. South End Press and Honor the Earth, 1999.

Lakhani, Nina. "Water-Guzzling Demands of Trump's Border Wall Threaten Fish Species." *The Guardian*, 29 Dec. 2019, www.theguardian.com/environment/2019/dec/29/trump-border-wall-water-fish-species-threatened.

Lovelock, James. *Gaia: The Practical Science of Planetary Medicine*. Oxford UP, 2000.

Margulis, Lynn. *Symbiotic Planet: A New Look at Evolution*. Science Masters, 1998.

Merleau-Ponty, Maurice. *The Visible and the Invisible*. Translated by Alphonso Lingis, Northwestern UP, 1968.

Morrison, T. "The Site of Memory." *Inventing the Truth: The Art and Craft of Memoir*, edited by W. Zinsser, Houghton Mifflin, 1995, pp. 83–102.

No More Deaths – La Coalición de Derechos Humanos. *Left to Die: Border Patrol, Search and Rescue, and the Crisis of Disappearance*, 17 Jan. 2018, www.thedisappearedreport.org/uploads/8/3/5/1/83515082/left_to_die_-_english.pdf.

Plumwood, Val. *The Eye of the Crocodile*. Australian National UP, 2012.

Powys Whyte, Kyle. "Indigenous Experience, Environmental Justice and Settler Colonialism." *Nature and Experience: Phenomenology and the Environment*, edited by Bryan E. Bannon, Rowman & Littlefield International, 2016, pp. 157–73.

Pugliese, Joseph. *Biopolitics of the More-Than-Human: Forensic Ecologies of Violence*. Duke UP, 2020.

Pugliese, Joseph. "More-Than-Human Lifeworlds, Settler Modalities of Geno-ecocide and Border Questions." *Journal of Global Indigeneity*, vol. 5, no. 2, 2021, pp. 1–34.

Sagan, Dorian. *Biospheres: Metamorphosis of Planet Earth*. CIP, 2021.

Spicer, Edward. *Cycles of Conquest: The Impact of Spain, Mexico, and the United States on the Indians of the Southwest, 1533–1960*. U of Arizona P, 1962.

Sundberg, Juanita. "Diabolic Caminos in the Desert and Cat Fights on the Rio: A Posthumanist Political Ecology of Boundary Enforcement in the United States–Mexico Borderlands." *Annals of the Association of American Geographers*, vol. 101, no. 2, 2001, pp. 318–36.

Sundberg, Juanita, and Bonnie Kasserman. "Cactus Carvings and Desert Defecations: Embodying Representations of Border Crossings in Protected Areas on the Mexico–U.S. Border." *Environment and Planning D: Space and Society*, vol. 25, 2007, pp. 727–44.

Todd, Zoe. "An Indigenous Feminist's Take on the Ontological Turn: 'Ontology' is Just Another Word for Colonialism." *Journal of Historical Sociology*, vol. 2, no. 1, 2016, pp. 4–22.

Varela, F.G., et al. "Autopoiesis: The Organization of Living Systems, Its Characterization and a Model." *BioSystems*, vol. 5, 1974, pp. 187–96.

Vernadsky, Vladimir I. *The Biosphere*. Translated by David B. Langmuir, Copernicus, 1998.

Villegas, Selso. "Let's Talk About Water in the Desert!" Interview by Gilbert Lujan Rivera Jr. Indst-37-rivera, jr.pdf, n.d., www.google.com/search?q=tohono+o%27odham+water+resources&rlz=1C5CHFA_enAU995AU995&oq=Tohono+O%E2%80%99odham+water&aqs=chrome.1.69i57j0i1312j0i390.4706j0j7&sourceid=chrome&ie=UTF-8.

Vincent, Eve, and Timothy Neale, editors. *Unstable Relations: Indigenous People and Environmentalism in Contemporary Australia*. U of Western Australia, 2016.

Watson, Irene. "Buried Alive." *Law and Critique*, vol. 13, 2002, pp. 253–69.

Whitman, E. "Proposed Arizona–Mexico Wall Threatens Southwest's Last Free-Flowing River." *Phoenix Times*, 5 July 2019, www.phoenixnewtimes .com/news/border-wall-would-threaten-southwes ts-last-free-flowing-river-11321738.

Wolfe, Patrick. "Settler Colonialism and the Elimination of the Native." *Journal of Genocide Research*, vol. 8, 2006, pp. 387–409.

Yetman, David, et al. *The Saguaro Cactus: A Natural History*. U of Arizona P, 2020.

Joseph Pugliese

Just keep swimming.
— *Dory*, Finding Nemo

Blood. Pee. Cum. Sweat. Water really makes us wet.
— *Ecosexual activist chant*, Water Makes Us Wet

This essay prioritizes pools as watery sites of queer and ecological worldbuilding that have thus far resided on the periphery of the blue humanities, which has consistently prioritized the ocean or the sea as its primary motivation for theoretical investigation.[1] Pools offer a scalar reinvention of the blue humanities and provide a distinct aperture by which to envisage water's queer relationality. Looking through and thinking with this aperture, we constellate a queer network of popular media — including film, documentary, young adult fiction, and graphic narrative — to explore a *queer hydropoetics* that illustrates how pools, as contained and recreational bodies of water, repeatedly surface in the contemporary imaginary as vexed locales in which queer affirmation, intimacy, and attachments bubble forth. Hydropoetics attends to water's form and formalism, the ways in which the shape and movements of water reconfigure our own aesthetic language. Whereas other frameworks for hydropoetics have favored poetic representations of natural bodies of water, we offer an exploration of hydropoetics that is attentive to pools across other media, with a particular emphasis on the popular forms that permeate our quotidian lives and consciousness, to invite a more expansive poiesis of multivalent and multimedia queernesses and their environmental corollaries.[2]

Just Keep Swimming? Queer Pooling and Hydropoetics

Jeremy Chow and Maite Urcaregui

Through queer hydropoetics, we showcase how queerness, water, and aesthetic form come together to collectively animate opportunities for rejecting the normativity of terrestrial forms so that we might perceive our environmental surrounds differently. The queerness that water offers, these media remind us, is constantly abounding, in-flux, and potentially lurking right in our own backyards (in the particular case of pools). Like queerness, water's disorienting movements invite us to reorient and "rethink the phenomenality of space," as Sara Ahmed proffers (6). At the same time, we recognize that the queer possibilities pools promise are shaped by the same power dynamics that make pools accessible to few.

We are not interested in a singular or celebratory queer reading of water or hydropoetics, which may run the risk of environmental utopianism or homonormativity. Rather, as the examples explored here suggest, we are invested in a hydropoetic hermeneutic that is polyphonic and, in turn, averse to stable signification. Queer hydropoetics is first and foremost a mode of reading environmental attunement and aqueous adjacency that is committed to visualizing queer identity formations, ruptures, and relations that abjure terrestrial or normative taxonomies. Pools produce one means by which to assess this mode that can inspire new queer ecological readings and forms of elemental being.

Our focus on pools articulates an "educated hope" and a vested interest in the popular as a realm of queer possibility.[3] Pools are significant vestiges within American popular culture and consciousness. As we explore later in this essay, even the alliterative allure of the pool party, a trope that emerges across popular culture forms and genres, is suggestive of the hydropoetics and queer politics that these seemingly "contained" spaces invite. Pulled from popular culture's depths, our title echoes a catchy soundbite begat by Disney/Pixar's *Finding Nemo* (2004): "Just keep swimming. Just keep swimming. Just keep swimming, swimming." Dory, a blue tang voiced by Ellen DeGeneres,[4] repeats this phrase as she accompanies Marlin, a clownfish seeking to recover his son Nemo, who has been abducted from the Great Barrier Reef by a Sydney dentist and amateur angler. Jack Halberstam uncovers how Dory, a perennially forgetful fish, "represents a different, a queer and fluid form of knowing, that operates independently of coherence or linear narrative or progression" (54). Dory's reminder to "just keep swimming" does not, in fact, propel her into the progress narrative of (hetero)normative success – a narrative that, despite its insistence on heterosexual, monogamous pairings, relies on the "bootstraps" ideology of individualism. On the contrary, Dory's repetitive refrain moves her into more collective modes of belonging and kinship, as she becomes Marlin's partner in his search for Nemo, and her forgetfulness models recursive pathways of (un)knowing – what Halberstam identifies as an opportunity to "dwell in the murky waters of a counterintuitive, often impossibly dark and negative realm of critique and refusal" (3).

This essay plays with Dory's aperçu to further query how the promises of and failures to just keep swimming unfurl queer alliances and worldbuilding that employ water's waves to rail against forms of heteronormativity. If Dory invites us to "just keep swimming" and Steve Mentz has proposed a "swimmer poetics" as a literary and environmental mode that unveils the disorienting risks of swimming that ultimately realize that "being in the water means knowing that stability cannot last," then we investigate what happens when the promise of swimming fails ("After Sustainability" 589–90)? When we can no longer stay afloat? And what of queer worldbuilding that becomes suspended in the contained aquatic spaces of pools?

This essay represents a desire – a longing – to queer the blue humanities and suture it to queer ecology. Queer ecology, an interdisciplinary field in its own right, has long theorized the ways in which heteronormativity has flooded environmentalism and, in reaction, articulated the connections and disconnections between environmental thinking and queer studies. As Catriona Sandilands-Mortimer and Bruce Erickson reason, queer ecologies promote "a new practice of ecological knowledges, spaces, and politics that places central attention on challenging hetero-ecologies from the perspective of non-normative sexual and gender positions" (22). How might, queer ecology asks, we apprehend the sinews of queer positionalities and ecological knowledge to dispossess any residual heteronormative commitments that might efface identity and difference? In painting queer ecological thought blue, we join Sandilands, Stacy Alaimo, and Jeremy Chow and Brandi Bushman, scholars who imagine the roles that affect, transcorporeality, and eroticism, respectively, play in joining queer ecology and the blue humanities. We extend this work by focalizing our attention on pools within popular media as sites that further invigorate a queer blue ecology.

Pools have received minimal attention within the blue humanities because they are perceived as artificial, constructed, and thus not natural, yet it is in these very features that we find productive affinities with queerness, a mode of social difference that has likewise been relegated to the margins because of its "unnatural nature." As intimate bodies of water that straddle the public and the private, pools provide apt environs from which to explore how "tacit scenes of sexuality" are indeed constructed by and implicated in public imaginations of sexuality and the material realities they subtend (Berlant and Warner 548). While pools are sometimes celebrated as places of community gathering and engagement, pools – both public and private – have historically been sites of segregation and exclusion on the basis of race, gender, and class in the United States context in which we work and write.[5] Given this history, we do not presuppose that pools are the exclusive liquid territories of queer promise. In fact, their often-chlorinated waters, an agglomeration of different chemicals, illustrate the complex and at times conflicted queer entanglements we hope to draw out. Rather than viewing the use of chemicals like chlorine as a hygienic shock that disavows or sanitizes queerness, we contend that this aqueous amalgamation makes pools places of queer phenomenological encounters. Consider one such sensory experience that is too often downplayed: scent. The smell of pools is *not* in fact a result of chlorination; the smell we most associate with pools is a result of chlorine's admixture with bodily chemicals, namely urine, sweat, feces, and other fluids, as well as artificial additives such as lotions and sunblock.[6] The almost never heeded recommendation to wash one's body in soap and water *before and after* swimming is an explicit endeavor to minimize this sensory overload. As the distinctive smell of a pool, often misattributed to chlorine, relays: pools, in their

queer possibility, are always already intermixed sites that enfold the human body, its natural emissions, and bio-chemicals through and with water.

Our attention to queer bodies in and of water is also an attention to the material, multisensory substance of queer aesthetic form across media. By "envisioning form expansively, as the sum total of formal structure, artistic technique, and plasticity of medium," as Kadji Amin et al. maintain, we might understand artworks "*in their multifaceted materiality*, as a sensuous mode of relation to their audiences" (228). Pools are not simply symbolic or metaphoric sites of queerness; their physical form shape modes of queer identification, relationality, politics, and aesthetics. The multifaceted materiality of pools – their movements, smells, textures, and even chemical makeup – and the bodies within them inform a formal analysis that attends to the social and the political through aesthetics and vice versa. The sight and smell of chlorinated water, the shimmering scales of light on its rippling surface, the waves that bodies create when submerged together, these are some pool aesthetics that we examine as we assemble a fluid media network of queer forms. One of these queer and fluid forms is our own collective prose style. As Jennifer DeVere Brody affirms, "aesthetic style is deeply political" (6). Readers will encounter numerous, sometimes groan-inducing, puns as we deliberately play with the boundaries of academic writing and the pleasures to be found therein. Indeed, groaning can be a queer affect that is just as likely to signal pleasure as it is resistance, or perhaps both. We unapologetically swim in wordplay as a means of performing our own queer hydropoetics on the page.

Pooling together a multimedia network of queer hydropoetic forms, we first turn to the independent film *Saved!* (2004) to address how pools and immersive play provide opportunities for coming out. For Dean, Mary's gay boyfriend in the film, the swimming pool becomes the space in which he can affirm his queer sexuality. We follow with a discussion of the documentary *Water Makes Us Wet*

(2019) by ecosexual filmmakers Beth Stephens and Annie Sprinkle to magnify how pools enliven a queer erotic praxis that is environmentally conscious. We close with Gabby Rivera's young adult novel *Juliet Takes a Breath* (2019) and its graphic novel adaptation, written by Rivera and drawn by Celia Moscote (2020), wherein Juliet Milagros Palante fashions her own queer of color politics at a pool party. Recognizing water as a complex site that affords and forecloses queer possibility, we offer fluid forays into popular culture to locate queer identity, pleasure, and politics in the shallows and depths promised by pools.[7] Our analysis of pools, as intimate bodies of water that straddle the public and the private, queerly reorients the blue humanities to consider closer proximities and smaller scales of water's queer potentiality.

diving in, coming out

Saved! (2004) throws audiences into the deep end of water's queer possibility. The film follows Mary (Jenna Malone), who enters her last year at a conservative Christian high school unknowingly expecting her gay ex-boyfriend's baby. Mary becomes pregnant the first time she and Dean (Chad Faust) have sex after he comes out. According to Mary's evangelical reasoning, which positions heterosexual sex as an antidote to queer attachments, their consummation will cure Dean of his "faggotry" and rectify his putative moral failings. (Spoiler: it doesn't. There's nothing to rectify, and the film makes this clear.)

Dean and the film's queerness come out underwater. Mary and Dean stage a game in which they share confessions while submerged in a backyard pool. "Two weeks before summer vacation ended, everything changed," Mary narrates over the opening credits. "My boyfriend and I played this game of telling each other secrets underwater." As the two descend beneath the turquoise waters for yet another round, Dean exclaims, "I thiilllinnk I'mmm gaaay [*sic*]" (see Figure 1).

In this moment, *Saved!* employs subtitles, used nowhere else in the film, to telegraph Dean's queer confession. While subtitles typically clarify comprehension and articulation for audiences when aural comprehension is hindered, here, both Dean's and water's queerness belie comprehension as they exist outside of the boundaries of legible and enforced heteronormativity.

Saved!'s subtitles acknowledge how water's elemental body contours and contorts the very structure of language, forcing it to concede to its fluid properties. The subtitles in this screenshot thus accord hydropoetic and hydro-narratological effects. We draw here from econarratology, what Erin James and Eric Morel describe as "the paired consideration of material environments and their representations and narrative forms of understanding," to consider how aqueous environments shape narrative forms (1). The queer hydro-narratology revealed by *Saved!*'s subtitles encodes the language of coming out, which for Dean is exclusively made possible and defined by aqueous submersion. These subtitles are queerly (de)constructed: the font curves and swirls as if italicized by the submarine suspension that captures Dean in the still in Figure 1. The deliberate misspelling of "thiilllinnk" (think) betrays the ways that the pool's fluidity shifts language and orthography in ways that make apprehension nearly impossible. The subtitles visually and aesthetically perform the fluid forms of knowing and forgetting that Dory models in her repetitive refrain, "Just keep swimming." Water provides a space for Mary and Dean to give queer form to their shared misrecognition. Summer Kim Lee offers queer form as moments of "wrong impressions" that "dwell in this ambivalent pause, this intimate yet estranging space nestled between subject and object" (261). A queer hydro-narratological form gives fluid structure to these ambivalent pauses, unsettling linguistic and orthographic hegemony.

The pool not only provides form and function to Dean's coming out; it also demands a phenomenological recalibration, a suspension in queer time and space. In response to his submerged secret, Mary flails in the water asking "Whaaat?" Dean responds, "Gay!" Aghast,

Fig. 1. Dean's underwater coming out in *Saved!* Brian Dannelly, director, *Saved!* (United Artists, 2004).

Mary questions, "Gay???" Dean nods. Mary repeats again, flummoxed, "What?" Whether it is the pool's waters or Dean's declaration that baffle Mary is unclear, and this is the point: in their jointure – chlorinated waters and queer coming out – the two perform a phenomenological resistance unique to the pool's intimate enclosures. Though the pool's waters initially obscure Dean's confession, where gay is elongated to include three a's, Dean's subsequent confirmation renders "gay" in its normative orthography. This confirmation of queer identity follows only after the two have been sufficiently submerged. That is, while the shifting of atmospheres and settling into aqueous surrounds might first humorously warp the orthography of the confession, once the two attempt to suspend themselves within water's fluid body, queer identity is affirmed. Water's queer potentiality is not just a mere cannonball into a pool with quick extraction. *Water's queerness demands dwelling with (in) liquidity.* The hydropoetics of this moment – the queerly rendered subtitles, the atmospheric waters, the close shot of Dean's face – moves the viewer to a similar state of suspension as we witness Dean's coming out as if also underwater. In his endeavor to just keep swimming underwater, we experience Dean's disclosure and confirmation of his sexuality, which is otherwise impossible for him to make outside of the pool, where the fundamentalist Christian community intends to erase him from sight and mind; indeed, Dean is sent away to a correctional school and only reappears when he and his queer kin crash the cliched conclusion of many a coming-of-age film: the prom.

As the two surface, the shock of Dean's coming out induces Mary's panic and bodily injury. There is an attempt on Mary's part to quickly exit the aqueous space, which is now contaminated with a queer confession that disrupts her heteronormative commitments and "lifestyle." Her abrupt ascendency results in a head-on collision with the pool's ladder, which leads to a minor concussion. The pain registered is a radical one that injures her body, her faith, her emotional state, and her psyche. The pool, as a site of coming out, then is a location that simultaneously threatens and awakens Mary. The broken illusion of her Christian heteronormative orthodoxy coincides with the head trauma she experiences in attempting to eject herself from the pool that is now suffused with the open secret of Dean's queer affiliation – one and the same. While Dean extricates himself quickly from the water's depths – his catharsis enacted – Mary wallows in the pool as she must now reckon with heteronormative disruption. The pool thus homes the radical disassociation of queerness from heteronormative bonds in that Dean can seamlessly traverse the liminality of the terrestrial/aqueous atmospheres, but Mary, still buoyed to heteronormativity, fails to successfully tread its fluid environs.[8] The pool's waters subtly yet graphically delineate the boundaries of queer acceptance and those who seek, as comes shortly after, to re-educate and "straighten" queer desires.

Mary's concussion spurs an aqueous vision wherein she is appointed a Christian directive, as she understands it, from God. "Maybe it was because I was drowning," Mary's voiceover returns, "or the shock of Dean's confession, but at that moment, I had a vision." Jesus' hunky carpenter doppelganger (crown of thorns intact) appears to Mary within the same queer waters in which Dean has just come out and tasks her with helping Dean: "Dean needs you now," Jesus says in a characteristic orb of light, "You must do all you can to help him." Mary misunderstands this calling to mean that she must actively dissuade Dean from his queer endeavors by offering up her "virginity" as an alternative. Unsurprisingly, she becomes pregnant with Dean's baby, an immaculate conception, at the same time Dean is expelled from the community. Mary's body is martyred to recuperate the flock that is now out one gay sheep.

While the film never returns to the pool, the opening of *Saved!* signals one facet of water's queer potentiality, a submerged space of coming out and the queer affirmation and disruption that ensue, and represents different modalities of successful and unsuccessful swimming. Mary's original commitment to the fundamentalist indoctrination that she has been spoon-fed (and ultimately rejects by film's end) forecloses the possibility of her swimming. Therefore, she identifies her hallucination of a hunky Jesus as a result of her drowning. Orthodoxy and its commensurability with anti-queerness drown here. The pool's queer ecological utopianism rejects Mary, who, even in her attempts at allyship, becomes an embodied weapon by which to induce alleged curative therapies. For Dean, on the other hand, who swims successfully in this scene, the pool makes possible the confession and confirmation of his queer identity in ways that evangelical terrestrial spaces inhibit. To just keep swimming, as Dean models, is to inhabit pools as sites of queer affirmation whose elemental and formal properties cannot but feel like queer sanctuary precisely because they are not beholden to the strictures or frameworks of terrestriality.

hydrophiliacs unite!

Beth Stephens and Annie Sprinkle's documentary, *Water Makes Us Wet: An Ecosexual Adventure* (2019), what might be read as a sequel to *Goodbye Gauley Mountain: An Ecosexual Love Story* (2013), further locates pools' glistening waters as homes for queer, specifically lesbian, desire and sex. Married collaborators Stephens and Sprinkle have long advocated for "ecosexuality" as a necessary pillar of queer identity and politics (what they suggest could be LGBTQIA2SE+); to boot, the documentary's closing shot features the couple with fellow ecosexuals-in-arms as they participate in the San Francisco Pride Parade – historically one of the first gay liberation marches, following New York City's 1969 Stonewall Riots, which we return to later. As Sprinkle and Stephens describe, ecosexuality assumes myriad definitions and positions, which include but are not limited to:

> 1. a person who finds nature romantic, sensual, erotic, or sexy, which can include humans or not. 2. A new sexual identity (self-identified). 3. A person who takes the Earth as their lover [...] 5. An environmental activist strategy. 6. A grassroots movement. 7. A person who has a more expanded concept of what sex and orgasm are beyond mainstream definitions. 8. A person who imagines sex as an ecology that extends beyond the physical body. (*Assuming the Ecosexual Position* 2)

Or put more succinctly by the narrator of the documentary, trans activist Sandy Stone, who ventriloquizes Earth, ecosexuality demands we realize "Earth is lover."

Sprinkle and Stephens, as ecosexual performance artists, enfold the environment into their entwined aesthetic and erotic praxes. The ecosexual outlook that the two champion acknowledges nonhuman environmental agents as possessing agencies (oftentimes erotic ones) that titillate the artists' erogenous work. From 2008 to 2014, Sprinkle and Stephens have been eleven-times wed: to the sun, to the moon, to the snow, to the earth in a Californian redwood forest, to the sea in Venice, to a lake in Finland, to the Appalachian Mountains, to black coal and rocks in Spain, and to the soil in Austria ("Ecosex Weddings"). These matrimonial performances recognize components of the Earth as agentive and thus queer the heteronormative histories of marriage to better realize polyamorous and polymorphous modes of recognition and care.[9] As Stone narrates (as Earth) towards the conclusion of the film: "I like that you try to pleasure me. It feels good. I need that. We need that." The Earth, in this way, is just as capable of endowing as well as experiencing erogenous pleasures, a recognition of the trans-corporeal nature of ecosexuality, and understands these pleasures as necessary for life.

Water Makes Us Wet explores how aqueous aesthetics and erotics inform the political mission of ecosexuality. The documentary envisions a Californian interstate journey in which Stephens and Sprinkle explore the Golden State's climate-change-induced water worries: massive droughts and desiccated reservoirs, water waste and wastewater, the bureaucratic greed that monopolizes water and drinking rights, and the erosion of aqueous agencies that ecosexuals uplift. Alongside this leitmotif, Stephens and Sprinkle repeatedly return to human-made pools for interviews, family gatherings, and sexual encounters. Pools provide a more intimate and immediate space from which the couple reflect on their queer attachments to waters of all kinds. Within their ecosexual commitments, recognizing water's queerness goes beyond an exploration of queer sexuality. It demands we witness water's queer valences and uphold queer liberation and environmental activism as two intersecting missions in queer political activism. Ecosexuality, in other words, emboldens and empowers an environmental advocacy that refuses to posit the Earth as object and instead heralds its sensuous subjectivity.

The moments of pool interaction in the documentary double down on its cultural association as a site of erotic play and fun. In one of the opening shots, Stephens and Sprinkle splash naked in their own backyard pool; the sounds and splashes of water's movement provide a backdrop as the couple's orgasmic utterances fill the aural soundscape. Sprinkle, held in Stephens's arms, spins in the pool moaning in ecstasy. The shot is overlaid with iridescent rays flickering across the water. The cinematography reveals the various queer textures and layers of swimming pool enjoyment, locating lesbian love and sex in the pool and filtering it through an aqueous aesthetics. As an introduction to *Water Makes Us Wet*, these opening shots remind audiences of water's queer filiation and its induction of sexual pleasure. To just keep swimming here invites audiences to plumb the erotic depths of pools that make possible the intersecting eroticisms of queer human and nonhuman bodies of water.

This aqueous eroticism follows the filmmakers as they retrace their familial histories. Sprinkle, a former sex worker (even her stage name conjures up fluidity), returns to her family pool in Granada Hills, California, which she describes as "my happy spot." This pronouncement coincides with Sprinkle's admission that the pool was the site of her "first blow job." Sprinkle remarks coquettishly, "I loved it wet." These quips, like the opening shots of the documentary, dramatize a vital contingency among pools of water and human bodies as co-constitutive entities, invoking Astrida Neimanis's ethic of "bodies of water" that encompass "environmental waters, feminist theory, and our corporeal implication in both" (6). The documentary's pools recognize and extend the aqueous makeup of human bodies and the Earth (both roughly 70 percent), which situate scales for imagining water's feminist and queer potentiality – materially, locationally, and semiotically. Indeed, the film closes with Stephens, Sprinkle, and ecosexual activists chanting at San Francisco

Pride: "Blood. Pee. Cum. Sweat. Water Really Makes Us Wet!" These bodily fluids are not possible without water, the lifeblood of sexual intimacy.

For Sprinkle, the pool as a "happy spot" metaphorizes vaginal, clitoral, and other erogenous pleasures that, within the purview of the documentary, do not exist separate from aqueous environs. Whereas in *Goodbye Gauley Mountain*, the two fondle, caress, and sexually engage other environmental interactors (mud, rocks, vegetables, and streams), *Water Makes Us Wet* explores environmental sexual playfulness exclusively within the parameters of aquatic locales.[10] This pattern recognizes water's placement within erogenous entanglement as an opportunity to rethink and unsettle notions of sex as strictly penetrative. If, as one interviewee posits, water is a bodily lubricant, then it opens up "an ecology of sex" that does not mandate penetration as the primary vehicle for embracing pleasure. To assume that sex is beholden to penetration is to concretize allegiances to hetero-reproduction, in which sex is bound to what Lee Edelman has termed "reproductive futurism."[11] Water's queerness envelopes and elicits polymorphic pleasures from both within and without, entangling human and non-human animacies and agencies in the process. In the words of interviewee Donna Haraway, water's ecosexuality finds a "way of soliciting each other into thinking and feeling differently [...] into a polymorphic sensuality that is for and of the earth." To "love it wet" is to confirm the pleasures that bodies in and of water can jointly endow.

Yet, hydromania comes with a price. Following Sprinkle's nostalgic reflection on her childhood pool, the documentary confronts audiences with statistics that reveal the financial and environmental costs of pool maintenance, particularly in California – a state that is, as of early 2022, experiencing extreme drought (roughly 90 percent at least), which affects more than 37 million residents (out of approximately 39.5 million people statewide) (Drought.gov). In times of extreme drought, "water is inadequate for agriculture, wildlife,

and urban needs; reservoirs are extremely low; hydropower is restricted" (Drought.gov). These conditions likewise induce and exacerbate a year-round fire "season." *Water Makes Us Wet* reveals that California boasts roughly 1.2 million residential swimming pools, of which 250,000 are in Los Angeles County, each requiring roughly 30,000 gallons of water to fill. These statistics reveal how socio-economic status and privilege contour pools, who has access to them, and the pleasures they avail. The cost of a pool, particularly with the soaring water costs in California among realized Anthropocentric fears of water wars, ultimately implies that pool play and its potential erotics are bound by economic regimes unattainable to most. While prior to these statistics Stephens and Sprinkle wade in the familial pool, following these disclosures, the two are seen only sitting on the pool deck. The shame of aqueous enjoyment is thus felt both statistically and representationally. Yet, the film stops short of interrogating Sprinkle's own "happy spot," her family pool in Granada Hills, a suburb of Los Angeles, where the number of private schools rival those of public and the median home price is over $930,000.[12] Only through impersonal statistics and subliminal shame does the documentary seem to recognize that one person's wet dream might come at the expense of a collective future.

Water Makes Us Wet, to this end, features two conflicting yet interconnected representations of how we might just keep swimming. First, to just keep swimming is to embrace aqueous eroticisms of human, queer, and more-than-human kinds. Second, to just keep swimming under the watchful eye of drought metrics is to commit a form of potential ecocide in which human-made pools contribute to the human-induced effects of Anthropocentric climate change. To just keep swimming, in this latter case, is to abnegate local, national, and global efforts that seek to ameliorate climate change, especially through a mindfulness of water and who has access to it. To just keep swimming is to, as a result, recognize the cost of water's queer potentialities and pleasures. Pools exist in a tenuous limbo: they enfold environmental agency and queer subjectivity in a politicized erogenous praxis, and, at the same time, they are shaped by exclusionary geographies that displace minoritized communities and exacerbate environmental racism and colonial extraction. The pool's queer eroticism potentially bungles environmental advocacy, but holding these realizations in collective tension elucidates the non-innocent and polyphonic modes that underline the possibility of hydropoetics. Though the documentary only briefly touches upon these furtive ironies, through the lens of ecosexuality, the queer promise (and its attendant futures) of just keep swimming is jeopardized in the face of the Anthropocene and its attendant crises.

pool parties and politics

In Gabby Rivera's *Juliet Takes a Breath* (originally published independently in 2016 and later rereleased by Dial Books in 2019), submersion in water, ironically, provides the protagonist a place to breathe, as the title suggests, from which she explores a queer of color erotics and politics.[13] The young adult novel follows Juliet Milagros Palante, a nineteen-year-old Nuyorican lesbian from the Bronx, who travels to Portland, Oregon, to undertake a summer internship. During her internship, she works as an assistant to Harlowe Brisbane, the White lesbian and polyamorous author of Juliet's favorite book, *Raging Flower: Empowering Your Pussy by Empowering Your Mind*.[14] Soon after she arrives in Portland, however, Juliet learns that it is not the queer haven she expected and that Harlowe is not the queer feminist idol she needs. In fact, Harlowe epitomizes the ways in which White women and queer White people use their gender and sexual identity as a band-aid for their racial privilege (and their uses and abuses of it). Harlowe's vision of "sisterhood," an often cited and co-opted term within feminist discourse, is one that invisibilizes difference and structural inequalities – erasing the intellectual labor and experiences of women of color and rendering trans and gender nonconforming people outside of feminist politics and community. In short, hippie Harlowe reeks of White feminism and trans exclusionary radical feminism.[15]

Much of the novel traces Juliet's queer of color *bildungsroman* as she confronts and navigates the ways that #solidarityisforwhitewomen.[16] Harlowe frequently abnegates solidarity, positioning herself as a White savior figure and appropriating the labor, experiences, and knowledge of women of color for her own fame and profit. In a climactic moment, Harlowe tokenizes Juliet at a public reading, the culmination of Juliet's internship, by misrepresenting her as "[growing] up in the ghetto" and "[fighting] for her whole life to make it out of the Bronx alive and get an education" (Rivera 206). Harlowe manufactures a narrative, one that relies on and reifies racist imaginaries of Latinx urban communities, to signal her own falsified virtue and wokeness. What she instead reveals is just "how little effort white women have made to understand and combat their racism," as the Combahee River Collective voice in their 1977 statement (27). After being put on display in Harlowe's performance of "wokeness," Juliet leaves Portland to spend time with her Titi (Aunt) Penny and cousin Ava in Miami, and the two provide Juliet with a very different version of queer kinship.

While in Miami, Juliet and Ava attend "The Clipper Queerz" pool party, a celebration exclusively for queer and trans people of color, where one can get a fresh fade before jumping in for a swim, which is exactly what Juliet does. At the pool party Juliet experiences a vision of solidarity that is more than virtue signaling or performative politics and instead stems from intersectional, collective struggles for racial and gender justice. Juliet's description of the party portrays the pool as shimmering with possibility: "The Clipper Queerz party stretched out before us in all its radical glory. Lit from the bottom, the underground pool shimmered" (Rivera 237). The pool's shimmering depths give aquatic form to what Macarena Gómez-Barris understands as "the sexual underground," "submerged spaces of queer and trans social life and cultural production not easily absorbed by the nation-state" (50). The pool provides a place where the Clipper Queerz – queer and trans people of color who have been marginalized both within hegemonic society as well as the queer community and thus are more vulnerable to state violence – can gather and organize in and through pleasure. It is a pool party after all, and, in a pool, bodies come together in fluid ways, creating movements (in both the embodied and political valence of the term) that might circumvent the state and its violently imposed normativity. Submerging oneself in, rather than swimming through, these underground waters give access to alternative modes of being from which they might "rethink the meaning of politics" (Gómez-Barris 67). Juliet notes that the pool is "lit from the bottom," as it elicits and enlivens these underground perspectives that center and celebrate those who are most marginalized – a political model that, rather than purporting to "trickle down," builds power from the bottom up, creating a collective swell.

Luz Ángel, the trans Latina woman who organizes the event, clarifies how these (pool) politics diverge from mainstream queer politics and traverse racial and national borders:

> We're here to chill, get sick haircuts, and dance. But let's not forget our fallen camaradas who've been brutalized by police and lovers or left for dead in the street. My fellow trans women, I will not forget you! We will not forget your names. We will not forget being discarded by our families, being homeless, and used and taunted. Bullied, murdered, oppressed for being brown, Black, Asian, for being queers, faggots, dykes, genderless renegades, trans warriors, for all our glory. We are not like those fake, fancy gays from *Queer as Folk* or *Will and Fucking Grace*! And we will never be them. We will never assimilate. Basura! The capitalist system that favors whiteness and wealth over all has denied us the right to live well, to be well, and to love. We won't let them win. We will riot and party and honor our ancestors and no one can stop us. Glory be to la madre, Sylvia Rivera; la Virgen de Guadalupe; and la reina, Selena Quintanilla-Pérez. (Rivera 240)

While the Clipper Queerz brings together a collective of queer and trans people of color, they are not asked to prioritize their gender or sexual identity over other aspects of their experience. Luz Ángel articulates a multi-racial coalition of "queers, faggots, dykes, genderless renegades, trans warriors" working across forms of difference "for the glory of all." Luz Ángel's speech also critiques the way that police violence is wielded against communities of color to protect "whiteness and wealth" and how trans women of color have experienced the brunt of this violence. She positions queer and trans liberation as fundamentally interconnected with struggles against racist and capitalist oppression. This coalitional view diverges from Harlowe's Whitewashed notion of "sisterhood," a term she appropriates from women of color, that requires an essentialized gender or sexual identity to take precedence over all other forms of social difference. Luz Ángel's speech, in its intersectional critique and coalitional call, recalls Audre Lorde's contention that those who experience oppression along multiple axes cannot "afford the luxury of fighting one form of oppression only" ("No Hierarchy" 9).

The pool party decries the increasingly mainstream brand of queer assimilationist respectability politics that colludes with racism, capitalism, colonialism, and state violence. These mainstream politics are perpetuated through popular portrayals of "fake, fancy gays" on shows like *Queer as Folk*, *Will and Grace*, and, we might add, *The Ellen DeGeneres Show*. Roderick A. Ferguson historicizes this mainstreaming of queer liberation; he argues that the gay (Ferguson decidedly does not index it as "queer") rights movement's emphasis on access to forms of capital and state recognition, such as marriage, increasingly narrowed the inherently intersectional politics of early queer activism, which was and continues to be led by queer and trans women of color (*One-Dimensional Queer* 8). Luz Ángel emphasizes an intersectional understanding of power and identity as foundational to the Clipper Queerz's politics, concluding her speech by saluting their ancestors, placing

Sylvia Rivera, co-founder of Street Transvestite Action Revolutionaries (STAR) and leader of the 1969 Stonewall riot (the first Pride) alongside Marsha P. Johnson, in conjunction with prominent Latinx cultural figures like la Virgen de Guadalupe and Selena Quintanilla-Pérez, the "Queen of Tejano music." The Clipper Queerz refuse to divorce queer liberation from its multidimensional origins. The queer future imagined at the pool party recasts coalition as a collective struggle that must attend to the embodied consequences of structural violence and their unequal distribution. Just as this essay pools together a variety of queer forms across genre and media, in her speech, Luz Ángel identifies multiple sources of inspiration that complicate any notion of a smooth or singular current of queer politics, emphasizing instead multi-generational, multi-racial, and transnational routes of kinship.

By refusing to "just keep swimming" alongside the queer mainstream, the Clipper Queerz theorize a counterhegemonic coalition that locates itself in poolside pleasures and politics. While private pools might provide exclusive locales of leisure for "fake, fancy gays," in *Juliet Takes a Breath*, the Clipper Queerz remake the private pool (the party takes place at an unidentified house) into a space of public protest and radical joy, calling out the ways that policing and capitalism favor "whiteness and wealth over all" and deny all others "the right to live well, to be well, and to love" (Rivera 240). For the Clipper Queerz, rioting and partying are two prongs of the same political praxis, as they "chill, get sick haircuts, and dance" while commemorating those they have lost to police, intimate, and social violence. By reorienting and repurposing the "private" pool to publicly proclaim the right to live and love free from violence, the Clipper Queerz enact and embody how "*Cuir* and trans life in the Américas finds its source of critique and pleasure within new avenues of political access, as well as in the submerged space of the sexual underground" (Gómez-Barris 67). The pool provides a space of submergence through which queer pleasure and politics

emerge as fundamentally intertwined. In this intermingling, the hydropoetics of *Juliet Takes a Breath* echo ecosexuality's call that the environment is inseparable from the politics of pleasure.

At the pool party, Juliet begins to mold and embrace her own version of queerness that refuses to conform to White hegemonic notions of femininity and respectability. Toward this project of self-fashioning, she embraces more than the Clipper Queerz's political vision: she also gets a haircut, more specifically an undercut, that quintessential lesbian coif. Juliet is initially reluctant to cut her hair because she is "afraid of looking like a dyke" (Rivera 245). In response to this, the stylist, whom Juliet has a crush on and refers to endearingly as Blue Lips because of their blue lipstick, asks "Are you a dyke?" When Juliet responds, "I think so," Blue Lips gently reminds her that "no matter what you do with your hair, you're gonna look like a dyke" (245). Rather than offering Juliet the assurance of conformity or assimilation, Blue Lips challenges Juliet's monolithic view of what a lesbian looks like and the presumption that avoiding such optics is desirable. While the ability to pass as heterosexual might provide a modicum of protection (mostly for those who already experience privilege along other axes of identity), it does so at a cost. As Lorde points out, when she asserts that "your silence will not protect you," conceding to power does not guarantee safety (*Sister Outsider*). Recognizing the personal and political power of self-definition, Lorde attests,

> I have come to believe over and over again that what is important to me must be spoken, made verbal and shared, even at the risk of having it bruised or misunderstood. That the speaking profits me, beyond any other effect. (*Sister Outsider* 40)

Juliet's poolside haircut does more than transform her physical appearance. It marks a transformative moment of queer identification, self-definition, and relationality that she chooses for herself even at the risk of misunderstanding or violence. Gazing at her newly shaved head,

Juliet reflects, "I looked fierce, fucking gay as hell, queer even. Shit maybe I was queer too. Whatever I was or however I decided to identify, the cut was rad" (Rivera 247). Juliet's queer transformation is not the typical makeover montage that reinforces racist, cissexist, and heteropatriarchal beauty standards that pervade popular media. Here, to just keep swimming means to dive into water's queerness and to swim against heteronormativity to find a more fluid and authentic expression of self. The pool provides the backdrop for Juliet's exploration of a more flexible understanding of her gender, her sexuality, and the ways she performs them, and the party introduces her to a community of other queer folk navigating the same choppy waters.

Juliet's poolside transformation, while politically charged, also enlivens her queer relationality and erotics, further demonstrating the way these experiences swirl together. She describes the sensuous experience of the haircut, saying,

> I liked the feel of their hands on my head, the pressure of the clippers, the hum of them and the care put into the cut. The energy focused on me was the good kind, the kind that didn't expect anything back. (Rivera 246)

The electric buzz of the clippers seems to emanate from Blue Lips, the hum of *them* referring simultaneously to the clippers and to the person that artfully wields them. This delicious hum entangles subject and object, human and nonhuman in a moment of queer animacy that, as Mel Chen contends, "has the capacity to rewrite conditions of intimacy, engendering different communalisms and revising biopolitical spheres" (3). Enlivened by the queer animacy of the haircut, Juliet and Blue Lips later strip down to their underwear and jump into the pool, where they kiss.[17]

The graphic novel adaptation of *Juliet Takes a Breath* (2020), drawn by Celia Moscote and written by Rivera, portrays their kiss in a series of three asymmetrical, wordless panels (see Figure 2). While the panels do not contain dialogue or narration (the "SPLASH" acts more as an onomatopoeic visual device that marks non-verbal diegetic sound), the pause and direct gaze of the second panel suggests the mutuality of the kiss, and, because affirmative verbal consent is imperative, in the novel, Juliet confirms that the kiss is indeed consensual, noting, "And when they kissed me, I kissed back" (Rivera 248). In these panels, Juliet's fresh undercut and Blue Lips' locks (also undercut) take on the blue and green color of the waves around them and their skin matches the warm pink and brown hues of the surrounding sunset sky. Their bodies take on the elemental qualities of the surrounding environs, which animates and enlivens their erotic encounter. In the final panel, gentle waves splash and move around them as they kiss. Water or sweat or both drip off them, their skin a glistening reminder of water's hydroerotic potentiality that we see in *Water Makes Us Wet*. Rather than a private encounter, Juliet's kiss takes place in public among a queer community whose play, pleasure, and partying put the pool's water (and its political possibilities) in motion.

While Juliet and Blue Lips float suspended, kissing in the water, the waves that surround them undulate from those who swim around them, a gentle reminder that in this place, in this pool, they are safe, seen, and in community. Just as "a life is thrown into relief as queer through its commitment to unauthorized or unorthodox relations and the transformative potential they represent," as David J. Getsy contends of queer form, the queer potentiality of Juliet's and Blue Lips' kiss is thrown into relief against the animated movements of the pool, which contextualize their intimate encounter within a collective project of queer world-making (254). Here, this community of queer and trans people of color allows Juliet to pause, to take a breath, and to be supported in a moment of fluid suspension. The collective takes on and up the work of swimming and, in doing so, supports Juliet's queer explorations. To just keep swimming, in Moscote and Rivera's capable hands,

Fig. 2. Juliet and Blue Lips kissing in the pool at the Clipper Queerz party. Celia Moscote and Gabby Rivera, *Juliet Takes a Breath* (Boom! Box, 2020), n. pag.

is to uphold queer of color coalitional activisms and eroticism.

queer pooling

The three interconnected, medial vignettes we have waded into exemplify what we identify as opportunities for "queer pooling." Through this blue media ecology, we have explored how contained bodies of water – namely human-made pools – home narratives of coming out, queer eroticisms, and trans-corporeal and coalitional politics. The etymology of "pool" indexes a longer genealogy of queer possibility that we interrogate by way of conclusion. *The Oxford English Dictionary* first locates "pool" within Old English (with curious cognates in Middle Dutch, Middle Low German, Early Irish, Old Cornish, and Old Icelandic) to define "a small body of still or standing water, esp. of a natural formation." Oftentimes, in these cognates, the pool is a hole, a ditch, a bog, a pond, or a pit. A pool thus performs a linguistic synecdoche for any number of bodies of water that enfold crude puns (as with hole, ditch, or pit) as well as ecological systems (like bogs and ponds) with exceptional physical and chemical properties. Yet through the late medieval and early modern period, the word takes on amorphous, antinomic definitions: both "a small shallow accumulation" as well as "a deep and still place in a body of water." Even more, pooling can refer to a collective of individuals and a means of gathering that collective (to pool energies, for example); therein lies another wave of queer pooling that invigorates our discussion. Pools, by definition, play with the irregularity and unquantifiable depths, forms, and accumulations, which we see readily available to queer the proximities, scales, orientations, and coalitions of the blue humanities.

As a research methodology, queer pooling promiscuously collects and coalesces different and sometimes divergent sites of study to attend to their ephemeral entanglements. Like Dory, we forgetfully swim between fields and disciplines, bringing the blue humanities to bear on queer ecologies and forms, to unlearn and imagine anew the queer world-making that pools might avail. Elemental pooling facilitates Dean's self-revelation, the activist erotics of ecosexuals and hydrophilics, and Juliet's transformational dive into a queer of color collective. We recognize pools not merely as sites of queer happenings but also as lubricious locales from which to theorize aquatic queer worlds and futures – not without risks and always with pleasure (and its politics) in mind. Queer pooling lingers in, seeps into, and soaks these contradictions. We locate water's and our own queer work in pools, intimate enclosures where human and elemental agents intermingle to create new environments and/with queer possibilities. These intimate locales and queer forms invigorate the blue humanities and encourage us to imagine how we might swim against the turbulent riptides of hegemony, or, refuse to swim altogether and embrace sublime suspension.

disclosure statement

No potential conflict of interest was reported by the authors.

notes

1 For frameworks that motivate the blue humanities, see John Gillis, Steve Mentz ("Toward a Blue Cultural Studies"), Elizabeth DeLoughrey, Stefan Helmreich, and Hester Blum.

2 See, for example, John Charles Ryan, Joshua Bennett, Catriona Sandilands, and Édouard Glissant on hydropoetics.

3 Our use of "educated hope" invokes the work of queer of color theorist José Esteban Muñoz who, drawing from Ernst Bloch, called for "a mode of hoping that is cognizant of exactly what obstacles present themselves" to sustain queer futures (207).

4 After a period of exile following her public coming out on *Ellen* in 1994, in the 2000s, US mainstream media positioned DeGeneres as an iconic lesbian figure. As a White woman who represents corporate and commercial success, she provided a version of queerness that did not threaten the heteronormative versions of success that Halberstam critiques. In recent years, she has become a failed queer figure for many, though not in the ways Halberstam celebrates, because of the abuse, harassment, and discrimination she perpetuated in the workplace.

5 Throughout the first half of the twentieth century in the United States, public pools were sites of *de jure* and de facto racial segregation, often enforced through White terror and violence. In the latter half of the twentieth century, this exclusion morphed into the private pool as many White families fled integrating cities and invented the suburbs. See Jeff Wiltse and Cathy Park Hong for social and poetic histories of these dynamics, respectively.

6 See Chris Wiant and Erika Englehaupt who dispel pool myths, especially as they play into concerns over chlorine use, hygiene, and public health.

7 While we create a network of only four works, the ripples of this project invite further diving. Consider queer cult films, such as *Get Real* (1998), *Henry Gamble's Birthday Party* (2015), *Beach Rats* (2017), *Getting Go* (2019), *Ammonite* (2020), and *Luca* (2021), as well as graphic narratives such as Alison Bechdel's *Fun Home* (2006), Marnie Galloway's *In the Sounds and the Seas* (2016), Alice Oseman's *Heartstopper* series (2016–), Molly Osertag's *The Girl from the Sea* (2021), and Kat Leyh's *Thirsty Mermaids* (2021), all of which invite textures of queer pooling.

8 This radical dissociation from heteronormative bonding coincides with Joshua J. Weiner and Damon Young's "queer bonds": forms of queer sociality that "come into view through the isometric tension between queer world-making and world-shattering, naming a togetherness in failures to properly intersect, the social hailing named by recognition as well as its radical occlusion" (223–24). See also Chase Gregory on how queerness signifies directional pulls (and bonds) that structure the field of inter- and intra-generational queer studies.

9 While we recognize the polyamorous and polymorphous queer possibilities of these human/non-human unions, we also note how they reinforce marriage (and the protections it provides) as the basis of legal recognition and interpersonal accountability. Like Lisa Duggan, we too understand "marriage as a much too narrow and

confining status to accommodate our elaborate, innovative forms of intimacy, interconnection and dependency" (n. pag.).

10 For other queer ecological readings of *Goodbye Gauley Mountain*, see Nicole Seymour and Jeremy Chow.

11 Edelman uses this term to describe an anti-social thesis that rails against the heteronormative logics in which reproduction is always the valuation of sex, futurity, and progress.

12 This number is based on information offered by *Redfin* as of September 2022. See "Granada Hills Housing Market."

13 Roderick A. Ferguson argues that "the decisive intervention of queer of color analysis is that racist practice articulates itself generally through gender and sexual regulation, and that gender and sexual differences variegate racial formations" and traces its theoretical genealogy to women of color feminisms (*Aberrations in Black* 3).

14 While *Juliet Takes a Breath* is fictional, Rivera has discussed how she borrowed from her own experience of moving to Portland to pursue an internship. While it is important to recognize the text as fiction and to avoid eliding Rivera's aesthetics with her autobiography, we mention this to draw attention to the racism, sexism, and homophobia that plague the publishing industry. See Audie Cornish.

15 Rafia Zakaria uses the term "white feminist" to refer to

> someone who refuses to consider the role that whiteness and the racial privilege attached to it have played and continue to play in universalizing white feminist concerns, agendas, and beliefs as being those of all of feminism and of all feminists. (ix)

According to *The Trans Advocate*'s Cristan Williams, within feminist and trans discourse, the term "trans exclusionary radical feminist" (TERF) "refers to a very specific type of person who wraps anti-trans bigotry in the language of feminism," often aligning their so-called radical views with extreme right-wing rhetoric (n. pag.).

16 The satirically serious hashtag #solidarityisforwhitewomen was started by feminist writer and activist Mikki Kendall on Twitter in 2013 in response to the "feminist" fragility of Hugo Schwyzer. See NPR Staff and Kendall.

17 Notably, another moment of queer intimacy is facilitated by water in *Juliet Takes a Breath* when Juliet has sex with Kira, another love interest, in the shower (Rivera 211–12).

bibliography

Ahmed, Sara. *Queer Phenomenology: Orientations, Objects, Others*. Duke UP, 2006.

Alaimo, Stacy. *Exposed: Environmental Politics and Pleasures in Posthuman Times*. U of Minnesota P, 2016.

Amin, Kadji, et al. "Queer Form: Aesthetics, Race, and the Violences of the Social." *ASAP/Journal*, vol. 2, no. 2, 2017, pp. 227–39.

Bennett, Joshua. *Being Property Once Myself: Blackness and the End of Man*. Harvard UP, 2020.

Berlant, Lauren, and Michael Warner. "Sex in Public." *Critical Inquiry*, vol. 24, no. 2, 1998, pp. 547–66.

Blum, Hester. "The Prospect of Oceanic Studies." *PMLA*, vol. 125, no. 3, 2010, pp. 670–77.

Brody, Jennifer DeVere. *Punctuation: Art, Politics, and Play*. Duke UP, 2008.

Chen, Mel. *Animacies: Biopolitics, Racial Mattering, and Queer Affect*. Duke UP, 2012.

Chow, Jeremy. "Masturbatory Ecologies: Pornography, Ecosexuality, and Perverted Environmental Justice." *Camera Obscura: Feminism, Culture, and Media Studies*, vol. 105, 2020, pp. 31–60.

Chow, Jeremy, and Brandi Bushman. "Hydro-eroticism." *English Language Notes*, vol. 57, no. 1, 2019, pp. 96–115.

Combahee River Collective. "The Combahee River Collective Statement." *How We Get Free: Black Feminism and the Combahee River Collective*, edited by Keeanga-Yamahtta Taylor, 2017, pp. 15–27.

Cornish, Audie. "Life, Love, Coming Out and Culture Shock in 'Juliet Takes a Breath.'" Interview with Gabby Rivera. *NPR*, 18 Sept. 2019, www.npr.org/2019/09/18/762046606/book-juliet-takes-a-breath.

Dannelly, Brian, director. *Saved!* United Artists, 2004.

DeLoughrey, Elizabeth. "Toward a Critical Ocean Studies for the Anthropocene." *English Language Notes*, vol. 57, no. 1, 2019, pp. 21–36.

Drought.gov. "Current U.S. Drought Monitor Conditions for California." 14 Sept. 2021, www.drought.gov/states/california.

Duggan, Lisa. "Beyond Marriage: Democracy, Equality, and Kinship for a New Century." *The Scholar and Feminist Online*, vol. 10, nos. 1–2, Fall 2011–Spring 2012.

Edelman, Lee. *No Future: Queer Theory and the Death Drive*. Duke UP, 2004.

Englehaupt, Erika. "Just How Much Pee is in That Pool?" *NPR*, 1 Mar. 2017, www.npr.org/sections/health-shots/2017/03/01/517785902/just-how-much-pee-is-in-that-pool.

Ferguson, Roderick A. *Aberrations in Black: Toward a Queer of Color Critique*. U of Minnesota P, 2004.

Ferguson, Roderick A. *One-Dimensional Queer*. Polity, 2019.

Getsy, David J. "Queer Relations." *ASAP/Journal*, vol. 2, no. 2, 2012, pp. 254–57.

Gillis, John. "The Blue Humanities." *Humanities*, vol. 34, no. 3, 2013.

Glissant, Édouard. *The Poetics of Relation*. U of Michigan P, 1990.

Gómez-Barris, Macarena. *Beyond the Pink Tide: Art and Political Undercurrents in the Americas*. U of California P, 2018.

"Granada Hills Housing Market." *Redfin*, www.redfin.com/neighborhood/1126/CA/Los-Angeles/Granada-Hills/housing-market. Accessed 9 Sept. 2022.

Gregory, Chase. "Critics on Critics: Queer Bonds." *GLQ*, vol. 25, no. 1, 2019, pp. 101–06.

Halberstam, Jack. *The Queer Art of Failure*. Duke UP, 2011.

Helmreich, Stefan. *Alien Ocean: Anthropological Voyages in Microbial Seas*. U of California P, 2009.

Hong, Cathy Park. "Minor Feelings: An Asian American Reckoning." UCSB Arts & Lectures, 10 Feb. 2022, University of California, Santa Barbara, Santa Barbara, CA. Lecture.

James, Erin, and Eric Morel, editors. *Environment and Narrative: New Directions in Econarratology*. Ohio State UP, 2020.

Kendall, Mikki. *Hood Feminism: Notes from the Women that a Movement Forgot*. Viking, 2020.

Kim Lee, Summer. "Wrong Impressions." *ASAP/Journal*, vol. 2, no. 2, 2017, pp. 261–64.

Lorde, Audre. *Sister Outsider*. Crossing Press, 2007.

Lorde, Audre. "There Is No Hierarchy of Oppressions." *Interracial Books for Children Bulletin: Homophobia and Education*, vol. 14, nos. 3–4, 1983, p. 9.

Mentz, Steve. "After Sustainability." *PMLA*, vol. 127, no. 3, 2012, pp. 586–92.

Mentz, Steve. "Toward a Blue Cultural Studies: The Sea, Maritime Culture, and Early Modern English Literature." *Literature Compass*, vol. 6, no. 5, 2009, pp. 997–1013.

Moscote, Celia, and Gabby Rivera. *Juliet Takes a Breath*. Boom! Box, 2020.

Muñoz, José Esteban. *Cruising Utopia: The Then and There of Queer Futurity*. New York UP, 2009.

Neimanis, Astrida. *Bodies of Water: Posthuman Feminist Phenomenology*. Bloomsbury, 2017.

NPR Staff. "Twitter Sparks a Serious Discussion About Race and Feminism." *Code Switch*, 23 Aug. 2013, www.npr.org/sections/codeswitch/2013/08/22/214525023/twitter-sparks-a-serious-discussion-about-race-and-feminism.

"Pool." n. *Oxford English Dictionary*, 2021.

Rivera, Gabby. *Juliet Takes a Breath*. Dial Books, 2019.

Ryan, John Charles. "Hydropoetics: The Rewor(l)ding of Rivers." *River Research and Applications*, vol. 38, no. 3, 2022, pp. 486–93.

Sandilands, Catriona. "Into this Blue: Betsy Warland's Queer Ecopoetics." *ISLE*, vol. 25, no. 1, 2018, pp. 186–205.

Sandilands-Mortimer, Catriona, and Bruce Erickson, editors. *Queer Ecologies: Sex, Nature, Politics, Desire*. U of Indiana P, 2010.

Seymour, Nicole. *Bad Environmentalism: Irony and Irreverence in the Ecological Age*. U of Minnesota P, 2018.

Sprinkle, Annie, and Beth Stephens. *Assuming the Ecosexual Position: The Earth as Lover*. U of Minnesota P, 2021.

Sprinkle, Annie, and Beth Stephens. "Ecosex Weddings." *Annie Sprinkle and Beth Stephens: The Collaboration*, 2021.

Stephens, Beth, and Annie Sprinkle. *Water Makes Us Wet: An Ecosexual Adventure*. Juno Films, 2019. Documentary.

Weiner, Joshua J., and Damon Young. "Queer Bonds." *GLQ*, vol. 17, nos. 2–3, 2011, pp. 223–41.

Wiant, Chris. "Busting a Chlorine Swimming Pool Urban Myth." *Water Quality and Health Council*, 27 July 2012, waterandhealth.org/healthy-pools/busting-chlorine-swimming-pool-urban-myth/.

Williams, Cristan. "TERF: What It Means and Where It Came From." *The Trans Advocate*, www.transadvocate.com/terf-what-it-means-and-where-it-came-from_n_13066.htm.

Wiltse, Jeff. *Contested Waters: A Social History of Swimming Pools in America*. U of North Carolina P, 2010.

Zakaria, Rafia. *Against White Feminism: Notes on Disruption*. W.W. Norton, 2021.

Jeremy Chow
Maite Urcaregui

⊘ OPEN ACCESS

In the summer of 2021, I returned to Amsterdam after a two-year research stay abroad. On my first walk through the city, I noticed how many of the famous canals and bridges were under construction. Some bridges were completely closed off and the streets along the canals were blocked by containers and heavy building equipment. The docks looked wavier than usual and large sheets of metal were erected in the water at about a two- or three-meter distance from the docks. The space between the dock and the metal was filled with sand. As in any expanding urban city, there is always construction. However, I had never seen anything like it. And why did it look like some of the streets were slanting and crumbling into the canal? Even the canal houses seemed wonkier than ever. Continuing on my walk, I found a sign explaining that the bridges and streets had been poorly maintained and were collapsing – sinking under the weight of water from below in a city built almost entirely on what they call "reclaimed land" as if it was supposed to be there all along – a wetland ecosystem turned into property.

I remember thinking to myself, "this is the end of the long 'Golden Age.' A beautiful yet morbid end of empire." My mind's eye pictured the signature houses along the Amsterdam canals – built with the money and resources from the colonies and slave plantations – crumbling into the water. Although centuries had gone into containing, capturing, and juridicalizing the water, the water's materiality remembered where it was and spilled out. Coming back to

A Sinking Empire

Mikki Stelder

reality I sighed and thought "those metal sheets, another quick-fix solution to postpone what might be the city's inevitable demise" as I scrutinized the rust chipping off the metal.

The metal sheets were placed to support the old brick structures and the marshy sand underneath them. The metal looked like an unmoving wave, leaving space between the familiar murky brown-green water and the dock. In those in-between zones, there was hardly any water, just sand. Sand blanketed by a small layer of liquid from the incessant summer

This is an Open Access article distributed under the terms of the Creative Commons Attribution-NonCommercial-NoDerivatives License (http://creativecommons.org/licenses/by-nc-nd/4.0/), which permits non-commercial re-use, distribution, and reproduction in any medium, provided the original work is properly cited, and is not altered, transformed, or built upon in any way.

rains and already getting sucked-up by layers of pulverized shells. As if the sand formed a dyke between land and water. The whole scene reminded me of seventeenth-century land "reclamation," or perhaps more pertinent "land-taking" projects occurring all across this Rhine River Delta. The Dutch were building land where there was none and claimed it as a nation – claiming possession over what was once wet. Dredging, dumping, draining. The water becoming more and more invisible, yet never truly gone. The riverbank, the shoreline coming and going, coming and going, coming.

In the sand, small shoots of native greenery were sprouting, interrupting the otherwise familiar shades of brown. A municipal sign instructed me "Please keep off. Newly sown flower beds." I felt cheated. The whole city was collapsing under the weight of its manmade land and the municipality tried to tell me this is some sort of community gardening project.

This summer scene captures a familiar trope running through the history of this liquid nation: the Dutch are always living under the threat of floods, while at the same time they have learned how to live below sea level – mastering hydraulic engineering and navigating the seven seas. All the while, promoting a Calvinist model of accumulation sold as a heroic tale of divine trade and navigation. A "Dutch East India Company mentality" our former Prime Minister J.P. Balkenende would like to "return to."[1] A model grounded in a system of conquest, slavery, and dispossession abroad and exploitation at home disguised as trade. A viable alternative to the Iberian mission. For centuries, the Dutch had been transforming their entire ecosystem by changing river deltas, tracts of sea, and bays into brackish water and erecting entire cities and agricultural land upon a historically marshy and riverine landscape. Today, the largest maritime business cluster *Maritime By Holland* claims that this same maritime sector functions as a "vibrant ecosystem" (Maritime by Holland).[2] Hydraulic engineering, land-

taking, extraction, and navigation have now become an ecosystem of their own – overriding the natural elements of land and water, but never fully. The supposed naturalness of this "vibrant ecosystem" rooted in a narrative of Dutch exceptionalism, which can be traced back to the beginnings of Dutch overseas expansion.

an amphibious nation?

The Netherlands is one of the most manmade countries on the planet. W.J. Wolff notes in his studies of Dutch wetlands from the Roman era to the present, "in the Middle Ages the Dutch population had mastered two technological innovations: drainage and embankment, which in the short term were beneficial to agriculture, but which after some centuries proved disastrous to the landscape" (6). As the Dutch increasingly became facilitators of large-scale European riverine inland trade, the factories up-river have left a definitive mark on the water quality. Together with today's large-scale agriculture and the bio-industry this gives the Netherlands Europe's poorest water quality today (European Environmental Agency, "Waterbase – Water Quality ICM").[3] Land-taking projects have continued to rise (European Environmental Agency, "Land Take in Europe").[4] And yet, the water continues to be in excess of these ambitions.

Sometime after my first encounter with the sinking bridges, I attended a talk on US marshlands by Amelia Groom. She noted that in Amsterdam "[i]t takes ongoing management to push the swamp away. Land reclamation fights the swamp reclamation. The swamp remembers where it was" (Groom). The swamp then shores up against and spills out of illusions of containment.

In the Netherlands, impending or imagined floods are always on the horizon. If you remove the dykes, dams, and dunes, Rosello notes, "[t]he Netherlands are an archipelago" (207). This permanent instability informs locally constructed meanings and imaginaries that seem to hover over stable definitions of the nation state. "My fragile land," Rosello writes, "is worried what the planet will do to it. And perhaps, it should consider what it is doing to the water" (209). In similar vein, Māori scholar Alice Te Punga Sommerville asks for a reversal of familiar scripts that understand the ocean as a threat to the land and asks us to consider that the land and particularly imperial and capitalist nations residing thereon pose a danger to the ocean ("The Great Pacific Garbage Patch" 345).[5] Rosello notes that if the Dutch have a "contemporary poetics and politics of water, it is surely more of the order of constant negotiation and intimate cohabitation than a clear inside-out model" (214). Such "intimacy" is not of the romantic kind, but rather part of a carefully constructed and maintained liberal humanist illusion of Man in control of nature.[6] But what shores up against such a construction? And how does water's materiality spill out of its legal, ontological, material, and epistemological confinements?

Amsterdam, Rosello writes, is "amphibious." The city exists in an intimate relationship between water and land (214).[7] It is worth exploring this amphibiousness from multiple angles. On the one hand, amphibious simply means suited for living on land and in water. However, this understanding of amphibiousness neglects the larger geopolitical and historical context that condition this (self-)perception of the Dutch state. Rather than living on land and in water, Dutch maritime and hydro technologies are premised on an antagonistic relation to water aimed at drainage, containment, dumping, and control.[8] On the other hand, the word amphibious describes a particular form of assault. An amphibious assault characterizes military forces landing from the sea. The Dutch were infamous for such amphibious assaults as they once were the largest commercial-cum-military fleet in the world. Although the ocean formed a threat, it also facilitated imperial expansion. It is Renisa Mawani who calls for a turn to "the *aqueous and amphibian legalities* through which settler colonial power continues to expand and flourish" ("Law, Settler

Colonialism" 126; my emphasis). In other words, the amphibious character of Dutch relations to water is no innocent one and warrants historicizing and denaturalizing. What is perhaps particular about Dutch (settler) colonialism and state formation is that it has become attached – metaphorically and materially – to the control and containment of elemental phenomena. And this local narrative has deeply impacted global maritime legalities and oceanic imaginaries. As Vishwas Satgar reminds us, imperial expansion is accompanied by "imperial ecocide" – "the destruction of conditions that sustain life such as ecosystems, the commons, as well as the destruction of actual human and non-human life forms, to ensure capitalist expansion" (55). And I would like to argue that this includes relations to and imaginations of our ecosystem.

The trope of the Dutch (nation) as amphibious is mobilized to support an antagonistic relation to the water that has informed Dutch self-perception and its global business models. Embanking, draining, containing, and dumping are profitable. Rather than having both lungs and gills then, do we the Dutch not understand ourselves as the perfect mediator between land and water? Manager, rather than frog? And what narratives and histories does such a self-perception rely on and erase?

conquest of maritime imagination

In this meditation on water, I explore what I am thinking of as the Dutch *conquest of maritime imagination*, which includes epistemological, legal, cultural, economic, and political visions of the ocean, deeds performed at sea, how they are imagined and their impact. Such a maritime imagination includes the ocean as a "legal archive," which Mawani describes as not only made up of rules and laws, but often also of a collection of hegemonic narrations of the past that are not always already connected to legalities ("Law's Archive"). In re-activating the word "conquest," I am deeply influenced by Tiffany Lethabo King's use of the term to draw attention to the ongoing violence of conquest in everyday life. Conquest here includes not only the land, but also forms a conceptual terrain to think together the ongoing genocide of Indigenous people, the ongoing assaults on Black lives, and the ways in which ideologies of conquest seep into humanist theories (King, "New World Grammars"; *The Black Shoals*). To me, this includes the violent control and occupation of what the relation to the planet might look like, which is consolidated in law, politics, philosophy, culture, and economics, in which the survival of Black and Indigenous peoples and the planet was but an "afterthought" of this white conquistador vision (Maynard and Simpson 23).

Thinking about conquest and oceans, it is imperative to turn to the work of early modern legal scholar Hugo Grotius – founding father of international law and Dutch state and empire ideologue. What kind of maritime imagination did Grotius's work inaugurate? What conditioned his conquest of maritime imagination? And, at the same time, how does the water continue to spill out of and shore up against his reductive fictions? Thinking about spilling out and shoring up, I am particularly inspired by King's use of the term "shoal." For King, the shoal is a liminal space, "a location of suture between two hermeneutical frames that have been conventionally understood as sealed off from each other" – land and sea – "that cannot be reduced to the ocean, the shore, or an island." The shoal "has the potential to be something else that cannot be known in advance" (King, *The Black Shoals* 7–8).[9] In other words, the place where water and land meet at the shoreline undermines the epistemological, political, legal, material, and metaphorical separation of the two and demands I ask how the elements appear and speak back within the legal archive.

Grotius's deliberation on the status of the seas has been much discussed ever since he first published *Mare Liberum* in 1609. In this anonymously published manifesto and his manuscript *Commentary on the Law of Prize and Booty*, or what he referred to as *De rebus Indicis*, or *On the Affairs of the Indies*, Grotius harnessed the element of water to present a peculiarly Dutch model of aquatic conquest that continues to impact international maritime legal regimes and imaginaries.[10] In particular, it is his construction of the ocean as common property of mankind that continues to structure contemporary negotiations over the status of the sea.

Mare Liberum constitutes the most famous early modern European text deliberating the status of the seas. The text was commissioned a few years prior to publication by the Directors of the Chamber of Zeeland to respond to a dispute between the Dutch and the Portuguese over the capture of the Portuguese carrack *Sta. Catarina* by Dutch captain Jakob van Heemskerck and his crew off the coast of present-day Singapore (Ittersum, "Hugo Grotius in Context"; *Profit and Principle*; "The Long Goodbye"; Borschberg; Mawani, *Across Oceans of Law*). This (in)famous text deliberated the status of the sea – based on a combination of Natural, Divine, Roman, and civil law – in order to dismiss Portuguese claims of dominion and possession in Southeast Asia and the Indian Ocean. From the nineteenth century onward, Grotius was hailed as a founding father of an international law of the seas, free trade, and navigation alongside Francisco Vitoria and Alberto Gentili (Mawani, *Across Oceans of Law* 43). Over the past two decades however, legal historians and political theorists have started to question this innocent celebration of Grotius and have shown how *Mare Liberum* was as much a dispute over the status of the seas as it was a dispute over the *Sta. Catarina* case (Ittersum, "Hugo Grotius in Context"; *Profit and Principle*; "The Long Goodbye"; Borschberg; Mawani, *Across Oceans of Law*).[11] They have also shown that although Grotius was unique in his insistence that one could trade with non-Christians whom he consistently called "infidels," he did not "oppose colonization but merely presented another version, one that foregrounded land and sea" (Mawani, *Across Oceans of Law* 47). Grotius, Anthony Anghie argues, set up the very conditions of possibility for the colonization of lands and of law. Furthermore, he argues that the foundation of the United Dutch East India Company was just as important for the inauguration of the modern-colonial era as was the conquest of the Americas in 1492 (Anghie, "Toward a Postcolonial International Law"; "TWAIL and the Decolonisation of International Law").

Contrary to Chapter XII of *De Indis*, the unpublished (at the time) chapter out of which his manifesto evolved, Grotius had carefully erased any mention of the *Sta. Catarina* case or his comments on Dutchness in *Mare Liberum* (Armitage; Ittersum, *Profit and Principle*). As David Armitage notes, "[a]lthough *Mare Liberum*'s influence and importance were – and remain – independent of that larger commentary, they cannot be fully understood outside of the argument of which they formed a part" (6). Although the manuscript was first published in the nineteenth century, Martine Julia van Ittersum argues that the text must be considered a preliminary study for his most famous work *The Rights of War and Peace* ("Hugo Grotius in Context"; *Profit and Principle*). In other words, what a careful reading of *De Indis* as originating study notes is that his text was not simply informed by the *Sta. Catarina* case, but also by Dutch exceptionalism as much as Dutch colonial interest, while paving the more generalized conditions for a universal theory of property acquisition and defense that rested on a system of Indigenous dispossession and slavery (Stelder).[12]

A central element of Grotius's *Mare Liberum* concerned a deliberation on whether the sea can be considered property of a person or a state. This question was important as Grotius hinged his understanding of the human and of society upon a rigid understanding of individual freedom *as* the right to private property acquisition, extraction, and defense. For Grotius, private ownership was at the basis of a modern community. The emergence of a regime of private property had a teleological and developmentalist quality to it as it only emerged among supposedly developed nations

(Stelder).[13] The centrality of ownership that accompanied colonial ideology, as Robyn Maynard notes, constituted "a disregard for all living things *except for their value as property to be accumulated*" (Maynard and Simpson 23–34). Ownership erases other relations to the planet not resting on capitalist accumulation.

In order to unsettle Grotius's free sea doctrine, I am building on Renisa Mawani's (*Across Oceans of Law*) emphasis on Grotius's transformation of an elemental distinction into a juridical distinction and Samera Esmeir's understanding of *mare liberum* as an act of capture. I move away from the assumption that Grotius's principle rested on a distinction between what can and cannot be owned. In particular, I focus on Grotius's characterization of the ocean as *perpetual res nullius*, which constructs the ocean as a thing that cannot have one singular owner, unless the singular owner is mankind. For Grotius, the ocean remained very much within the orbit of property – an elemental division between land and sea that determined acts of possession, use, and (non)sovereignty. He captured the ocean in the service of white European male "humanity," which deeply impacted imperial relations to the ocean for centuries to come and undergirded an anthropocentric notion of the commons that perceives the globe as a thing or "resource" in the service of humankind. How might conquest be a productive lens to re-read the Grotian project?[14]

In this essay, I center the work of Grotius to consider the political stakes of ontological assessments of the ocean within the context of Dutch imperialism. It is not the paradox between Grotius's depiction of the ocean as common possession or the strategic exceptions to his own framework that interest me here. Neither is it the important observation that Grotius understood the ocean as common and contributed to colonial and capitalist ideologies, nor that the Dutch hold a particular relation to the water. Rather, it is the interplay between water's materiality – described by Grotius and always on the Dutch horizon – and colonial-capitalist attempts to subject it to a logic of property that structures this essay. I seek to problematize the very logic of property that conditions Grotius's legal prescription of the ocean as common and will show how it does not escape this logic. Grotius's legal fiction of the ocean as *perpetual res nullius* does not form an exception to territorial, individual, or state conceptions of property, but rather preconditions it – renders the globe capturable. In doing so, I seek to re-frame Grotius's work in order to problematize and historicize the Dutch built environment, but also open the door to reconsider contemporary questions of colonial-capitalist resource extraction, transportation and trade, and racist renditions of navigation. Furthermore, historicizing the Dutch built environment through a meditation on Grotius's maritime imagination I think through how the water shores up against and spills out of Grotius's legal fictions in the hope to shed light on the limitations of contemporary legal and political debates on oceans that center its status as "common heritage of mankind." My question is not "how do we more evenly divide and regulate resources offered to humanity by the ocean?" – be they for horizontal or vertical extraction – but rather what relations to the water do "we" need to envision and have been envisioned by people and communities outside of Eurocentrism that do not depend on racial capitalist notions of the human and the biosphere that subject water and oceans to the logic of (common) property?[15] Water's materiality inevitably belies the epistemological, legal, and colonial-capitalist grids that have thingified oceans. In this essay, I provincialize Grotius's text in order to unsettle its global reach and universalizing tendencies.

turning water into property, or land-taking

In a discussion of a controversial Dutch (anti-)immigration test video, Rosello hones in on the trope of the Netherlands as a powerful seafaring nation living with the constant threat of the rising sea. Rosello writes, "the unexplored quality of the relationship between colonization and seafaring expertise leads to an ambiguous non-condemnation and relegation of the past as a whole, as if no distinction could be made" (214).[16] With the end of formal colonization, it seems as if the heyday of Dutch seafaring is but a distant yet glorious memory that disconnects colonial violence from the Dutch business ethos. Rosello writes, "a centuries-old history of how the Dutch have successfully mastered the liquid element is consigned to history books, while geography is entrusted with the preferred ideological narrative of vulnerability and dikes" (214). Such a narrative positions the Dutch as masters of the elements who have somehow managed to turn their vulnerability into a strength. In this trope, water serves as a mediator between history and geography, while keeping the two seemingly distinct.

In the seventeenth century, land-taking projects accelerated when the nascent and growing Dutch Republic commenced its imperialist expansion. The Dutch used the capital that they had garnered from their overseas ventures and inter-European trade for land-taking and embankment projects (Wolff 7). A growing population also demanded more energy sources and therefore small-scale peat extraction gained industrial size in the seventeenth century and continued well into the twentieth century when oil and coal began to provide cheaper alternatives (7–8). Dutch imperial interest abroad supported the growing population at home and enabled the transformation of the waterscape in the service of early modern mashup of industrial and merchant capitalism.

A walk through the city offers reminders of this history everywhere. In the Amsterdam City Hall, across from my home, an underground barometer tracks the ebb and flow of the canals. Boat tours will inform the visitor that Amsterdam's rich history of trade and the battle against the sea have made the city what it is today. Arriving at Schiphol Airport, the sign "Welcome Below Sea Level!" will great new arrivals. Such narratives establish a relation to the water that is at once belligerently mercantile and innocent. Deploying the term "innocent" I am referring to a specific iteration Gloria Wekker has called "white innocence," which forms a central paradox in white Dutch self-perception (5). This is a self-perception of the Netherlands as a small country, liberal, humanitarian, and free from race or gender as a means to deny the existence of structural racism-sexism. The possibility that four hundred years of colonialism have deeply affected contemporary social relations is hereby disavowed (17–19).

Flying into national airspace from the south, you first witness the grand dame of Dutch water management, the Delta Works – an intricate system of mega dams and dykes controlling the ebb and flow of the North Sea – the first of its kind. Its patented technology a ready export product to other coastal nations facing rising sea levels. Flying further north, your plane will land amid neatly aligned parcels of green, bordered by a grid-like structure of canals on all sides, which the Dutch call the *polder*, the epitome of land-taking projects.

In her book *Capitalism and Cartography in the Dutch Golden Age*, Elizabeth Sutton addresses the relation between Dutch land-taking projects (both from Indigenous peoples and from the sea), mapmaking, and the political and legal ideology of Hugo Grotius. She describes how seventeenth-century Dutch mapmaking reveals an intimate connection between water and land grounded in claims of possession and control. From the seventeenth century onward, rich Dutch East India Company (VOC) merchants invested in land reclamation projects in the province of Holland displacing local fishers. Land was made and settled with farmers for agricultural production to support the emergence of a new urban class of Amsterdam merchants (Sutton 15, 22).

The Beemster Land Reclamation Project started in 1608 and became the first large-scale corporate and privatized land reclamation investment scheme in the province of Holland (Sutton 3). It coincided with Hugo Grotius's initial writings on property and its relation to the state, the individual, and the overseas (Sutton 36). This system of capital accumulation, Sutton notes, was supported by

geographic developments and mapmaking, which Grotius furthered through "rational juristic thought" (Sutton 6). In particular, it was Grotius's legal system that provided the grounds for claiming sovereignty, dictating ownership, legitimating taxes, and defending military maneuvers. Land-taking helped further stratify regimes of ownership and control. In this Calvinist setting, the ethos of capitalism reigned supreme (Sutton 8). The rationalization of water and sea power in the service of capital and imperial expansion was not far at hand. The Dutch Calvinist work ethos provided a "providential blessing" to these endeavors that rendered ownership, profit, and accumulation acceptable, and it also provided a context in which the idea that humans naturally compete for resources first became naturalized (8–9).

Sutton describes how a similar model of land-taking and water management was imported into Dutch colonial settlements to create grid cities, such as in "New Netherlands" (Mannahatta) and "Mauritsstad" (Recife) (31). Also in Suriname, extensive tracts of forests were razed to the ground and turned into *polders* with the use of enslaved African and Indigenous labor to build Suriname's infamous sugar plantations. These grid-like structures were not only implemented to dictate white ownership and conquest, but also to prevent fugitivity and revolt of the enslaved. At the same time, the constant ebbing and flowing of Suriname's wetlands into the dense rainforest were mobilized by Maroon communities to stay hidden from slave catchers (de Kom; Robinson 138–40).

In Manhattan, the Dutch used water and flood control within the grid-like structure in the service of military control and divisibility. Influential seventeenth-century figures, such as master surveyor Simon Stevin, believed that surveys of hydraulics and navigation were fundamental to Dutch state formation (Sutton 34–36). These land and water claims were, as Sutton argues, supported by maps that "visually engaged Grotius's theory of possession" (19). On such maps ownership was depicted by showing how land was controlled by hydraulic technologies used for commerce and government (19). For Sutton, building on water allowed the Dutch to reclaim land as *res nullius* and develop it (86). These structures were not simply made to protect from floods, but instigated new forms of capitalist and colonial management that enabled the rise of the Dutch empire in the long seventeenth century. These land-taking projects, although profitable, proved detrimental to the environment, while at the same time supported a larger political ideology of both local and imperial expansion. Land-takings foreclosed other relations to the environment that might have rested on cohabitation. Embankment and enclosure have always been practiced, but in the early seventeenth century the Dutch introduced a profitable model of land reclamation on a colonial-capitalist scale that rested on an antagonistic and appropriative relation to the water that it continues to export across the globe today. This relationship further rested upon a particular juridicalization of water and of Dutchness that sutured the nation-building project to the ocean.

"those true sons of the sea"

For Grotius, van Ittersum notes, the Dutch were "merchants not conquerors." His ideology of empire was therefore maritime (Ittersum, "The Long Goodbye" 387). This did not mean that Grotius was not interested in colonial settlement; he simply rescripted it (Mawani, *Across Oceans of Law* 47; van Ittersum, "Hugo Grotius in Context" 535). Free trade and navigation on the high seas, and especially Indigenous resistance to the natural right to free trade and navigation became ways for the Dutch to justify Indigenous dispossession (Stelder). Conquest, then, was still at the heart of merchant capitalism.

Grotius turned the Dutch relation to the water into a juridical text. In order to do so, he relied as much on an ontological description of the elements as he did on an ontological description of Dutchness – and both seem intimately related. In the concluding chapter of *De Indis*, Grotius eagerly asked his readers "What may be hoped for the Dutch, those true sons of the sea?" (*Commentary on the Law of Prize*

and Booty 481). With this question, he concluded his five-hundred-page discourse on just war doctrine, natural rights theory, prize law, and Dutch teleology. In his future-oriented vision, Grotius proselytized the transformation of the barely sovereign United Provinces into a powerful Dutch maritime empire and prophesized a time of splendor for those "true sons of the sea."[17] In this scenario the ocean is feminized as an object in the service of the masculine sons of the sea. Writing at the advent of what historians call the Dutch Golden Age, Grotius's dreams would come true not much later with the violent acquisition of Dutch power around the globe.

In Chapter XV, the young jurist described the ontological precedents that made the Dutch more suitable to oceanic commerce than any other nation. He described the size and speed of Dutch vessels as more apt to "meet every martial and maritime emergency" (Grotius, *Commentary on the Law of Prize and Booty* 479). On the contrary, he described Portuguese vessels as an extension, or prosthesis of Portugueseness. Their ships were, in his words, "slow-moving hulks [...] inadequate for strife against the winds [...] fitted to be conquered rather than to conquer" (479). He then continued to describe why the Dutch are more apt to navigate the world ocean. He wrote:

> Dutch people – reared amid their own waters beneath a frosty, wind-swept sky, under the light of Northern stars, and in an amazing number of cases accustomed even from childhood to spending more time upon the ocean, than on land – are just as familiar with the sea as they are with the soil. (479–80)

Grotius wrote that the Dutch could endure the cold "extremely well," could go without food for long periods of time, and were "thoroughly accustomed to the hardships attended upon extended journeys such as [voyages to the Indies]" (480). The Dutch were more apt than any nation to take to the seas. Grotius contrasted a cold, masculine, restrained, Calvinist pragmatism with the Portuguese, who – he writes – were, "enervated by warmth," "wasted with debauchery," "effeminate," and "accustomed to luxury" (480). In other words, Grotius constructed a context in which the Dutch relation to the elements provided an ontological, elemental, and material justification for Dutch conquest and piracy. For Grotius, the Dutch were the superior maritime race; it was God's purpose to "select the Dutch in preference to all others [...] and reveal the glory of our race to the farthest regions of the world" (496).

Although the ocean could not be owned by a state or individual, it was navigable by especially European, and – for Grotius – Dutch ships. It was God's ocean, and not the Iberian Christianizing mission or the papal bull, that granted the Dutch access to the resources of the world. Mawani further argues that the ship itself constituted a juridical form, which "produced the foundational and legal distinction between land and sea" (*Across Oceans of Law* 49).[18] For Grotius the lightness and velocity of Dutch ships are exemplary of a new mode of maritime capital's circulation and justification. The ship becomes a prosthetic of Dutchness to be projected and mapped onto the globe. To prevent the Dutch from navigating their ships across oceans would be in violation not just of natural law, but of nature herself (Grotius, *Commentary on the Law of Prize and Booty* 303).

Grotius's thinking about the ocean belongs as much to the realm of imagination as it does to the realm of materiality and it draws attention to the ways in which the mutable myth of the freedom of the seas is implicitly bound to ideas of Dutchness and Dutch interest. According to Alison Rieser, the Dutch "crafted legends and patriotic explanations for the superiority of the Dutch brand and its economic model," which turned *mare liberum* not only into law, but also into a convenient truth, legend, and social technology to protect Dutch hegemony (211, 216). These legends did not simply craft explanations; they provided the ontological and epistemological backbone of Grotius's legal framework. They now provide the opportunity for unpacking Dutch exceptionalism and its subsequent claims to

the sea as myth, history, economy, law, and destiny, denaturalizing the universalization of the world ocean as a free sea. Erasing the *Sta. Catarina* case from his *Mare Liberum* allowed his work to become instrumentalized by other imperial states. However, this did not mean that the text is not rooted in Grotian ideas about Dutch exceptionalism that "rationalized accumulation and colonial ownership" (Sutton 14).

ocean as *perpetual res nullius*

In Chapter XII of *De Indis*, Grotius deliberated on the status of the sea. For him, the sea, like the air, is the "common *possession* of all men and the private possession of none" (*Commentary on the Law of Prize and Booty* 321–22; my emphasis). After this initial statement on the juridical status of the sea, he begins to nuance his argument. The reason for the ocean to be the common possession of all men is that it "is so vast no *one* could possibly take possession of it" (322; my emphasis). Furthermore, it is made to serve the rights of navigation and of fishing (322).

For Grotius, both the ocean and the shore are common *property* to all under natural law and the law of nations. It is at this point in *De Indis* that Grotius makes an important observation or statement about the status of the sea. He writes,

> [n]evertheless, even though the said things [the sea and the shore] are correctly called *res nullius* in so far as private ownership is concerned, they are very different from those which are also *res nullius* but which have not been assigned for common use: e.g. wild beasts, fish, and birds.[19] (Grotius, *Commentary on the Law of Prize and Booty* 322)

He further specifies that items belonging to the latter class can be rendered private ownership through the act of possession, whereas

> items within the former class [of *res nullius*] have been rendered *forever exempt* from such [private] ownership by the unanimous

agreement of mankind, in view of the fact that the right to use them, pertaining as it does to all men, can no more be taken from humanity as a whole by one individual than my property can be taken from me by you. (322–23; my emphasis)

In other words, the ocean indeed falls within the class of *res nullius*, even as it remains *exempt in perpetuity* from private ownership – *perpetual res nullius*.

He specifies that if any of the things just mentioned do become "susceptible to occupancy in accordance with nature's plan," they *can* become private property of the person(s) occupying it as long as it does not impede common use (Grotius, *Commentary on the Law of Prize and Booty* 323). In this section, Grotius opens the door to ongoing Dutch coastal land-taking projects at home and abroad, while at the same time he provides the legal parameters for just invasion and occupation of [parts] of an overseas shore. He even went as far as to argue that acts of occupation can be both acts of a private individual and of a nation, even as the sea and the shore frequently resist such occupancy (324–25). Moreover, Grotius argued that possession of the shore can only occur when the site remains occupied. However, the sea might reclaim that part of the shore.[20]

In this section, I am particularly interested in Mawani's reading of Grotius's manifesto as she contemplates his deliberation on the elemental distinctions between land and sea. Mawani writes,

> *Mare Liberum* might also be read as an aesthetic meditation on the high seas, one that was informed by an element-turned-legal distinction between land and sea. For Grotius, it was the physico-material properties of oceans, their expansiveness, and ceaseless change – that rendered them to be juridically different from *terra firma*. (*Across Oceans of Law* 43)

It was this elemental distinction "that determined the legal questions of occupation and possession" (43). The sea's very livingness as churning, ebbing, and flowing made it uncapturable. Land could be bordered and cultivated, so Grotius argued, and thereby possessed by an individual or a state. In a similar way, inland waters were subject to occupation and possession. For Mawani, Grotius's text offered a different worldview in which imperial sovereignty was repositioned via the ocean as central (43). Grotius decidedly understood the ocean in liquid terms and "liquids cannot be possessed except by means of that whereby they are limited" (46).[21]

Grotius's thinking about the ocean as facilitator of traffic and trade was sutured to political, epistemological, and legal ideas about Dutch exceptionalism that attempted to turn the globe into a colonial-capitalist ecosystem replete with its own Calvinist rationalization. This reductive understanding of the ocean has created what Esmeir describes as "an oceanic image [where] nature has ordained commerce between peoples and put oceans to facilitate this traffic and trade" (84).

For Grotius, the ocean was unknown yet knowable at the time of writing his text. He was convinced that marine science could make it known and enable capitalist expansion across the globe, providing the conditions for one of the first encounters between natural law and natural science. Esmeir writes, Grotius's vision "facilitated the production of an enlarged surface of the world as an object to be *captured* through European navigation and trade" (82; my emphasis).[22] Where most Grotian scholars have argued that Grotius described the sea as free from ownership, what is striking is that Esmeir uses a language of capture to describe the world-making event of the text. For Grotius, capture was necessary to establish ownership. In a world where the ocean is imagined as capturable – yet can never be legally owned by an individual or a state – other visions for the world and the sea are lost (Esmeir 83).[23] Esmeir calls this the "coloniality of the Free Sea," which she describes, "lies not only in its solicitation by the VOC to expand Dutch trade to the East Indies but in its productive power, which persists today in the field of international law" (85). Such a "vision" does not simply produce the ocean as supposedly free and common to all; it provides, "the constitutive center for staging an enlarged world [...] a unified world and, more significantly, spatial-political possibilities for capturing it and intervening in it" (85). The force of the text therefore does not only include the imposition of an elemental-juridical framework that demarcates the land from the sea, it equally constructed an imposition of a particular maritime imagination where navigating the ocean became a way to enforce said legal and epistemological order, which attempted to capture the ocean as an element in the service of global racial capitalism. What made this world capturable, I argue, was Grotius's construction of the ocean as *perpetual res nullius*. It is this thingification of the ocean that both enabled the consolidation of European maritime colonial expansion for centuries to come and the transformation of coastal regions at home and in the colonies into arable land to facilitate plantation and urban expansion. Grotius's colonial-capitalist worldview does not only undergird private possession, but also produces an anthropocentric notion of the commons through the logic of ownership that forecloses other, non-exploitative relations to the sea.

The distinction between the land and the sea then does not rest upon a distinction between what can and cannot be owned, but rather on a temporal distinction between different stratifications within a larger regime of ownership. In this move, Grotius reduced the turbulent, vast, unknowing sea into the status of a thing – property, yet common. Although Grotius hinged his conception of the human on becoming propertied and defending private property, the ocean itself becomes the private property of all mankind to be defended by the Dutch, thereby excluding those considered non-human, including racialized, gendered, and more-than-human life forms. In this at once juridical, ontological, and epistemological gesture Grotius reduces the ocean's life-giving force to the status of a thing in the service of merchant men and the corporate state. This relation between land and sea conditioned the emergence of global racial capitalism as different

stratifications within a regime of property acquisition and defense. It conditioned a system in which the climate, to speak with Christina Sharpe, is "anti-Black" as much as it is anti-Indigenous (106). Grotius's rendition of the winds and the weather facilitated and justified the trans-Atlantic, Pacific Ocean, and Indian Ocean slave trade and Indigenous dispossession based on a logic of accumulation in the service of free trade and navigation. Supporting acts of bodily, sovereign, and elemental dispossession and possession, Grotius's narrative is thus not simply legally "effective"; it creates the discursive conditions upon which the elements can be imagined and harnessed in the service of anti-Black, anti-Indigenous, and environmental violence – genocide and ecocide.

Mawani argues that the freedom of navigation in Grotius only included European men. In extension, the ocean is then not free from possession, but the common possession of white European men. At the same time, even Grotius's own writings continue to underscore the ephemerality of these collective and private acts of occupation and possession as the ocean "cannot easily be built upon nor enclosed" (*Commentary on the Law of Prize and Booty* 325).[24] It might not be a foreign enemy, but rather the ocean itself that remembers where it was – reclaims what has been deemed ownership of Man by European men.

The sea itself becomes an active actor in Grotius's writings, who much like man, "diverted [things] from other uses and made its own, such as the sands of the sea, of which the portion merging onto the land is called the shore" (*Commentary on the Law of Prize and Booty* 322). Because the shore, as it were, was claimed as part of the property of the ocean, the shore as a whole could not be subject to private possession. He even went as far as to argue that where the sea seems "to resist possession like a wild beast who can no longer be considered property of its captor after retaining its natural liberty," the shore "returns to the sea, under the principle of *postliminium*" (324). Here he seems to imply that the ocean, under *postliminium*, has a right to "recover what has been lost or stolen" (178). In Book II, Chapter II of *The Rights of War and Peace*, Grotius further asserts that certain "Banks of Sand" cannot be owned not simply because the sand returns to the ocean, but because they are "incapable of Culture, and serve only to supply Men with Sand, but can never be exhausted" (430).[25] Although Grotius perhaps meant that the shore could not be cultivated, it might be productive to read uncultivated and uncultured together through the larger prism of conquest as they both facilitated colonial expansion and plantation slavery. This section is one of the most direct ways in which Grotius assigns the sand to its inexhaustible use for land-taking projects. The shore then, as R.P. Anand notes, "derives its character from the sea, and it is not considered part of the land" (84).

The shore was the first point of contact after a long conquistador voyage. For Grotius the shore constituted neither land, nor water, its ground too unstable to fall under the category of landed sovereignty. According to R.P. Anand, the understanding of the shore as a space where foreigners could erect trading posts within which they followed their own legal customs, much like upon ships, constituted an appropriation of Indian Ocean understandings of the free sea, which quickly led Europeans to conquer foreign territories (82–89). At the same time, Grotius's descriptions of the shore are reminiscent of a Dutch shoreline. Here, the beaches are wide, sandy, low – a significant visual difference between ebb and flow where the sea continues to swallow up large tracts of sandy beach only to reveal it again when the tide recedes. At that time, the seawater would shore up all the way to Amsterdam. Even today, the city's waters are brackish. The place where ocean and sand engulf each other, to think with King, "has the potential to be something else that cannot be known in advance" (*The Black Shoals* 7–8). Contours and boundaries that cannot be fixed challenge the territorial sovereignty of the nation state. It is such possibility that escapes and, at the same time, undergirds the Grotian imaginary and Eurocentric relations to the water.

Grotius's conception of the shore as taken and given by, or perhaps belonging to the ocean, reveals that his understanding of the elemental-cum-juridical distinction between land and sea is not as clear cut as he claims it is. On the one hand, this allows him to claim the shore as common as a means to enable Dutch ships to penetrate distant shores. On the other hand, this leaves me space to consider the ocean from a different vantage point. It is particularly his understanding of the shore as a hybrid, or perhaps amphibious (legal) zone between land and sea that reveals the conceptual ambivalence of Grotius's argument. In this hybrid space, the brackish waters flowing through the Amsterdam canals reveal an interplay between saline and fresh water that creates its own ecosystem that is neither strictly oceanic, nor strictly riverine – a transitional zone where two different bodies of water meet. Grotius's argument opens the door to amphibious assaults and to the ongoing Dutch creation of land onto the sea, but also shows that the sea continues to take back – flood and immersion on the horizon. Such an image of the shore as a liminal space shows that the elemental and juridical distinction between land and sea, or between different bodies of water cannot be as easily drawn.

I find Grotius's idea of the ocean taking back, reclaiming itself, helpful as it spills out of and shores up against his own attempts to capture the surface of the world for navigation and trade, and the ocean as a resource for humans. Water reclamation demands a different relation to the water, one not premised on conquest. Clearly, this did not prevent the Dutch from expanding their empire. However, looking at the metal sheets along the Amsterdam canals it seems there are limitations to capturing and juridicalizing the water. The blue planet speaks back to regimes of property and capture – it speaks through rising sea levels and ocean acidification. What interests me here is not simply that Grotius developed strategic exceptions to his idea of the ocean as common property by suggesting that it could, at times, become the private possession of an individual or state, albeit temporarily, but that he described the ocean as an active agent, even with the right to *postliminium*. The ocean can take back what was taken – rendering unstable any claims that can be made, any boundary that might be drawn. Nowhere do we perhaps see this more clearly than in dammed and controlled coastal environments where the water continues to reclaim itself, such as the city of Amsterdam. When sand no longer holds the weight of brick and metal, water refuses a long history of racial capitalist violence. When water trickles through, the city sinks. Even the sand itself is part of an intricate play between water, movement, shell, rock, and crustaceans. The city is built on the pulverized remains of bazillions of ancient exoskeletons. The ocean's materiality is always already in excess of Grotian legal claims.

The ocean resists its thingification in the service of global capitalism. It devours ships; it reclaims land for itself; it coughs up sand when it wants to; it regurgitates our pollution and spits it out as acid rain. It is the ocean's "more-than-wet-ontology" that trickles into Grotius's legal imaginary (Peters and Steinberg), even as he seems to erect a juridical fortress and impose a perspective of the ocean that turns it into an element in the service of European navigation and maritime supremacy.

negotiations for the planet

Grotius's conquest of maritime imagination continues to pervade our international legal imaginaries. The horizontal and vertical stratification of the ocean into different juridical zones in the United Nations Law of the Seas Convention based on the Common Heritage of Mankind principle is but one symptom of the reduction of the ocean to *perpetual res nullius*.[26] The "common heritage of mankind principle" resulted from the efforts of newly found and decolonized nation states, and was, as Henry Jones remarks, "revolutionary." As a result of Third World Movements, it positioned the ocean as "a resource belonging to all, and to be exploited for the benefit of all" (Jones 316). Unfortunately, it also proved itself, much in the spirit of Grotius's free sea

doctrine, susceptible to cooption by the free market principles of First World States (Jones 314). For Esmeir, this failure, even though its potential was great, was because the ocean remained captured within the logic of the nation state (83). I would like to add that in the face of climate catastrophe, the failure of the common heritage and free sea principles lies in the fact that they subject the ocean to a logic of property, a resource to be exploited by (hu)mankind. It is particularly Indigenous thinkers, writers, and organizers who demand a different relation to the biosphere and resist elemental separation and compartmentalization – the "deathwork of 'unmaking water'" (Perera 59) – but whose demands fall flat within a worldview that is premised on accumulation and perceives the world as (common) property (Aikau et al.; Perera; Te Punga Sommerville, *Once Were Pacific*; Hau'ofa; Christian and Wong).[27]

Thinking with the work of Indigenous studies scholar Mishuana Goeman (Tonawanda Band of Seneca), King argues, "through European colonialism, European conceived scales – units of accumulation – have been imposed on the biosphere, turning the environment into separate spaces such as 'reservations, nation states, continents [and] hemispheres,' in addition to land and water" (*The Black Shoals* 94; Aikau et al. 94). Such "scalar fragmentation" continues to affect contemporary relations to the ocean and erases other modalities of relating to water. It is particularly early modern European humanism that has actively sought to undo the ocean's "more-than-wet ontology" through the imposition of scalar and legal fragmentation. What water studies calls water's "more-than-wet ontology" has been part and parcel of Indigenous and Black histories, thought, and scholarship for centuries, which destabilizes some of the claims made within the field that seeks to script itself as "new."[28]

For Grotius, there seems to be no contradiction between the elemental livingness of the ocean and its ongoing thingification in the service of conquest-as-free-trade. Such conquest includes a conquest of the imagination, which includes the ontological, epistemological, elemental, and legal myths that have been scripted to support racial capitalism's conquistador ideology. What becomes clear is that capitalism can only acknowledge livingness in its very thingification. This is perhaps capitalism's greatest failure and achievement as its vision for the biosphere continues to dominate negotiations over, or should I say *for*, the planet while the planet is pushing back against such a reductionist vision. In other words, capitalism can only continue to exist through its naturalization, while global climate catastrophe reminds us that the elements continue to exceed it. What Surabhi Ranganathan describes as international law's "extractive imaginary" starts with Grotius and does not just relate to things taken from the ocean, be they fish or other marine "resources," but also to the movement and circulation of ships and their owners upon it and what remains in excess of such reductive fictions.

conclusion

The more the world is forced to come to terms with climate catastrophe, the more I am reminded that water cannot be controlled or owned. The ocean demands that I come to terms with spill, draught, acidification, and flood, and the unevenly felt effects of climate catastrophe outside the neoliberal onslaught of sustainability for capitalist growth. The properties of the ocean are in excess of its status as common heritage, or should I say, common property of mankind.[29]

A few months after my first walk through the city, the aquatic community gardens now aligning the water's edge show that another relation to water is possible. At the same time, they are exemplary of a new turn in the logic of capitalism – sustainability, a discourse that has been coopted by the state and industry and "now refers primarily to the *economic* sustainability of capital accumulation itself" (Coulthard 77). New seeds are sown, but to what extent is this a rupture with the not-so-distant past? The little sprigs and bushes sprouting up from the expanded

sandboxes are but a temporary solution masked as a contemporary turn in Dutch water management policy geared towards neoliberal sustainability and so-called "resilience" (i.e., AquaConnect). This illusion of sustainability is more about sustaining a Dutch way of life than about degrowth or decolonization – a politics and poetics of water that does not operate in the service, or under the protectorate of Dutch mankind. I would like to keep asking with Rosello and Te Punga Sommerville what we are doing to water. If I want to move away from a colonial understanding of the planet, it is imperative to move away from a Grotian maritime imagination that positions the ocean as common property to be exploited in the service of capital accumulation – a relation to the commons that ultimately remains anthropocentric in nature.

The sinking city built on uprooted underwater old growth – traded handsomely across European states – serves as a reminder of a logic David Harvey has called the "spatial fix" aimed at control rather than cohabitation – the reification of a capitalist relation to nature. A spatial fix describes "capitalism's insatiable drive to resolve its inner crisis tendencies by geographical expansion and geographical restructuring" (24). At the same time, the water itself spills out. Today, whenever those old-growth underwater structures come in touch with oxygen they start to tilt making the canals look like rows of dancing houses. The water spills out – a reminder that we must cohabitate with it as it refuses to bend and submit to its canalization, dredging, and management.

The limitations of a Grotian maritime imaginary that continues to capture dominant international legal, cultural, economic, and political deliberations begs the question how "we" can rethink elemental relations, refuse the logic of property, and abolish a Grotian maritime imagination. Where do I think from? How do I write about water and act upon water so as not to perpetuate its status as a commodity? What might this mean for contemporary deliberations on the status of the sea that seem to suggest that an "Area" of the ocean can be protected, while another "Area" is being prepared for the largely unknown project of deep-sea mining by the world's richest and most powerful corporations and corporate states supported by the International Seabed Authority as "steward"?[30] I place the "we" between quotation marks here, because the uneven responsibility for and effects of the long environmental crisis of the "racial capitalocene" (Vergès) "we" find ourselves in must be contemplated as "we" try to form and understand alternative, future, and existing relations to the biosphere that do not rest on thingification.

In this essay, I tried to find a way to write about how water speaks back to its legal, epistemological, material, ontological, and political confinement by thinking through the idea of water reclaiming itself in the face of its juridical and political thingification in the service of global racial capitalism. In doing so, I juxtaposed Grotius's legal thinking about the ocean, Amsterdam's sinking city scape, and land-taking projects to better understand how the ocean both spills out and shores up against the modern-colonial legal-elemental fictions that subject it to a carceral logic of property.

In May 2022, I was asked to join a panel on "brackish methodologies" that centered on the Dutch waterscape. On the panel, I was joined by benthic ecologist Arie Vonk. What struck me was how much of our thinking about water was alike. Where I talked how Dutch maritime imaginaries turned colonial capitalism into its own ecosystem, he studied the benthic ecosystem in the Netherlands and talked about the environmental damages that occur as a result of damming, reclaiming, and confining water. He described how, contrary to Dutch strategies of separating and compartmentalizing the environment, marking hard separations between land and sea, organisms in brackish estuaries embrace their conditions, moving in and along the ecosystem. Land-taking and marine engineering create a static ecosystem where benthic ecosystems depend on the movement of salt and fresh water, and sand. His work as a researcher to protect and understand this ecosystem collides with the maritime capitalist ventures of the Dutch. We joked about this manmade land. He said, "It is so typically Dutch! We don't like a tree in some place, we put it somewhere else. We need land? We take it from the water!" According to his expertise, it would perhaps not be such a bad idea to imaging embracing the natural dynamics of the ecosystem to live *with* it in different ways.

disclosure statement

No potential conflict of interest was reported by the author.

notes

This project has received funding from the European Union's Horizon 2020 Research and Innovation Programme under the Marie Sklodowska-Curie grant agreement No. 838904. I would like to express my deepest gratitude to Renisa Mawani for her valuable feedback and support. Thank you to the Law of the Seas Workshop and Elspeth Probyn in particular for her comments on the very first draft. To Erika Doucette for listening and thinking through various instantiations of this article with me. To the two anonymous reviewers and editors for their generous suggestions.

1 In 2006, former Dutch Prime Minister Jan Peter Balkenende expressed the desire during a political debate to return to a "VOC mentaliteit," or "Dutch East India Company mentality" (Groenendijk).

2 Maritime by Holland is the website of the Dutch Maritime Cluster commissioned by the Dutch Ministry of Infrastructure and Water, which connects the different onshore and offshore maritime sectors in the Netherlands. In the NL Portal website commissioned by the Dutch Ministry of Infrastructure and Water Management, we learn that "more than 12,000 maritime companies create €18.5 billion in added value, with employment amounting to some 167,000 jobs. The indirect added value represents an additional €4.3 billion and 90,000 jobs" (NL flag).

3 This includes both effects on the water table, which has to remain low for Dutch mass farmers

to work the land but has adverse effects on the ecosystem (including humans) increasingly leading to droughts, and the water quality through dumping toxic waste from factories and farms (that operate much like factories these days).

4 In this essay I will use the term "land-taking projects" to refer to what is conventionally called land reclamation. I do this to destabilize the clear-cut distinction between land and sea and the relation between conquest, capital accumulation, and land reclamation.

5 In particular, Te Punga Sommerville is talking about the long history of the Pacific Ocean garbage patch.

6 For more on the intimacies of liberal humanism, see Lowe.

7 Rosello builds on Ciriacono's comparative study of land reclamation in early modern Venice and Holland. In this book, Ciriacono briefly mentions the amphibian state as metaphor. It remains disconnected from the larger context of nascent European imperialisms.

8 In the early 2020s, we see a self-acclaimed "paradigm shift" from an explicitly antagonistic relation to the water to one that centers the concept of "resilience" with the commencement of the Aqua-Connect Project. However, this project still operates exclusively from an anthropocentric purview that privileges the capitalist economy – industry and agriculture (AquaConnect).

9 For King, the shoal is a particularly useful conceptual terrain to destabilize the suture between blackness and liquidity and between indigeneity and land, and to suggest an alternative way to understand the relation between Black and Native Studies.

10 Grotius referred to his manuscript as *De rebus Indicis*. It is only much later that the text became known as *De Iure Praedae* or *Commentary on the Law of Prize and Booty*. Following Eric Wilson, I will use the title *De Indis* to draw attention to the coloniality of the text (Wilson, "On Heterogeneity and the Naming"; *Savage Republic*).

11 It must be noted that he receives a far less critical reception in the Dutch context itself, where he continues to be portrayed as somewhat of a folk hero.

12 His work formed the theoretical ground for the works of Adam Smith, Johan and Pieter de la

Courts, Edmund Burke, Thomas Hobbes, and John Locke (Sutton 38). And, as van Ittersum cautions, "Dutch ways of understanding empire were crucially important to neighboring imperial powers" ("A Miracle Mirrored?" 98).

13 Grotius "radically re-defined property" as a private affair (Sutton 69). This partitioning between what is mine and what is yours depended on an intimate Dutch relationship to the land and the water (55). The grid-like structure of the *polder*, for instance, informed Grotius's writings in *Jurisprudence of Holland* and helped explain his understanding of private property (67). In *The Rights of War and Peace*, Grotius notes that in the Americas Indigenous people have not yet achieved this level of development as they still seem to live in a state in which all things are held in common (421). His understanding of property is therefore racialized.

14 Turning to conquest, I am inspired by King's call to turn to the idea of conquest as ongoing and central to the project of liberal humanism (*The Black Shoals*).

15 This is a very tentative "we," Indigenous, Black, and decolonial scholarship has continued to call for and nurture relations to the biosphere that refuse Eurocentric imaginaries and do not rest on a logic of accumulation (i.e., Satgar; Simpson; Coulthard; Maynard and Simpson; Walcott; Vergès; Christian and Wong).

16 Rosello is particularly addressing how the Netherlands is narrated in a video used as part of the controversial entrance/integration test for newly arriving migrants. Rather than hone in on the use of sexuality in the test (as done by Judith Butler and others), Rosello picks up on the sea and the water as a central element of narrating national history and belonging.

17 At the time of writing, the United Provinces had not yet been recognized as a sovereign state among European powers as it was still at war with its Iberian sovereign (van Ittersum, *Profit and Principle*; Porras).

18 Furthermore, she writes, ships were "colonial laboratories" (Mawani, "Law, Settler Colonialism" 123). In particular, she argues, they were "places of confinement and conviviality where legal idioms, practices, and forms of violence were not only enforced, but also deliberated, disputed, and often extended to *terra firma*" (Mawani,

Across Oceans of Law 49). This is also why Grotius could position the *Sta. Catarina* case as a legal precedent for larger deliberations over the status of the sea.

19 For Grotius, items which can be considered *res nullius* also include non-Christian prisoners of war and uncultivated lands, which opened the door to the transoceanic slave trade and Indigenous dispossession.

20 Interestingly, Grotius does not give the enslaved the same right as wild beasts or oceans, as the enslaved must not resist or escape (Stelder).

21 Mawani cites here from Grotius's response to William Welwod ("Defence of Chapter V").

22 She also laments how this was not overcome in the 1982 United Nations Law of the Seas Convention, even as those negotiations were heavily impacted by the Bandung alliance and newly decolonized states at the negotiation table.

23 For instance, Steinberg writes that Grotius asserted that "the sea is definitely not *res nullius*," but that there is a duty, especially for more powerful nations, to preserve access to resources and navigation to all, even as the resources taken from the ocean do not have to be equally divided (Steinberg 93). Steinberg even insists Grotius developed an "activist regulatory form of stewardship" in which a few major users operate as the main stewards (93–94). Steinberg places Grotius's notion of the ocean within the realm of states, emphasizing *use* rather than *possession*, but what he bypasses is that Grotius does indeed describe the ocean as *res nullius*, albeit unpossessable by an individual/state. Grotius's ocean does not only remain within the realm of states as Steinberg contends; it also remains within a logic of property acquisition and defense.

24 In Book II, Chapter II in *The Rights of War and Peace*, he does further specify instances where parts of the ocean and sea lanes might be captured.

25 It must be noted that in the colonial context the supposed absence of "culture" within non-European peoples often provided the grounds for racist civilizationalist arguments used to justify conquest.

26 For a comprehensive overview of the concept, see Baslar.

27 Perera extends the work of Deborah Bird Rose in relation to Indigenous struggles over the river Murray in South Australia to the ocean. "To unmake water is to 'impair […] water's living presence and at the same time work […] at killing the human capacity to understand water in its living complexity' (Rose, 2007: 12)" (Perera 59).

28 See, for instance: Glissant; Hau'ofa; Te Punga Sommerville, *Once Were Pacific*; Chang; Stephens and Martínez-San Miguel; LaDuke; Simpson; Mulalap et al.; Christian and Wong; Perera; King, *The Black Shoals*; Sharpe. Conventionally, within water studies I would use Peters and Steinberg's "more-than-wet-ontology" to speak about the ocean's materiality. However, understanding the ocean's relation to the rest of the biosphere has been part and parcel of particularly critical Indigenous studies scholarship and knowledges for centuries. Although the spiritual and theoretical dimensions of such relations are particular to specific Indigenous cosmologies, I draw inspiration from these writings as they refuse the violence and epistemologies of racial capitalism and imperial ecocide.

29 This is a reference to the "common heritage of mankind" principle described in the 1982 United Nations Law of the Sea Convention and its 1994 Amendment.

30 On the one hand, recent UN negotiations over the status of the sea have called for more Marine Protected Areas (MPAs), while on the other hand, the International Seabed Authority has now granted permits to mine other parts of the deep sea, which UNLCOS 1994 amendment refers to as "The Area." For more on the ISA and deep-sea mining, see Silva; Zalik.

bibliography

Aikau, Hōkūlani K., et al. "Indigenous Feminisms Roundtable." *Frontiers*, vol. 36, no. 3, 2015, pp. 84–106.

Anand, R.P. *On the Origin and Development of the Law of the Sea: History of International Law Revisited.* Martinus Nijhoff, 1983.

Anghie, Anthony. "Toward a Postcolonial International Law." *Critical International Law,* edited by Prabhar Singh and Benoit Mayer, Oxford UP, 2014.

Anghie, Anthony. "TWAIL and the Decolonisation of International Law: Part 1." Ben Beinart Memorial Lecture, University of Cape Town South Africa. *YouTube*, 23 Nov. 2017, www.youtube.com/watch?v=riLgiqJetTc. Accessed 29 Sept. 2022.

AquaConnect. "Pathway to Impact." *AquaConnect*, July 2021, www.aquaconnect.nu/about-aqua-connect/. Accessed 28 Sept. 2022.

Armitage, David. "Introduction." *The Free Sea*, translated by Richard Hakluyt, with William Welwod's Critique and Grotius's Reply, edited by David Armitage, Liberty Fund, 2004.

Baslar, Kemal. *The Concept of the Common Heritage of Mankind in International Law*. Martinus Nijhoff, 1998.

Borschberg, Peter. "Hugo Grotius, East India Trade and the King of Johor." *Journal of Southeast Asian Studies*, vol. 30, no. 2, Sept. 1999, pp. 225–48.

Chang, David Aiona. *The World and All the Things upon It: Native Hawaiian Geographies of Exploration*. U of Minnesota P, 2016.

Christian, Dorothy, and Rita Wong, editors. *Downstream: Reimagining Water*. Wilfrid Laurier UP, 2017.

Ciriacono, Salvatore. *Building on Water: Venice, Holland and the Construction of the European Landscape in Early Modern Times*. Berghahn Books, 2006.

Coulthard, Glenn Sean. *Red Skin, White Masks: Rejecting the Colonial Politics of Recognition*. U of Minnesota P, 2014.

de Kom, Anton. *Wij Slaven van Suriname*. 1934. Atlas Contact, 2020.

Esmeir, Samera. "Bandung: Reflections on the Sea, the World, and Colonialism." *Bandung, Global History, and International Law*, edited by Luis Eslava et al., Cambridge UP, 2017, pp. 81–94.

European Environmental Agency. "Land Take in Europe." *European Environmental Agency*, Prod-ID: IND-19-en, 13 Dec. 2019, www.eea.europa.eu/data-and-maps/indicators/land-take-3/assessment. Accessed 1 Apr. 2022.

European Environmental Agency. "Waterbase – Water Quality ICM." *European Environmental Agency*, Prod-ID: DAT-240-en, 10 May 2021, www.eea.europa.eu/data-and-maps/data/waterbase-water-quality-icm-1. Accessed 1 Apr. 2022.

Glissant, Édouard. *Poetics of Relation*. Translated by Betsy Wing, U of Michigan P, 1997.

Groenendijk, Peter. "Balkenende gelooft nog steeds in VOC-mentaliteit." *Algemeen Dagblad*, 30 Oct. 2016, www.ad.nl/rotterdam/balkenende-gelooft-nog-steeds-in-voc-mentaliteit~a76d00a3/?cb=3fa5c002d81eacd2c89335914af1a2d4&auth_rd=1. Accessed 26 Sept. 2022.

Groom, Amelia. "Wetlands." Studium Generale, Rietveld Academy of Fine Arts, 16 Mar. 2022. Unpublished lecture (shared with author).

Grotius, Hugo. *Commentary on the Law of Prize and Booty*. Translated by Gwladys L. Williams, edited and with an introduction by Martine Julia van Ittersum, Liberty Fund, 2006.

Grotius, Hugo. "Defence of Chapter V of the *Mare Liberum*." *The Free Sea* by Hugo Grotius, translated by Richard Hakluyt, edited by David Armitage, Liberty Fund, 2004, pp. 77–130.

Grotius, Hugo. *The Free Sea*. Translated by Richard Hakluyt, edited by David Armitage, Liberty Fund, 2004.

Grotius, Hugo. *The Rights of War and Peace I, II, III*. Edited and with an introduction by Richard Tuck, translated by Jean Barbyrac, Liberty Fund, 2005.

Harvey, David. "Globalization and the 'Spatial Fix.'" *Geographische Revue*, vol. 2, 2001, pp. 23–30.

Hau'ofa, Epeli. *We Are the Ocean: Selected Works*. U of Hawai'i P, 2008.

van Ittersum, Martine Julia. "Hugo Grotius in Context: Van Heemskerck's Capture of the *Santa Catarina* and its Justification in *De Jure Praedae* (1604–1606)." *Asian Journal of Social Science*, vol. 31, no. 3, 2003, pp. 511–48.

van Ittersum, Martine Julia. "The Long Goodbye: Hugo Grotius' Justification of Dutch Expansion Overseas, 1615–1645." *History of European Ideas*, vol. 36, no. 4, 2010, pp. 386–411.

van Ittersum, Martine Julia. "A Miracle Mirrored? The Reception of Dutch Economic and Political

Thought in Europe in the Seventeenth and Eighteenth Centuries." *BMGN – Low Countries Historical Review*, vol. 127, no. 4, 2012, pp. 83–99.

van Ittersum, Martine Julia. *Profit and Principle: Hugo Grotius, Natural Rights Theories and the Rise of Dutch Power in the East Indies 1595–1615*. Brill, 2006.

Jones, Henry. "Lines in the Ocean: Thinking with the Sea About Territory and International Law." *London Review of International Law*, vol. 4, no. 2, 2016, pp. 307–43.

King, Tiffany Lethabo. *The Black Shoals: Offshore Formations of Black and Native Studies*. Duke UP, 2019.

King, Tiffany Lethabo. "New World Grammars: The 'Unthought' Black Discourses of Conquest." *Theory and Event*, vol. 9, no. 4, 2016.

LaDuke, Winona. *All Our Relations: Native Struggles for Land and Life*. South End Press, 1999.

Lowe, Lisa. *Intimacies of Four Continents*. Duke UP, 2014.

Maritime by Holland. "Introduction Movie Maritime by Holland." *YouTube*, 23 Oct. 2013, www.youtube.com/watch?v=SsuoqYrGDBE. Accessed 1 Apr. 2022.

Mawani, Renisa. *Across Oceans of Law: The Komagata Maru and Jurisdiction in the Time of Empire*. Duke UP, 2018.

Mawani, Renisa. "Law's Archive." *Annual Review of Law and Social Science*, vol. 8, 2012, pp. 337–65.

Mawani, Renisa. "Law, Settler Colonialism, and 'the Forgotten Space' of Maritime Worlds." *Annual Review of Law and Social Science*, vol. 12, 2016, pp. 107–31.

Maynard, Robyn, and Leanne Betasamosake Simpson. *Rehearsals for Living*. Haymarket Books, 2022.

Mulalap, Clement Yow, et al. "Traditional Knowledge and the BBNJ Instrument." *Marine Policy*, vol. 122, 2020, pp. 1–10.

NL flag. "The Dutch Maritime Cluster." *NL flag*, n.d., nlflag.nl/business-nl/dutch-maritime-cluster. Accessed 1 Apr. 2022.

Perera, Suvendrini. "Oceanic Corpo-graphies, Refugee Bodies and the Making and Unmaking of Waters." *Water*. Spec. issue of *Feminist Review*, vol. 103, 2013, pp. 58–79.

Peters, Kimberley, and Peter Steinberg. "The Ocean in Excess: Towards a More-than-Wet Ontology." *Dialogues in Human Geography*, vol. 9, no. 3, 2019, pp. 293–307.

Porras, Ileana. "Constructing International Law in the East Indian Seas: Property, Sovereignty, Commerce and War in Hugo Grotius' De Iure Praedae – The Law of Prize and Booty, or 'On How to Distinguish Merchants from Pirates.'" *Brook Journal of International Law*, vol. 31, 2006, pp. 741–804.

Ranganathan, Surabhi. "Ocean Floor Grab: International Law and the Making of an Extractive Imaginary." *European Journal of International Law*, vol. 30, no. 2, May 2019, pp. 573–600.

Rieser, Alison. "*Clupea Liberum*: Hugo Grotius, Free Seas, and the Political Biology of Herring." *Blue Legalities: The Life and Law of the Sea*, edited by Irus Braverman and Elizabeth R. Johnson, Duke UP, 2020.

Robinson, Cedric. *Black Marxism: The Making of the Black Radical Tradition*. U of North Carolina P, 2020.

Rose, Deborah Bird. "Justice and Longing." *Fresh Water*, edited by E. Potter et al., Melbourne UP, 2007.

Rosello, Mireille. "Becoming UnDutch: 'Wil je dat? Kun je dat?'" *The Postcolonial Low Countries: Literature, Colonialism, Multiculturalism*, edited by Elleke Boehmer and Sarah de Mul, Lexington Books, 2012, pp. 188–221.

Satgar, Vishwas. "The Anthropocene and Imperial Ecocide: Prospects for Just Transitions." *The Climate Crisis: South African and Global Democratic Eco-Socialist Alternatives*, edited by Vishwas Satgar, Wits UP, 2018, pp. 47–67.

Sharpe, Christina. *In the Wake: On Blackness and Being*. Duke UP, 2016.

Silva, Mariana. "Mining the Deep Sea." *E-flux*, no. 109, 2020, pp. 1–9.

Simpson, Leanne Betasamosake. *As We Have Always Done: Indigenous Freedom Through Radical Resistance*. U of Minnesota P, 2017.

Steinberg, Philip E. *The Social Construction of the Ocean*. Cambridge UP, 2001.

Stelder, Mikki. "The Colonial Difference in Hugo Grotius: Rational Man, Slavery and Indigenous Dispossession." *Postcolonial Studies*, vol. 25, no. 4, 2022, pp. 564–83, https://doi.org/10.1080/13688790.2021.1979297.

Stephens, Michelle, and Yolanda Martínez-San Miguel. *Contemporary Archipelagic Thinking: Toward New Comparative Methodologies and Disciplinary Formations*. Rowman & Littlefield, 2020.

Sutton, Elizabeth. *Capitalism and Cartography in the Dutch Golden Age*. U of Chicago P, 2015.

Te Punga Sommerville, Alice. "The Great Pacific Garbage Patch as Metaphor: The (American) Pacific You Can't See." *Contemporary Archipelagic Thinking: Toward New Comparative Methodologies and Disciplinary Formations*, edited by Michelle Stephens and Yolanda Martínez-San Miguel, Rowman & Littlefield, 2020.

Te Punga Sommerville, Alice. *Once Were Pacific: Maori Connections to Oceania*. U of Minnesota P, 2012.

Vergès, Francoise. "Racial Capitalocene: Is the Anthropocene Racial?" *Futures of Black Radicalism*, edited by Gaye Theresa Johnson and Alex Lubin, Verso, 2017.

Walcott, Rinaldo. *On Property*. Biblioasis, 2021.

Wekker, Gloria. *White Innocence: Paradoxes of Colonialism and Race*. Duke UP, 2016.

Wilson, Eric. "On Heterogeneity and the Naming of *De Indis* of Hugo Grotius." *JPIL*, vol. 1, no. 1, 2006, pp. 72–115.

Wilson, Eric. *Savage Republic: De Indis of Hugo Grotius, Republicanism and Dutch Hegemony within the Early Modern World-System (c. 1600–1619)*. Martinus Nijhoff, 2008.

Wolff, W.J. "Netherlands-Wetlands." *Hydrobiologia*, vol. 265, 1933, pp. 1–14.

Zalik, Anna. "Trading on the Offshore: Territorialization and the Ocean Grab in the International Seabed." *Beyond Free Trade: Alternative Approaches to Trade, Politics and Power*, edited by Kate Ervine and Gavin Fridell, Palgrave Macmillan, 2015.

Mikki Stelder

water and the war

In August 1995, the World Bank vice president Ismail Serageldin stated that "the wars of the [21st] century will be about water" (163; see Shiva vii). It was not a prediction. It was a declaration. A declaration of war. A war being fought for access to natural resources and the way to manage them. But the war reaches back, and in depth, to mobilize other historical strata. It began 500 years ago with colonialism, with the imposition of new property relations, with the imposition of the state and the parallel depoliticization and atomization of the social. However, under the surface of a war for access to and appropriation of land, water, and natural resources, another war was taking place – that between incompatible legal and economic systems. One war follows a well-known script: with greater or lesser violence, it will accompany the struggle for the appropriation of increasingly scarce resources. Instead, the other "war" has always opened, and can open up, new scenarios and put an end to the colonial, appropriative parable. This article investigates the tensions between these incommensurable trajectories.

The Cochabamba water war in 2000 was the first water war of the twenty-first century that aimed to restore another practice of democracy and different property relations.[1] The fact that Cochabamba's war was over water is critical. Indeed, it is not merely the subject of a dispute concerning ownership. A Cochabamba woman stated, "If God gave us water, no human being should take it away" (Farthing and Kohl 8–11). Irrigators used similar language: "Water is *Pachamama* [Mother Earth] and *Wirakhocha* [Creator God] that is

Social Property in The Cochabamba Water War, Bolivia 2000

Massimiliano Tomba

neither person nor spirit but rather the land that gives us life and its blood that is the water that allows for human life" (Hines 173). In Andean culture, the land is not thought to be a natural resource at the service of indigenous people, but as their Mother Earth, "which is why they give their lives to defend her" (Blanco 172). Water and land constitute a single entity that cannot be appropriated because, to use Western categories, it is not an object that stands before a subject. Although improper, it could be said that it is another subject with whom one relates. In the indigenous Andean culture, the term used to characterize this nexus of reciprocal relations is *"ayni,"* which implies a dialogue and reciprocal bond.

In the rural areas of Cochabamba, the attempt to privatize and commercialize water violates customs and traditional norms. Here, *usos y costumbres* refers to practices that repeat and characterize everyday life; practices based on an intimate knowledge of the territory and the social context; practices which are accepted as endogenous and not imposed from the outside (Perreault 839). However, to these three dimensions it must be added that *usos y costumbres* are dynamic, that is, they are reconfigured in their encounter with other unprecedented practices, situations, and legal systems. As stated by an irrigator and activist closely associated with the Cochabamba Departmental Federation of Irrigator Organizations (FEDECOR):

> *Usos y costumbres* are closely related to an historical process, they have much to do with Andean culture, and also reflect processes of struggle between [*campesino*] communities and hacienda owners, for example [...] In this sense they are not static, they are dynamic. (Perreault 840)

A dynamic conception of customs and traditions has to be understood in relation to concrete historical struggles.

During the 2000 water war mobilizations in Bolivia, a factory workers' manifesto read: "We don't want private property nor state property, but self-management and social property" (Dwinell and Olivera i47). The water war fought in Bolivia in 2000 gave us the term social property (*propiedad social*). Social property is not a new concept of ownership, but a practice that aims to restore another practice of democracy and different property relations in relation to water, to infrastructure for its distribution, and more. It is from the practices that emerged during the water war that I intend to start in order to extract legal and political concepts and categories and to rethink not only the essential question of water, but, more generally, an alternative political and legal framework. My intention is neither to make the water war an episode in a series of anti-globalization struggles, nor to judge the water war on the basis of pre-established models of efficiency and socio-ecological or organizational

limitations (see, for example, Marston). It is not a matter of working with theoretical models to measure the distance or proximity between social practices that were in place in the water war and forms of neoliberal governmentality.

The perspective needs to be reversed. It is about extracting theory from practice – extracting from concrete social practices new concepts that require thinking about. It is about being schooled by Bolivian "water warriors (*guerreros del agua*)" and learning from them how the notion of social property has operated, operates, and can operate in social practices that are incompatible with the legal edifice based on the binary of public and private. As Oscar Olivera, activist and spokesperson for the water war, stated, the events of 2000 had to do with more than just water. The water war was an experiment "to unprivatize the very fabric of society" (Olivera and Lewis 47). What does it mean to go beyond the horizon of water? It means that the practice of social property does not have water as its own object because it dismantles the relationship between individual will and the object, which is fundamental in modern political theory. Social property places water in relation to a multiplicity of relationships of use, rights, and obligations between users. Priority is given to this network of obligations. Not the object – be it the water, the land, or the Earth. The water war has reopened a field of possibilities in which legal systems, property relations, and forms of life that are incompatible with the designs of the modern Western state are taking shape.

This article deals with these possibilities. In the first part I reconstruct the socio-historical and legal context in which the water war arose. In the second part I show the limits of the state's legal perspective on water defense. In part three I present the possibilities that water warriors have opened up in terms of reconfiguring the social, an alternative legal system and property relations. It is not a matter of choosing between the Western and indigenous legal systems. This is just another binary. The task of theory is to work in their

the social–historical context

If the long history of the water war overlaps with 500 years of colonialism, its short prehistory can be identified in the World Bank intervention and presidential Supreme Decree 21060 of 1985 that, in order to stop inflation, paved the road to privatization of state-owned companies. In reaction, in 1986 the miners' union organized a March for Life that involved thousands of miners until the military intervened to halt the march. What should be emphasized is that the intervention of the state not only served to suppress any resistance, but also paved the legal ground on which privatizations could be carried out. The latter aspect was explicitly carried out by Law 2029 of 1999, which gave the monopoly of water resources to the international consortium *Aguas del Tunari*. Law 2029 shows a dynamic characterized by three dimensions: the state intervenes by imposing a monopoly on resources; in this way, it attacks social and legal systems of self-management of resources at the community level; the social is thus leveled, paving the way for massive privatizations, free to impose themselves in a civil society of private individuals. It is important to keep this intertwining in mind because it shows that state intervention, its monopoly, and privatizations are not terms in opposition to each other. This script has been re-enacted countless times in the modern history of colonization within and outside Europe.

Law 2029 shows this intertwining of nationalization and privatization. Article 29 states:

> No natural or legal person, public or private, civil association with or without profit aims, anonymous society, co-operative, municipal or of any other nature, may provide services of water supply and sanitation in concession zones, without a concession issued by the Basic Services Superintendency.

In this way the state imposes its monopoly on water. The irrigators, who use their infrastructures for water distribution, are granted temporary licenses. But in fact, in a short time, they risk seeing their alternative systems of water supply, which are regulated according to *usos y costumbres*, become illegal. The attack, as pointed out by the *Coordinadora de Defensa del Agua y de la Vida* (Coalition in Defense of Water and Life),[2] is on each autonomous use of water, on communal or associative forms of organization, peasants and indigenous people that, through mutual aid systems, have their own water infrastructures. Under the state monopoly, not only are infrastructures snatched from the hands of communities, but the practices of self-management and water regulation become illegal. At the same time, Article 72 of Law 2029 stated that users "are obliged" to connect to the company network, undermining *de jure* and de facto any residue of legal autonomy. A juridical model that synchronizes alternative and, from the state's point of view, anachronistic legal systems was imposed. On this new legal basis, Article 19 of Law 2029 could be implemented: "The State will promote the participation of the private sector in the water supply and sanitary sewerage services." This led to the concession contract with the *Aguas del Tunari* consortium which established that the concession-holder had the following rights and duties with an "*exclusive nature*: transport and storage, distribution and marketing of drinking water from treatment plants or water wells to the users in the concession area" (Título II). Annex 5 of the contract made explicit the handing over of water resources from the state to the private company according to the same monopolistic logic present in Law 2029. Annex 5 also states that "the use of alternative sources will not be allowed." As if this were not enough, Annex 5, Numeral 1.3 established that if users own alternative water sources, for instance a well, the concession-holder had the right to install a metering system and the installation costs would be at the expense of the user (cited in Gutiérrez et al. 142). The logic of privatization went so far as to prohibit "the peasants from constructing collection tanks to gather water from the rain" (Olivera and

Lewis 9). Since rain, as such, could not be privatized, the law simply prohibited collecting it. If in Cochabamba the collection and distribution of water developed in community forms, through committees with a two-year term, and in harmony with customs and traditions, then Law 2029 declared these autonomous systems *illegal*. This is how legal synchronization of the state works.[3]

The price of water increased as much as 200 percent and *Aguas del Tunari* began to take control of community-owned water distribution infrastructures. But this privatization process would not have been possible without Law 2029 and without the state power to make decisions about the country's water resources. Law 2029 and its application show that the opposition is not between state and private. It is a clash between a legal system of individual private rights and a system of collective and community rights. This clash takes place on legal and extra-legal grounds. The water warriors defended systems of regulation and self-management of water, which from the point of view of the state are illegal, but which are in fact part of a different legal order, not compatible with that of the state. To demolish this alternative legal order, the state used both the violence of the law as well as military and police violence of a state of emergency.

After a number of protests and struggles, on 11 April 2000, the Bolivian government was forced to repeal Law 2029 and issue a new law, number 2066, which reformed thirty-six sections of the previous act. Law 2066, in addition to keeping open the possibility of creating a national water council, recognized traditional *usos y costumbres* and the presence within the territory of local units of popular participation (Assies 30). Law 2066 can be defined as a compromise between community practices of water use, supply, and management based on "natural authorities" and "socially established norms" (Art. 8, z) and the "original dominion of the state" (Art. 28). Although the *Coordinadora* won the battle against water privatization by forcing the *Aguas del Tunari* company to leave the country, at that point a new level of discussion and conflict regarding

the future of the municipal water supply company (SEMAPA) was opened. It must immediately be said that the *Coordinadora*'s attempt to restructure SEMAPA on the basis of customs and traditions – on the basis of the practice of social property and social control – failed (Spronk 8–28; Razavi 1–19). The *Coordinadora* tried to transform SEMAPA into a sort of social enterprise, a water management system organized on the basis of local authorities revitalized in social practices (Linsalata 180). Raquel Gutiérrez Aguilar rightly observed that "current law [...] allow[s] no room for social property and only recognizes classical forms of ownership: public or private, each with its variants (state, municipal, cooperative, corporate, individual)" ("The Coordinadora" 60).

Little could be done within the existing legal framework. There were at least two main obstacles on the path to real reform and social reappropriation of SEMAPA. On the one hand, the practice of social property was incompatible with both the regime of private property and state property; on the other hand, the forms of local authority and self-government were incompatible with the notion of unitary state sovereignty. Different, incompatible legal systems were set up against each other. The water war, its history and its aftermath, show that these systems cannot coexist side by side for long. SEMAPA returned to public hands under the control of municipal government.[4]

While the water war halted the march of privatization, bringing back state public property was no longer an option. As noted by Oscar Olivera, "nationalization, in the end, prepared the condition for the denationalization of our collective wealth. The opposite of the cataclysmic privatizations and de-nationalization of transnational capitalism is neither state capitalism nor state property" (Olivera and Lewis 156). This *neither–nor* logic is critical. The Cochabamba water war shows the alternative to the state property–privatization binary opposition. For this reason, Cochabamba, beyond the duration of its success, shows the possibility of disrupting that apparent dichotomy between state public and private that continues to haunt modern history. This alternative, which has been labeled as social property, is the *practice* of undoing the entanglement that characterizes the concurrent birth of the state and private property.

ownership and social property

The modern concept of ownership was defined in the *Code Napoléon* (1804), which has served as a model for countless civil codes in many countries, not only in Europe. Its definition of private property has become classic: "Property is the right of enjoying and disposing of things in the most absolute manner" (Art. 544). The French Revolution and the *Code Civil* sanctioned a new demarcation between public power and private property: "Property belongs to the citizen, empire to the sovereign" (Blaufarb 208). This notion of property, based on an individual's free will to make use and abuse of the object, is at the root of many ecological disasters.

Today, not only has private property become an unquestionable dogma, but its constitutive categories have been naturalized to the point that, even when trying to think of an alternative, it operates according to modern property grammar. At most, ownership changes, so that the private individual is replaced by the nation state, or the territories stolen from indigenous peoples are returned in the form of property titles. The language of the Indigenous and Tribal Peoples Convention Article 14 of ILO Convention No. 169 ("Indigenous and Tribal Peoples Convention") shows the problem well. The first paragraph of Article 14 speaks of recognition of the "rights of ownership and possession of the peoples concerned over the lands." But the second paragraph clarifies the meaning of that recognition and the dependence of the property on the government that shall "guarantee effective protection of their rights of ownership and possession." Finally, the third paragraph clarifies that the entire dynamics of property relationships takes place in the state legal system: "Adequate procedures shall be established within the national legal system to resolve land claims by the peoples concerned." At the basis of this and other articles remains the dominant Western legal grammar according to which it is not the single local authorities but the authority of the government that guarantees property and settles any conflicts. In 2004, the Bolivian Constitutional Court refused to recognize "indigenous claim to communal property on the grounds that it violated the right of private property, ruling that 'customary law … is not applicable to resolve a possible conflict of the right of property over land'" (Hammond 678).[5] From the state perspective the verdict is right. The two legal grammars, that of customary law and that of right of property, are mutually incompatible. The "solution" of constitutionalizing customary rights, water rights, and land rights only expands one pole of the tension: that of state sovereignty. This is a path that, even if pushed toward global constitutionalism, would only expand and intensify the categories of state sovereignty beyond the nation state – toward a public monopoly of power in charge of a supposed "Federation of the Earth."[6]

The experiment that took place in Cochabamba teaches us that the real issue about water and earth is not their protection through their encapsulation in some pompous catalog of inalienable rights or in the preamble of a national or global constitution. Even though in 2009 the Bolivian Constitutional Assembly made an effort to constitutionalize the protection of Mother Earth; even though Art. 2.6 of the 2010 "Law of the Right of Mother Earth" proclaims that the

> exercise of the rights of Mother Earth requires the recognition, recovery, respect, protection, and dialogue of the diversity of feelings, values, knowledge, skills, practices, transcendence, transformation, science, technology and standards, of all the cultures of the world who seek to live in harmony with nature,

in 2011 the Morales government, without prior consultation with the local populations, decided to build a 190-mile road through the Isiboro Sécure Indigenous Territory and National Park (TIPNIS) (Delgado 373–91; Calla 77–83). Fernando Vargas, a TIPNIS indigenous leader, accused Morales of not being "a defender of Mother Earth, or indigenous peoples." He added that "[t]his is the beginning of the destruction of protected areas in Bolivia and indigenous peoples' territory" (Collyns). The government's decision perhaps contradicts the spirit of the declaration of the Rights of Mother Earth, but the power of the state is not limited either by the Rights of Mother Earth or by the acknowledged local autonomies of indigenous peoples. This is why Evo Morales's victory in Bolivia in 2005 cannot be called a "victory." Rather, it is the beginning of the defeat of the experiment begun in Cochabamba. It is the re-enrollment of the experiences of local self-government, local authorities and forms of social property in the grammar of the state. The issue does not lie in identifying Morales's tactical errors, but in the incompatibility between the practices of self-management based on the political pluralism of local authorities and the grammar of the state.

The tension between unity and plurality is implicitly contained in the definition of Bolivia as a "Unitary Social State of Pluri-National Communitarian Law (*Estado Unitario Social de Derecho Plurinacional Comunitario*)." Article 2 does not hide the tension when it states that

> indigenous peoples and their ancestral control of their territories, their free determination, consisting of the right to autonomy, self-government, their culture, recognition of their institutions, and the consolidation of their territorial entities, is guaranteed within the framework of the unity of the State, in accordance with this Constitution and the law.

Plurality is recognized, but within the framework of the unity of the State and within the limits established by the constitution. Recognition means dependence on the state grammar of modern law.

Predictably, this tension extends through the various articles of the constitution. Articles 190 and 290 refer to indigenous autonomy, authorities, and jurisdictional functions, even including (Art. 290) the expression of their will through consultation, but always in accordance and harmony "with the Constitution and the law." This is the feeble voice of plurality. But in the constitution the baritone voice of the state is dominant. Article 378.I concerns the different forms of energy and strategic resources which are essential for the development of the country; the second paragraph clarifies that it is "the exclusive authority of the State to develop the chain of energy production in the phases of generation, transport, and distribution." Article 298.II leaves no doubt that the "central level of the State has exclusive authority" over natural resources, minerals, and water sources.[7] Article 349.I reiterates that "natural resources are the property and direct domain, indivisible and without limitation, of the Bolivian people, and their administration corresponds to the State on behalf of the collective interest." The Bolivian people, as a whole and unity, only exists through the state that represents the nation, which therefore has "direct domain" on natural resources. Indeed, if according to Article 356, "[t]he activities of exploration, exploitation, refining, industrialization, transport and sale of nonrenewable natural resources shall have the character of state necessity and public utility," then from the previous articles it follows that this character of necessity and public utility is decided by the state.

The TIPNIS case shows the constitutional tension between plurality and unity, between the state's sovereignty and local authorities. Although Article 30 of the 2009 Constitution of the Plurinational State of Bolivia lists a long series of rights granted to "rural native indigenous peoples," all these rights depend on the state to guarantee and protect them.[8] And in so far as they depend on the state, the state can also limit and suspend them. Therefore, what Evo Morales stated on 31 July 2011 is not in contradiction to the constitution:

We are going to do consultations, but I want you to know that they are not binding. [The road] won't be stopped just because they [the Indigenous peoples] say no. Consultation is constitutionalized, but is not binding, and therefore, the great desire we have for 2014 is to see the Villa Tunari – San Ignacio de Moxos road paved. (Qtd in Hindery 178)

Incidentally, it should be mentioned that while the *Anteproyecto de ley de la Madre Tierra* (*Draft Law of Mother Earth*) of 2010, drafted by indigenous communities, spoke of prior and binding consultation (*derecho de consulta y consentimiento previo y vinculante*), its translation into law (*Ley 300*, 2012) transformed that right into a vague consultative process.[9]

It is not a question of blaming Evo Morales for his inconsistency with regard to the promises he made in the election campaign or his references to *Pachamama*. Morales's language mirrors the grammar of the nation state. When he refers to the *bien común*, the common good of the country, he refers not only to the will of the majority, to which the minority must adapt, but also to the Bolivian people as a whole and unity, which he represented. As also reiterated by the vice president of Bolivia, Álvaro García Linera: "besides the people's right to land, the State – the State led by the indigenous-popular and peasant movement – has the right to prioritize the higher collective interest of all the peoples. And this is how we proceeded afterwards" (Svampa et al.). Linera's language, just like Morales's, is the language of progress and the state. What merges in this and other similar examples[10] is the clash between incommensurable juridical–political trajectories. Evo Morales and García Linera acted in the name of progress and superior national interest, which also includes indigenous peoples who opposed the construction of the road. Paraphrasing Rousseau, it could be said that within the framework of the modern concept of sovereignty, the particular will of the indigenous peoples has only one possibility, which is to conform to the general will of the state. If they refuse to obey, they will be "forced to be free" (Rousseau 58) – in the name of progress and superior national interest.

At least two considerations emerge from the legal grammar of the modern state: the first concerns the incompatibility between unity and monopoly of state power on the one hand and plurality of local authorities on the other; the second concerns the varied attempts to protect water and nature within a legal shell. It could be said that there is a direct proportionality relationship between the extension of a catalog of rights of subjects to be protected and the extension of the power called upon to perform this function. The 2010 UN Resolution 64/292 on "The Human Right to Water and Sanitation" confirms this grammar. Having acknowledged the importance of equitable access to water, the Resolution reaffirms "the responsibility of States for the promotion and protection of all human rights" and "calls upon states and international organizations to provide financial resources, capacity-building and technology transfer, [...] in order to scale up efforts to provide safe, clean, accessible and affordable drinking water and sanitation for all." This grammar neither excludes private sector management of water supply systems nor prevents the state, as happened in Bolivia, from claiming the right to regulate the use of resources for the general good. For this reason, "some indigenous-rights activists fear that a human right to water will provide additional leverage for states intent on wresting control of water resources from local communities" (Bakker 149).

The extension of rights and legal personhood to animals and nature, often hailed as a sign of legal progress, is an expression of a hypertrophic process of subsumption of the whole realm of life into the legal realm of the state. This extension does not constitute a paradigm shift in the state mechanism, but falls within the field of possibilities of modern power understood as a movement of depoliticization and colonization of the living transformed into a multitude of subjects to be protected. A real alternative must be devised beyond the constitutionalization of nature. It has to be devised in a completely different legal framework.

Like the one that emerged in the water war in Bolivia. Social property not only challenges the private/public binary. As a practice, it shows a third field of possibilities emerging in the tension between customs, authority, and the state. It is not a matter of picking sides for romantically good indigenous rights. It is not about emphasizing the potentially progressive role of modern law against backward and oppressive customs. It is about operating, as the water warriors did, in the tension between these terms. It is a tension that, while altering the terms at play, also opens up a third field of possibilities. It is time to investigate this field.

social property and the politics of presence

On 8 December 2000, the Cochabamba Declaration was drafted. The text is short. It is the result of discussions between different parties from different nationalities. The declaration can be read not as an epilogue to the water war, but as an attempt to keep that social and legal fabric of experimentation open. The attempt to point toward a common direction.

Article 1 declares that "water belongs to the earth and all species and is sacred to life." Article 2 defines water as a "fundamental human right and a public good." Water, continues Article 2, "should not be commodified, privatized or traded for commercial purposes." Article 3 affirms that "water is best protected by local communities and citizens." These three clarifications are part of a single constellation. Water cannot be commodified, privatized, or nationalized because it cannot be owned. It "belongs to the earth and all species and is sacred to life." One document of the *Coordinadora* articulated four forms of reappropriation: "reappropriate what is ours; reappropriate our rights; reappropriate the patrimony of the country; reappropriate the ability to say and to do, decide and execute the projects and plans that suit the people and the country" (*¡El agua es nuestra, carajo!*). In the phrase

"Reappropriate what is ours," the terms "ours" and "we" do not indicate a set of individuals, but relations and reciprocal obligations between users. This means that the "reappropriation" does not only concern water or a "common good," but a form of life. This is why the water war points in a direction that goes beyond water as a common good. The right as a guarantee of full access by individuals to the common good for the satisfaction of fundamental rights is not what is at stake.

In this legal configuration, the right to use water is not an individual or collective right guaranteed by the state. It is the common use, according to customs and obligations, by the users that define the juridical field of a legal system autonomous from the state. In this alternative juridical configuration, water is not the target of a subjective right to property. Rather, water, and the plurality of relations to water, has juridical priority. This is an inverse relationship to that of modern Western law. If the latter is prompted by the individual will of the subject who exercises the right to property over external things, the grammar of the right to life instead gives priority to the use and, therefore, to the *way* in which social groupings relate to a common resource, according to regulations that go beyond individual rights and are instead rooted in the *usos y costumbres* of the ancestors.

In this context, social property, far from being an absolute right of the subject, is reconfigured in the concrete relationships between users and resources. The use of common resources is part of the democratic practice of local self-government, in which communities and "citizens" decide and do, discuss and execute together.[11] In the practice of social property, property relations take place at a distance from the state and are part of democratic regulations at the local level. It could be said that dominium of ownership is dispersed to the extent that political power and authority are dispersed. It is the community, through its own institutions, that collectively discusses and decides on common and individual use, and on the most appropriate way to preserve common resources. In this way, users are bound to each other by reciprocal obligations, which also involve resources used in common. These become a subject among subjects and not, as happens instead in the modern concept of private property, an object of individual will.[12]

The Cochabamba water warriors showed in their practices that the alternative to private property is intertwined with alternative practices of democracy and government. There ensues a network of relations regulated by forms of self-government, in which rights do not precede, but follow use, and this, in turn, is regulated by a "system of reciprocal obligations" (Linsalata 102), which refers to existing forms in indigenous communities of the Andean area. Self-government, rights, obligations, and traditions constitute a set in which none of these elements has a real priority over the others or is subordinate to others. Restoring the proper use of water was a matter of *democracy*. Social property was not defined by ownership, but as a democratic practice based on the *relations of use* between the object and a plurality of users who, in addition to having rights, have reciprocal obligations. In this framework, the semantics of property cannot be reduced to ownership; rather, it is the expression of *proper* use relations in a community of users. Quarrels and conflicts continue to take place, but they concern the qualification of what is *proper use* instead of ownership.

In a public statement on 6 February 2000, the *Coordinadora* made it clear that the question of water, its use "according to traditional practices," is no different from the question of democracy, whose authentic meaning can be summarized in "we decide and do, discuss and carry out. We risked our lives in order to complete what we proposed, that which we consider just. Democracy is sovereignty of the people and that is what we have achieved" (6 February 2000, "Texts of the Coordinadora del Agua of Cochabamba"). But here, people, sovereignty, and democracy do not coincide with the concepts that bear the same name in the dominant canon of political thought. As it stood out in the 2000 Cochabamba Declaration,[13] saving water means different regulations based on local communities, customs, and traditions, and different practices of democracy. What is at stake is a practice of democracy which is not based on the state and the modern concept of representation. In another of the *Coordinadora*'s documents we read that "we are fed up with the simulation of democracy which only renders us obedient and impotent, and turns us into obliged voters" ("Texts of the Coordinadora del Agua of Cochabamba"). Undoing the "simulation of democracy" is something absolutely concrete. It is not a question of implementing democratic procedures within the existing constitutional framework. In the language of the insurgents and the *Coordinadora*, it is about "recovering the voice" of the people (see Olivera and Gutiérrez 166) to give rise to a correct practice of democracy (see Olivera and Gutiérrez 169). The theory of this "correct practice of democracy" must be extracted from the social practices of the insurgents and from the intersection of different traditions, from the women and the unionist tradition of the miners to the *usos y costumbres* of the peasants.

However, here we must also emphasize an asymmetry between the participation of women in protests and assemblies and those who instead went to negotiate with authorities. One woman complained that in "the countryside especially, machismo predominates" (Bustamente et al. 85). This culture also partly permeated the *Coordinadora*:

> Those who would lead, who would make up the commission that would be part of the Coordinadora, and who would come to represent the Coordinadora, were all men, and we women had to do other things, anything but be the leaders. (Bustamente et al. 85; also see Udaeta)

The struggle against the privatization of resources and the social fabric had to overcome this obstacle: women had occupied the public and political scene, but some roles related to representation and leadership, in terms of gender, reproduced the separation between public and private that was otherwise questioned in the water war. Indeed, if the binary between public and private also separates "the market and politics, instrumental rationality and bureaucratic organization from home and family, spirituality, affective rationality, and sexual intimacy," if this separation, in which "men figured on the public side, women on the side of the private" (Scott 13), is one of the pillars of the modern national state and private property, then privatization cannot be really challenged without also questioning gender inequality. Insofar as the experience of Cochabamba, like many other political experiences in which women are direct protagonists,[14] shows another way of doing politics and practicing democracy which are not based on the representation or charisma of a leader, the water war mobilization began to alter not only the social and political fabric, but also people's subjectivity, habits, and mentality.[15]

The practice of the insurgents during the water war teaches us that doing democracy and undoing privatization are entangled. The democracy in action of the insurgents of Cochabamba disrupted the division between the political and the social. A different democratic practice, articulated in a plurality of local assemblies, authorities, and forms of self-government develops on the basis of different property relationships. And vice versa. *Social property* requires a different vision of democracy. In the words of the insurgents, in Cochabamba an "extraordinary pedagogy of democratic assemblies" took place. It was not based on representative democracy, according to which a leader speaks on behalf of everyone, but on the exercise of "direct democracy" where the "power of decision-making is reappropriated by social structures, which, in their practice of radical political insurgency, derogate from the delegative habit of the state power and exercise power themselves" (Gutiérrez et al. 170). This political pedagogy began to produce a "different way of exercising and feeling political power" and gave rise to a "reconfiguration of the state and the way to practice political rights" (170).

If "representative democracy," which the *Coordinadora* defined as a "*simulación de democracia*," is based on the principle of people's sovereignty; if political representation is the representation of the invisible *unity*, of the impossible *whole* of the nation and of its fetishistic political *identity*, which become visible through representative artifice and through an exclusionary act; if "representative democracy" simulates democracy, because a leader or group of delegates speaks on behalf of the nation and *re-presents* it in the sense that it makes it visible, then the *politics of presence* is completely different. It is not based on a political identity to be produced. It is based on political presence in numerous local assemblies, communities, and associations. It is based on an expansive plurality because it is open to anyone who participates politically in the life of the assemblies. This democratic openness, which also questions property relations, is what the Cochabamba experiment has offered to political theory. In Cochabamba, unity is disarticulated in the plurality of groups and social strata that do not need to be re-presented, because they are present. What the *Coordinadora* called a "*correcto ejercicio de la democracia*" is another vision of democracy as a practice. The water war opened up a "space" of practical and theoretical experimentation. This "space" has been hidden by the dominant juridical forms, but it characterizes and has characterized human life in an incomparably more extensive way than the brief parenthesis of modern Western European property relations can represent.

This is the long war that underlies the water war. The conflict is not between privatization or nationalization of natural resources. Nor is it for a right of free access to available resources. The conflict takes shape between incompatible legal and political systems. In Cochabamba, democracy in action in a network of "assemblies and councils" (see Olivera) also reconfigures property relations, and creates space for the reconfiguration of institutions inherited, and constantly reinvented, from the past. What emerged in Cochabamba was a different legal trajectory based on the democratization and the common use of water and infrastructures, which from the state's point of view is illegal in many respects. This different trajectory was rightly presented in terms of a "Copernican inversion" that "involves displacing the centrality of 'state' and 'institutional power' as a privileged space for politics to instead situate it in the polyphonic and plural social capacity for insistently distorting the heteronymous political order" (Gutiérrez, *Rhythmos of the Pachakuti* xxii). Cochabambinos and Cochabambinas were not defending water as an object, but forms of life in common and a way of practicing democracy in the politics of presence.

Social property, the term that the experiment of Cochabamba has left us, is not the result of an appropriation or expropriation of common resources, infrastructures, or means of production, but the consequence of their democratic use, or what the insurgents called *autogestión*. The water warriors of Cochabamba, in their practices, recombine different historical layers and temporalities to shape another way of practicing property, democracy, and institutions articulated in a system of reciprocal obligations. In the words of an activist of the water: "we are learning how to fortify and consolidate an alternative to the system which we oppose" (Olivera and Gomez).[16] With the same modesty as the Cochabamba insurgents, we can say that it is a question of learning from their political and social experiments to start envisaging other democratic practices which are alternative to modern Western law and its proprietary forms.

disclosure statement

No potential conflict of interest was reported by the author.

notes

1 During one of my conversations with Marcela Olivera, she pointed out that, in the water war, terms like "recuperar" and "reconstituir" the social fabric were very common among people. The writing of this article owes much to Marcela, her generosity, and her political insights.

2 The *Coordinadora* arose spontaneously. At the beginning of the conflict, the activists of the *Coordinadora* sought refuge in a convent, and the nuns accepted. It was not clear who or what the *Coordinadora* was, so much so that people asked, "Where is '*la señora coordinadora*,' […] the brave female coordinator who is defending water" (Beltrán 35).

3 On the term "synchronization," see Tomba 9–10.

4 On the appropriation of water and SEMAPA by the state, see Crespo Flores.

5 The principle stated by the Court is that "customary law cannot violate the Constitution and the laws." This means that indigenous territories are not only not an autonomous jurisdiction from the state but are subject to forced institutionalization (*institucionalización forzada*) and state dominion of lands (see Chivi).

6 An example of this legal scaling-up is found in Ferrajoli.

7 Article 304, which should recognize rural native indigenous autonomies and authorities clarifies the extent of this authority: "Irrigation systems, hydraulic resources, sources of water and energy, *within the framework of State policy*, within their territory" (Art. 304.III.4).

8 Article 30 provides indigenous people the right to "self-determination and territoriality" (Art. 30.II.4), "the collective ownership of land and territories" (Art. 30.II.6), and "to be consulted by appropriate procedures, in particular through their institutions" (Art. 30.II.15).

9 On the impossibility to translate the indigenous legal system into the grammar of the state's liberal framework, see Bellina.

10 In 2007, despite the Ecuadorian government's declaration that it would have suspended the extraction of oil from a field within the Yasuni National Park, despite the attribution of legal rights to nature by incorporating *Pacha Mama* (Art. 71) in the 2008 Constitution, in 2013, Rafael Correa's government announced that, for economic reasons, the extraction of oil had become necessary.

11 As we can read in a statement of 6 February 2000 by the *Coordinadora*: "For us […] this is the

true meaning of democracy: we decide and do, discuss and carry out" ("Texts of the Coordinadora del Agua of Cochabamba").

12 These "ontological" differences at the basis of the subject–object and subject–subject relationship are primarily based on different property relationships.

13 An English translation of the Cochabamba Declaration is also available in Olivera and Lewis.

14 See, for example, the case of women in Turkey and Kurdistan (Üstündağ).

15

> After the Cochabamba Water War, when people returned to normal life, many women who had participated in the protests described profound changes in their identity as community members, especially relative to their participation in activities that would have been off-limits to them prior to the water war [...] participation cannot be mandated by decree; it is part of a profound cultural change that has to permeate all social actors. (Bennett et al. 121–22)

16 The article was provided to me by Marcela Olivera and is the English translation of "La crecida de las aguas. Los bienes comunes restablecidos por la gente en Bolivia" also published under the title "La crecida de las aguas. Los comunes y la visión Andina del agua restablecidos por la gente en Bolivia y los Andes," 2016, in desinformemonos.org/la-crecida-de-las-aguas.

bibliography

"Anteproyecto de ley de la Madre Tierra del Pacto de Unidad." *Somo Sur*, 7 Nov. 2010, www.somossur.net/documentos/AnteProyectoLMT_nov2010.pdf.

Assies, Willem. "David versus Goliath in Cochabamba." *Latin American Perspectives*, vol. 30, no. 3, 2003, pp. 14–36, https://doi.org/10.1177/0094582 × 03030003003.

Bakker, Karen J. *Privatizing Water: Governance Failure and the World's Urban Water Crisis.* Cornell UP, 2010.

Bellina, Agnese. "A Novel Way of Being Together? On the Depoliticising Effects of Attributing Rights to Nature." *Environmental Politics*. Currently under review.

Beltrán, Elizabeth Peredo. "Water, Privatization and Conflict: Women from the Cochabamba Valley." *Global Issue Papers*, no. 4, 2004, genderandsecurity.org/sites/default/files/Beltran_-_2004_-_Water_privatization_and_conflict_women_from_the_.pdf.

Bennett, Vivienne, et al. "Water and Gender: The Unexpected Connection that Really Matters." *Journal of International Affairs*, vol. 61, no. 2, 2008, pp. 107–26.

Blanco, Hugo. *We the Indians: The Indigenous Peoples of Peru and the Struggle for Land.* Merlin Press, 2018.

Blaufarb, Rafe. *The Great Demarcation: The French Revolution and the Invention of Modern Property.* Oxford UP, 2019.

Bustamente, Rocio, et al. "Women in the 'Water War' in the Cochabamba Valleys." *Opposing Currents: The Politics of Water and Gender in Latin America*, edited by Vivienne Bennett et al., U of Pittsburgh P, 2005, pp. 72–89.

Calla Ortega, Ricardo. "Tipnis y Amazonia: Contradicciones en la agenda ecológica de Bolivia." *European Review of Latin American and Caribbean Studies | Revista Europea de Estudios Latinoamericanos y del Caribe*, no. 92, 2012, pp. 77–83, https://doi.org/10.18352/erlacs.8405.

Chivi Vargas, Idon Moisés. "Justicia Indígena y Jurisdicción Constitucional. Bolivia 2003–2005." *Derechos Humanos y Acción Defensorial*, no. 1, 2006, pp. 45–71.

"Cochabamba Declaration." *Nadir*, 8 Dec. 2000, www.nadir.org/nadir/initiativ/agp/free/imf/bolivia/cochabamba.htm#declaration.

Collyns, Dan. "Bolivia Approves Highway through Amazon Biodiversity Hotspot." *The Guardian*, 15 Aug. 2017, www.theguardian.com/environment/2017/aug/15/bolivia-approves-highway-in-amazon-biodiversity-hotspot-as-big-as-jamaica.

Crespo Flores, Carlos. "Estatalizacion del agua en Bolivia." *El Libertario*, 15 Dec. 2011, periodicoelibertario.blogspot.com/2011/12/estatalizacion-del-agua-en-bolivia.html.

Delgado, Ana Carolina. "The Tipnis Conflict in Bolivia." *Contexto Internacional*, vol. 39, no. 2, 2017, pp. 373–91, https://doi.org/10.1590/s0102-8529.2017390200009.

Dwinell, Alexander, and Marcela Olivera. "The Water is Ours Damn It! Water Commoning in Bolivia." *Community Development Journal*, vol. 49, suppl. 1, 2014, pp. i44–i52, https://doi.org/10.1093/cdj/bsu014.

Farthing, Linda, and Ben Kohl. "Bolivia's New Wave of Protest." *NACLA Report on the Americas*, vol. 34, no. 5, 2001, pp. 8–11, https://doi.org/10.1080/10714839.2001.11722593.

Ferrajoli, Luigi. *Per una Costituzione della Terra: L'umanità al bivio.* Feltrinelli, 2022.

Gutiérrez Aguilar, Raquel. "The Coordinadora. One Year After the Water War." *¡Cochabamba!: Water War in Bolivia*, edited by Oscar Olivera and Tom Lewis, South End Press, 2004.

Gutiérrez Aguilar, Raquel. *Rhythmos of the Pachakuti.* Duke UP, 2014.

Gutiérrez Aguilar, Raquel, et al. *El Retorno de la Bolivia Plebeya.* Comuna-Muela del Diablo, 2000.

Hammond, John L. "Indigenous Community Justice in the Bolivian Constitution of 2009." *Human Rights Quarterly*, vol. 33, no. 3, 2011, pp. 649–81, https://doi.org/10.1353/hrq.2011.0030.

Hindery, Derrick. *From Enron to Evo: Pipeline Politics, Global Environmentalism, and Indigenous Rights in Bolivia.* U of Arizona P, 2014.

Hines, Sarah T. *Water for All: Community, Property, and Revolution in Modern Bolivia.* U of California P, 2022.

"Indigenous and Tribal Peoples Convention." *International Labour Organization*, 1989, www.ilo.org/dyn/normlex/en/f?p=NORMLEXPUB:12100:0::NO::P12100_ILO_CODE:C169.

"Law 2029." *Lexivox*, 1999, www.lexivox.org/norms/BO-L-2029.html.

"Law 2066." *El Servicio Estatal de Autonomías*, 2000, sea.gob.bo/digesto/Compendio11/O/160_L_2066.pdf.

Linsalata, Lucia. *Cuando manda la asamblea. Lo comunitario-popular en Bolivia: una aproximación desde los sistemas comunitarios de agua de Cochabamba*, tesis para optar por el grado académico de Doctora en Estudios Latinoamericanos, UNAM, 2014.

Marston, Andrea J. "Autonomy in a Post-Neoliberal Era: Community Water Governance in Cochabamba, Bolivia." *Geoforum*, vol. 64, 2015, pp. 246–56, https://doi.org/10.1016/j.geoforum.2013.08.013.

Olivera, Oscar. "After the Water War." *ROAR Magazine*, 9 Dec. 2015, roarmag.org/magazine/oscar-olivera-water-war-commons/.

Olivera, Oscar, and Luis Gomez, "The Rising of the Waters. The 'Commons' Re-established by the People of Bolivia." 2006, desinformemonos.org/la-crecida-de-las-aguas/.

Olivera, Oscar, and Raquel Gutiérrez. *Nosotros Somos La Coordinadora.* Quimantú, 2008.

Olivera, Oscar, and Tom Lewis. *¡Cochabamba!: Water War in Bolivia.* South End Press, 2004.

Perreault, Tom. "Custom and Contradiction: Rural Water Governance and the Politics of *Usos y Costumbres* in Bolivia's Irrigators' Movement." *Annals of the Association of American Geographers*, vol. 98, no. 4, 2008, pp. 834–54, https://doi.org/10.1080/00045600802013502.

Razavi, Nasya S. "'Social Control' and the Politics of Public Participation in Water Remunicipalization, Cochabamba, Bolivia." *Water*, vol. 11, no. 7, 2019, pp. 1–19, https://doi.org/10.3390/w11071455.

Rousseau, Jean-Jacques. *The Social Contract.* Oxford UP, 1994.

Scott, Joan W. *Sex and Secularism.* Princeton UP, 2018.

Serageldin, Ismail. "Water: Conflicts Set to Arise Within as well as Between States." *Nature*, vol. 459, no. 7244, 2009, p. 163, https://doi.org/10.1038/459163b.

Shiva, Vandana. *Water Wars: Privatization, Pollution, and Profit.* North Atlantic Books, 2016.

Spronk, Susan. "Roots of Resistance to Urban Water Privatization in Bolivia: The 'New Working Class,' the Crisis of Neoliberalism, and Public Services." *International Labor and Working-Class History*, vol. 71, no. 1, 2007, pp. 8–28, https://doi.org/10.1017/s0147547907000312.

Svampa, Maristella, et al. "El punto de bifurcación es un momento en el que se miden ejércitos," entrevista con Alvaro García Linera. *Rebelion*, 9 Feb. 2009, rebelion.org/el-punto-de-bifurcacion-es-un-momento-en-el-que-se-miden-ejercitos/.

"Texts of the Coordinadora del Agua of Cochabamba." *Nadir*, www.nadir.org/nadir/initiativ/agp/cocha/agua.htm.

Tomba, Massimiliano. *Insurgent Universality: An Alternative Legacy of Modernity*. Oxford UP, 2019.

Udaeta, Maria Esther, "Bolivia: La Vision y Participacion de las Mujeres en la Guerra del Agua en Cochabamba Bolivia." *Género en el PNUD – America latina genera*, 2014, americalatina-genera.org/wp-content/uploads/2014/07/637_Bolivia_vision_y_participacion_de_mujeres_-en_guerra_del_agua.pdf.

UN Resolution 64/292 on "The Human Right to Water and Sanitation." *United Nations Digital Library*, 2010, digitallibrary.un.org/record/687002/files/A_RES_64_292-EN.pdf?ln = en.

Üstündağ, Nazan. "Mother, Politician, and Guerilla: The Emergence of a New Political Imagination in Kurdistan through Women's Bodies and Speech." *Differences*, vol. 30, no. 2, 2019, pp. 115–45, https://doi.org/10.1215/10407391-7736077.

Massimiliano Tomba

[C]ertain conditions for knowing date from hundreds of millions of years ago.
— *Michel Serres*, The Incandescent

For 6 million years, the great Colorado River flowed 1,450 miles from the icepacks of the Rocky Mountains to the Sea of Cortez. In 1998, following just a few decades of intense water development, the "American Nile" dried up before it could reach its destination. What happens to time when rivers stop flowing to the sea? What happens to the perennial river model of time when it stops short of describing what it has always embodied, namely, the linear flow of time?

Mass-scale water development reached a turning point at the end of the nineteenth century when hydroelectricity became a viable source of energy. The proliferation of hydroelectric dams has considerably interrupted and redirected river flows ever since. As these structures transformed American and European landscapes, they began to appear in the writings of some of the first celebrated thinkers of the discontinuity of time. I focus here on Gaston Bachelard and Martin Heidegger and how they relied on hydroelectricity to elaborate less linear and more complex conceptions of time that are particularly apparent in their pioneering works on historical epistemology.

In his history of historical epistemology, Hans-Jörg Rheinberger locates the decisive moment of its foundation at the end of the nineteenth century, when scientists and philosophers began to question more forcefully the dominant ideas that all the sciences shared a common unity and that the production and progress of scientific knowledge resulted from the kind of continuous, cumulative, and

A Timeful Theory of Knowledge: Thunderstorms, Dams, and the Disclosure of Planetary History

Kieran M. Murphy

teleological process that was the hallmark of classical mechanical thinking. This questioning opened the way for more historical, social, and situated approaches in the study of knowledge formation that has characterized historical epistemology ever since.

Evidence against the unity of the sciences and the mechanical conception of knowledge production came in great part from the study of electromagnetism. Classical mechanics couldn't fully explain the strange behavior of recently discovered electromagnetic phenomena, prompting Michael Faraday and James Clerk Maxwell to elaborate a different vision of physics based on what is known today as field theory. In addition to undermining the unity of physics, electromagnetic phenomena powered new technologies like the telegraph that appeared to operate beyond the traditional flow of time. But the most transformative event to usher in the electric age occurred in 1896 when Nikola Tesla successfully lit up the city of Buffalo, NY, with hydroelectric energy generated by dynamos located at Niagara Falls. Tesla's achievement demonstrated that a massive amount of electrical current could be distributed almost instantaneously over long distances, making the power grid a reality.

The coming of age of hydroelectric technology played a prominent role in the rise of historical epistemology as a field of study that seeks to identify and explain temporal discontinuities. Bachelard's and Heidegger's references to hydroelectricity confirm this claim. They also provide an opportunity to extend the history of historical epistemology from the nineteenth century to deep time. Hydroelectricity essentially describes a relationship between water and electricity that nineteenth-century technology harnessed to change the world. But that relationship has a much older history that predates the human and that goes back at least to the apparition of thunderstorms on the planet.

Resituating the history of human knowledge within a much older natural history promotes "timefulness." To counter the presentism and short-term thinking that brought us disasters such as global warming, Marcia Bjornerud proposes to nurture timefulness through the teachings of geology, art, and non-modern folk wisdom where she finds accounts of time more attuned to the poly-temporality and wide-ranging rhythms of the planet and its inhabitants. Michel Serres has proposed a philosophy of deep time history based on such timeful articulations of human and nonhuman actors and of modern and non-modern modes of knowing. He urges to engage with landscapes (*paysages*) and seek how their seemingly disparate elements form a deeply connected geological, biological, and cultural network, where time percolates in all its multiplicity. Bachelard and Heidegger relied on hydroelectric landscapes to explore nonlinear time. Their compositions include thunderstorms, mountains, rivers, lakes, life, dams, and dynamos. Together, these varied yet connected elements offer rich environmental and conceptual terrains that I revisit to lay the groundwork for a deep time theory of knowledge. I conclude by discussing how such theory could promote timefulness by establishing less anthropocentric historical narratives – or what Dipesh Chakrabarty calls "planetary history" – on more suitable epistemological grounds.

bachelard's hydroelectric landscape: imagination, wonder, and the depth time

Hydroelectricity came of age in the nineteenth century due to the discovery of electromagnetic induction. In 1831, Michael Faraday unveiled this new phenomenon by showing that a magnet in motion induces an electric current in a nearby conductor. The dynamo is a turbine that converts motion into electric current via electromagnetic induction. In a hydroelectric power station, hydraulic pressure provides the force that makes the dynamos spin.

The discovery of electromagnetic induction triggered what Bachelard called an "epistemological break" in the history of science. In a 1952 interdisciplinary conference that included Erwin Schrödinger, Ferdinand Gonseth, and Jean Wahl, Bachelard found in the examples of the dynamo and hydroelectricity an effective way to convey his idea of "epistemological break" to a general audience ("La vocation scientifique" 15, 25–26).[1] Bachelard cited the poet and essayist Paul Valéry who had argued that if we had access to the place where the great pre-nineteenth-century minds reside, and were to give a dynamo to Archimedes, Galileo, Descartes, or Newton, they would not know what to do with it. They would spin the movable part, take the device apart, measure all its pieces, and never have a chance to penetrate its secret. The dynamo would confound them because these luminaries could only think of mechanical transformations. Such thinking could grasp machines such as the classical clock, lever, or balance but not the electromagnetic transformations at work in the dynamo. Bachelard added that pre-nineteenth-century thinkers would also be perplexed at the hydroelectric power grid. They would consider as inconceivable how a river in the Alps allows Parisians to light up their homes and make phone calls to people across the world.

The phenomenon of electromagnetic induction at work in a dynamo manifests a transformation of energy that eludes mechanical interpretation. The great achievements accumulated by Newtonian physics since the eighteenth century legitimized this mechanical worldview associated with industrialization and the flowering of bourgeois society during the nineteenth century. However, a significant component of the world continued to elude the Newtonian conception of nature. The application of Newtonian physics to electromagnetism yielded only limited results. The classical laws of electromagnetism, what we now call "Maxwell's equations," took form in 1861 thanks to the elaboration of a new physical concept that originated in the patterns formed by iron filings around a magnet.

Faraday called these patterns "lines of force" and thought that they represented electric and magnetic forces better than the Newtonian law of universal gravitation, which states that gravitational attraction occurs between separate objects without delay or apparent mediation. Faraday thought that the instantaneous force at work in Newton's atomist universe seemed too magical to be true and saw in the curved lines of force extending beyond the magnet a more accurate way to represent a force acting in space. Whereas space is absolute and plays no part in gravitational attraction, lines of force show that a magnet reconfigures the surrounding space to move iron filings or to attract other magnets

The concept of a magnetic field implies that objects are not really separate. They participate in the same continuum characterized by a malleable and active space that contains their potential for action. Now known as "field

theory," this new representation of the transmission of energy broke away from Newtonian atomism and prompted James Clerk Maxwell to develop a mathematical formalism compatible with a continuous physical reality. Besides the laws of electromagnetism, Faraday's lines of force helped Maxwell formulate the electromagnetic wave theory from which he predicted the existence of the radio wave and identified light as an electromagnetic phenomenon. In 1905, Einstein published his special theory of relativity, which builds on field theory and an asymmetry in Maxwell's interpretation of electromagnetic induction to show that time and space are indeed malleable. Einstein's special theory of relativity completed Faraday's critique of Newtonian physics and ended a theoretical system that had dominated the intellectual climate of the previous one hundred and fifty years.

Bachelard knew the instrumental role electromagnetic induction played in this epistemological break (*Le nouvel esprit* 42, 146–47). To understand how a dynamo works, scientists had to rethink their conception of reality and how to investigate it. Such a dramatic shift in the history of science did not simply depend on the inductive reasoning characterizing the empirical sciences. It also involved a cognitive leap, which, for Bachelard, was akin to an electromagnetic induction, and which he considered a crucial engine for both scientific and artistic insights (Alunni; Bontems 22–24, 124–26; Murphy 121–26). To clarify the nature of this cognitive leap I will turn to his works on the faculty of imagination and how he modeled it after the dynamo.

Gaston Bachelard defines imagination as the movement that, through distortion ("déformation") and unexpected association, alters the images of sense-perception (*L'air et les songes* 7–26). This movement is not simply random. The altered images manifest certain patterns that reveal the structure of imagination. To identify these patterns, Bachelard relied on literary authors and how their wide-ranging poetic images tend to cohere around the four elements: water, fire, earth, and air. Each element comes with its characteristic movement that impels imagination. For instance, in *L'air et les songes* (1943), Bachelard explores how aerial images move our thoughts upward, towards the weightless and ethereal. They set us free from the grips of gravity and the material world, revealing their affinity with the nature of imagination itself. Air and imagination partake in a liberating movement where Bachelard locates a primordial openness to rethink reality and its material foundation (*L'air et les songes* 15–16, 135–36, 281–303).

The elements inform images that can operate beyond mere re-presentations or metaphors. An effective poem is a "good conductor" that generates "a dynamic induction" in the reader. Our intimate relationship with each element "can determine a truly active participation that we would gladly call an *induction* if the word wasn't already taken by the psychology of reasoning [...] Only this material and dynamic induction [...] can transport our innermost being" (Bachelard, *L'air et les songes* 10–12). Elsewhere, Bachelard makes clear that the inducive power of images is akin to electromagnetic induction:

> Frequently, too, critics pay more attention to the word than to the sentence; they concentrate on the locution rather than the whole page. Their judgments are inevitably static, atomic. Few critics are prepared to test a new style by submitting to its *induction*. As I see it there ought to pass between writer and reader a kind of *verbal induction* sharing many of the characteristics of electromagnetic induction between two circuits. A book would then be a sort of psychic induction apparatus producing in the reader temptations to originality of expression.[2] (*Le droit de rêver* 181)

Electromagnetic induction is reversible. A dynamo easily converts into an electric motor. A dynamo harnesses movement to generate electric current, which, in turn, can be harnessed to generate movement. An effective literary work provides the platform where this reversible process takes place. To be moved to "originality of expression," the reader must be a good conductor who channels the electric

current generated by what had moved the writer's imagination in the first place. This "psychic induction apparatus" establishes an intimate link between writer and reader that doesn't derive from mimesis. As the material and dynamic foundation of imagination, water, fire, earth, and air provide the main sources of movement that power the dynamo-electric motor that allow writer and reader to be moved by the same elemental energy.

Within the elemental families of inductive imagery, the water–imagination interface functions like a hydroelectric power station where induction derives from rivers, lakes, springs, and seas. Bachelard mapped out how imagination harnesses these hydrological landscapes in *L'eau et les rêves* (1942) and *La poétique de la rêverie* (1968), privileging streams, lakes, ponds, and springs. He grew up among the fresh waters of his beloved Champagne region and, as he imparts to the reader, shares a stronger bond with them than the sea (Bachelard, *L'eau et les rêves* 11).

Bachelard is particularly drawn to the way a body of water reflects its surroundings. These reflections are not just flat mirror images. They acquire the depth of the aquatic medium (Bachelard, *L'eau et les rêves* 11, 74). In a lake, the world perceives itself, suggesting a primordial self-reflection that reappears in poetic images evoking Narcissus and the need to see beyond the surface of things (Bachelard, *L'eau et les rêves* 40–45; *La poétique de la rêverie* 170–73). In French, to reflect (réfléchir) also means to think. As poets have shown, lakes, ponds, and rivers are sources of reflection that have inspired a deeper engagement with the world. Such engagement is particularly apparent regarding time. Quoting Paul Claudel, Bachelard sums up: "l'eau ainsi est le regard de la terre, son appareil à regarder le *temps*" ("water is then the gaze of the earth, its device for looking at *time*"; my trans.; Bachelard, *L'eau et les rêves* 45).[3] Water flows like a river and abides like a lake, capturing both the transience and depth of time (11, 73–74; *La poétique de la rêverie* 173).[4]

The way lakes and ponds[5] reflect the depth of time reveals the important role one's early life plays in imagination and its dynamo induction. Contemplating reflections in deep, still waters generates an upstream flow towards a more remote reservoir of memories that filled up during childhood (Bachelard, *La poétique de la rêverie* 94–95). Bachelard characterizes childhood as an inner lake that remains throughout one's life a major distributary of imagination. The murky depth of childhood memories does not reflect clear events. The deepest reflections of the world into the lake of childhood cannot be dated. They operate beyond the chronological time of the calendar, clock, and history. They abide in the depth of time as states that later resurface due to the inductive power of a landscape or poetic image. One of these fundamental states is wonder. A child's openness to the world comes together with unadulterated wonder. This state of wonder lives on submerged in a lake-like depth of time from which, later in one's life, imagination draws to rethink reality and move beyond the surface of things.

Bachelard elaborated a historical epistemology that relied on electromagnetic induction and hydroelectricity to explain how imagination induces scientific and artistic insights. Imagination behaves like a power station where our intimate relationship with the elements makes the dynamos spin. Water, for its part, provides a reservoir of energy and imagery that has pushed the exploration of time further. The rise of modern hydroelectricity triggered massive water development that rendered time more malleable and less linear. The way dams abruptly interrupted rivers to create artificial lakes accentuated the temporal divide between flowing and still water. Artificial lakes submerged previously familiar areas that entered a state of limbo. Furthermore, the transformation of hydraulic pressure into electric current implied that time could possess contrasting properties. The large-scale manipulation of water that came along with hydroelectricity offered a material foundation for a more complex and multifaceted conception of time.

Bachelard invokes this profound shift in the hydrological landscape by considering the dynamo and hydroelectricity emblematic of the temporal discontinuity of an epistemological break, and childhood wonder a key reservoir of inductive power. The latter also points to the deep time perspective informing his historical epistemology. The childhood state of wonder reveals a deeper openness to the world due to a depth of time where the human and nonhuman converge in the reflective gaze of water. Although Bachelard contributed to reconceptualizing philosophy in terms of twentieth-century science, he also resorted to nonmodern elemental thinking to grasp the inductive power of imagination. To reduce water to the chemical formula H_2O would occlude hydrological landscapes and poetic images that remain crucial sources of scientific and artistic insights. The water–imagination interface channels a primordial state of wonder that manifests an aspect of deep time that cannot be reduced to a linear conception of time, which suggests an ever-expanding separation between the past and present. Childhood wonder reappears throughout one's life because it abides in a depth of time that allows for the past and present to occur simultaneously. Hydroelectricity helped Bachelard materialize a complex notion of time where the inductive power of imagination impels a historical epistemology marked by temporal discontinuities and the depth of deep time.

heidegger's hydroelectric landscape: river poiesis, erosion, and fluctuation

A contemporary of Bachelard and the transformation of the hydrological landscape, Martin Heidegger also relied on hydroelectricity to convey the discontinuities of his historical epistemology. I will focus on his influential 1954 essay "The Question Concerning Technology" and show how its form and content spring from a hydroelectric landscape. But first a few words should be said about Heidegger's philosophical style.[6] His terminology derives from his redefinition of traditional philosophical concepts in terms of their original, more layered Greek meanings. This strategy aims to recover a deeper relation to reality that, he contends, marked the advent of Western philosophy. To illuminate forgotten aspects of Greek concepts, he translates them into colloquial German words that evoke every-day meanings. He relies on etymology to form a tightly woven network of concepts that res-onates with the Greek originals and to justify puns and thematic riffs that, together with logical argumentation, play an integral part in his approach to revealing the essence of things. In "The Question Concerning Technol-ogy," the river combines with the related themes of mountains, erosion, wonder, and hydroelectric dams to create the main motif that sheds light on the essence of technology.

For Heidegger, the essence of technology is not fixed. It has a history. He contrasts the old waterwheel with the hydroelectric dam to show that the nature and function of modern technologies have little in common with ancient tools and machines. Whereas the water-wheel gears into the river flow, the hydroelec-tric dam forcefully stops and transforms it. The waterwheel operates according to what the Greeks called *poiesis*. The term applied to wide-ranging activities like midwifery and tending a field. In each case, *poiesis* described a type of production that gently follows or nur-tures a natural process without altering its course. In the Greek context, art is also a kind of *poiesis*. A stone already contains the figure that will guide the sculptor's hand. The stone itself is the product of a more primordial and self-emerging *poiesis* called nature (*physis*).

Humans help bring what nature produces into fruition. As they performed their comp-lementary role of *poiesis*, they developed what the ancient Greeks called *techne*. In contrast to the current use of the word technology, *techne* did not refer to manufactured objects but rather to knowledge and know-how. The crafts of a musician, architect, doctor, or philo-sopher are all types of *techne*. Heidegger situ-ates the origin of modern technology in one type of *techne* that came to dominate the others: the philosopher's art of reasoning,

which laid the foundation for science and the explosion of knowledge that marked recent history. The rise to prominence of science manifests a fundamental shift in the human engagement with nature. Scientists do not approach nature poietically anymore. Through the imposition of their rational and calculable order, they aggressively seek to penetrate and manipulate nature's secrets. Such approach cul-minated in the hydroelectric power station which, by damming up rivers, has transformed them into a mere reservoir of energy or, in Hei-degger's term, *Bestand*, which has been trans-lated as "standing-reserve" (Lovitt) and, more recently, "disposable" (Rojcewicz). This tech-nocratic practice presents a danger because it reduces the environment, including its human and nonhuman inhabitants, to something expendable.

Heidegger proposes to sum up the essence of modern technology with the word *Ge-stell* ("enframing" (Lovitt) or "all-encompassing imposition" (Rojcewicz)). Although human *poiesis* and *Ge-stell* are epistemologically different, they are forms of *techne*. The ancient Greeks called *aletheia* the kind of knowledge produced by *techne*. Translated as *veritas* in Latin, *Wahrheit* in German, and truth in English, the concept of *aletheia* has been central to the history of Western thought and its conception of knowledge. For Heidegger, the translations of *aletheia* have been misleading because they do not convey the word's negative meaning implied by the prefix "a-," which is privative and implies that revealing the essence of things always involves a tension between what comes in the open and what remains in the dark. *Veritas*, *Wahrheit*, and truth have lost this negative connotation.

The shift from a negative to a positive expression of truth manifests a change of atti-tude towards "being." In ancient Greece, and especially among pre-Socratic thinkers, truth is indissociable from being, or the fact that there *is* a world to apprehend in the first place. All beings partake in the world of being. Humans are the site (Dasein) where the essences of beings and, to some extent, being itself can be revealed. Yet, this power of revelation originates from being, which provides the overarching condition that determines what humans can and cannot grasp.

In his works on pre-Socratic *aletheia*, Heidegger shows that in Parmenides the dependence on being takes the appearance of a goddess named Aletheia who guides the thinker towards truth (*Parmenides* 1–6). The terms *veritas*, *Wahrheit*, and truth, do not evoke the divine and imply that human agency alone is responsible for knowledge. Heidegger underscores the divine conception of *aletheia* because it offers a less hubristic concept of truth where humans, as recipients of being, play a more receptive than active role in the production of knowledge. He finds another significant example of *aletheia* in Homer's *Iliad* when Nestor refers to a propitious sign that the Greeks received before their expedition to Troy, and that was sent by Zeus in the form of a lightning bolt (31–34). Here, the divine origin of truth takes the shape of an awe-inspiring yet natural phenomenon, lightning, which corresponds with another essential aspect of *aletheia*: god-sent truth appears in a flash that illuminates and blinds, reveals and conceals. Translators have rendered the tension between the positive and negative dimensions of the Greek and Heideggerian conception of truth with the terms "disclosure" and "unconcealment."

Heidegger also argues that the word *aletheia* contains an important allusion to the mythological field of Lethe (*Parmenides* 118–29). In the concluding lines of Plato's *Republic*, Socrates invokes the legend of the warrior Er to address the questions of anamnesis and what remains of human beings after death. Several days after he died in battle, Er mysteriously came back to life and shared what he saw during his time on the other side. To prepare their return to life, the dead visit several places until they go through fire and asphyxiating air to reach the desolate field of Lethe where the "Carefree" River flows. After drinking the river's water, the dead forget their previous life and, following a thunderstorm and earthquake, are transported back in the world of the living. What

remains from the previous life in the new life depends on how much Carefree water one drinks. The genuine thinkers who were receptive to the essence of being will drink the right measure, which lets them forget without losing their insightful disposition. The others will drink too much and continue to live their next lives in error.

Heidegger calls the insightful disposition of genuine thinkers "wonder" (Erstaunen). Like Aristotle, he contends that philosophy starts with wonder. And like Bachelard, he attributes an aquatic and temporal dimension to wonder. The word *Erstaunen* evokes and is probably etymologically related with the verb *staunen* (to dam), which appears in words like *stausee* (artificial lake, reservoir). In "The Question Concerning Technology," Heidegger asserts that to disclose the essence of technology is "to be in wonder at the approach of the earliest" (Rojcewicz 117–18). His disclosure of the essence of modern technology as *Ge-stell* derives from the deeper essence of *techne*, which in ancient Greece conveyed a knowledge production determined by *aletheia* and the self-disclosure of being. As his own demonstration illustrates, wonder taps into an upstream reservoir of forgotten knowledge to reveal the essence of things. Heidegger's historical epistemology hinges on a type of anamnesis where "the approach of the earliest," or the self-disclosure of being to the knowledge producer, evokes a relationship between a reservoir and its distributary.

In Plato's account of the field of Lethe, the passage from death to life and from unknowing to knowing entails the withdrawal of nature (*physis*) and one's past. Nothing grows in the field of Lethe. As a primordial expression of *aletheia*, nature's *poiesis* does not belong where beings fall into oblivion. Although the Carefree River seems out of place in the barren landscape of Lethe, it also participates in wiping nature out because, as Er reports, its water is uncontainable. The field of Lethe recalls a desert canyon or flooded area that was grounded down by a boisterous stream. This allusion to water erosion supports an epistemology where knowledge is submerged in the past and where the revelation of truth always coincides with a withdrawal of truth.

To recover the ancient, less presumptuous, and erosive meaning of truth, Heidegger translates *aletheia* with the German coinage *Entbergen*. The privative prefix "Ent-" means "to deprive of" or "undo." Its association with "Bergen" foregrounds the etymological root with "Berg," mountain. Entbergen – the revelation of truth – literally means to disinter, unearth, or dig up something that a mountain hides. *Poiesis* and *Ge-stell* characterize different kinds of digging up. Heidegger relies on mining terminology (*fördern*) to portray how *Ge-stell* ravishes nature through forceful extraction. He hopes that the logic of extraction provoked by the rise to prominence of *Ge-stell* and epitomized by a world dominated by technocrats will eventually pass. Since such deep historical change ultimately depends on what being has in store for us, he contends that his philosophy can only "prepare the way" for a return to a less reductive and more respectful engagement with the world that he perceives in *poiesis*. In "The Question Concerning Technology," he attempts to unearth the essence of technology through a poietic mode he calls "questioning." Each question leads to another question that slowly clears a path towards truth. It is "a way of thinking" that asks readers to follow the meandering movement of the entire essay without getting fixated on one of its parts. Through questioning, Heidegger seeks to generate a kind of flow that recalls that of a river. A stream does not flow in a straight line. It includes detours and bifurcations that are contingent on the shape of the landscape, the appearance of obstacles, and erosion. Unlike the fast pace and imposing extraction of modern mining, a river unveils what lies in a mountain by slowly eroding its slope. River *poiesis* is a slow grind that sometimes leads to the rush of a breakthrough.

By re-casting truth in terms of *aletheia* and *Entbergen*, Heidegger advocates for a kind of mining akin to panning or what promoters of "slow time" like Paul Harris call "rock fishing." What knowledge producers must patiently sieve through is contingent on what being allows them to grasp. Being works like a river that reveals what lies inside a mountain through erosion. Like the rocks uncovered by a river over time, the disclosure of being fluctuates. As manifestations of this disclosure, the contrasting epistemologies of *poiesis* and *Ge-stell* cannot be understood in terms of linear progress because the history of being clears its path like a primordial river percolates in a landscape: through erosion, fluctuation, detour, and bifurcation.

In "The Question Concerning Technology," Heidegger decries how hydroelectric dams impoverished the meaning of the great Rhine River, which, in Friedrich Hölderlin's romantic poetry, had embodied Germany's vital source of *poiesis* (Heidegger, "The Question Concerning Technology" 16). Heidegger often discussed the *poiesis* of Hölderlin's "river poetry" in other works, painting a different yet familiar hydroelectric landscape located upstream dams and dynamos.[7] Up in the mountains, thunderstorms swell rivers up. One of the planet's main sources of wonder determined the reception of the history of being: a relationship between water and the electricity (or "fire") from the sky. An elemental wonder for the hydroelectric sparked contrasting paths to knowledge. In Heidegger's historical epistemology, modes of knowing fluctuate yet continue to participate in *aletheia*, *Entbergen*, or truth. From the currents of river *poiesis* to the dams of *Ge-stell*, what supports this continuity in the otherwise nonlinear history of being is the thunderstorm found at the source of knowledge.

the disclosure of planetary history

My reading of Bachelard's and Heidegger's historical epistemologies has amplified their hydroelectrical, geological, and, more generally, nonhuman origins to lay the groundwork for a deep time theory of knowledge. Such a project promotes timefulness and is one of the prerequisites for bringing what Dipesh Chakrabarty calls "planetary history" into fruition. In *The Climate of History in a*

Planetary Age, Chakrabarty contrasts "planetary" with "global" history, which focuses on narratives of globalization from purely anthropocentric perspectives. These narratives have played a critical role in showing the interconnected economic, social, and environmental impacts of capitalism and modern technology. More recently, they have also revealed how humans became geological agents responsible for altering the course of natural history and causing climate change and mass extinctions. The emergence of a "geological consciousness" (Chakrabarty 215) signals "the arrival of a point in history where the global *discloses* to humans the domain of the planetary" (80, 207; emphasis in original). Drawing from Heideggerian parlance and historical epistemology, Chakrabarty characterizes "the domain of the planetary" as a disclosure of global history that reveals something "antecedent to the global" (207).

Chakrabarty locates the determining moment of this "approach of the earliest" in the rise to prominence of Earth system science (ESS). In the 1960s and 1970s, questions concerning the habitability of planets and the relative stability of Earth's atmosphere over deep time prompted James Lovelock and Lynn Margulis to consider Earth a whole, self-regulating system supported by living and nonliving actors. The Earth system implied the existence of various feedback loops responsible for its self-regulation. Their examination called for a new interdisciplinary field of study, combining findings and methodologies from geology, biology, chemistry, physics, and mathematics. Since its inception, ESS made significant contributions to the understanding of Earth's and other planets' atmospheres, and played a major role in identifying the origins and effects of anthropogenic global warming. Chakrabarty underscores that ESS has also offered planetary as opposed to global historical narratives. As a scientific discipline, ESS traces a history that is non-teleological and that does not make the human central to its narrative. ESS history renders manifest what is "antecedent to the global" because, for 4.5 billion years, the Earth system has pursued its course indifferent of and mostly unencumbered by human existence.

Along with the popularization of debates surrounding climate change and the "Anthropocene hypothesis," ESS participated in "the percolation of a geological consciousness into our sense of history." Chakrabarty draws from a modern portrayal of landscapes to highlight the value of this change and its political implications. Modern thought has traditionally assumed a reciprocal relationship between humans and Earth. Chakrabarty finds examples of this "structure of mutuality" (182, 186) across wide-ranging figures, including John Locke, Søren Kierkegaard, Edmund Husserl, Rabindranath Tagore, Joseph Stalin, Jawaharlal Nehru, Fernand Braudel, Bede Griffiths, and Martin Hägglund. In their descriptions, landscapes seem "unchanging," "given," or "for us."

For instance, Nehru, the anticolonial first prime minister of India, considered the Himalayan glaciers a kind of Heideggerian "standing-reserve" that would inexhaustibly drive India's development via the irrigation and power provided by big dams (Chakrabarty 106–07). In speeches, he promoted hydroelectric technology in lofty terms, calling dams "temples of modern India." Nehru's impassioned rhetoric appears misguided now that the glaciers are receding, and India's great rivers are drying up. Such development projects participated in the mid-twentieth-century global modernization rush that worked hand in hand with the reduction of landscapes to a mere background for human intervention and short-term planning.

From the deep time perspective of planetary or Earth system history (they are essentially the same for Chakrabarty), landscapes are constantly changing and clearly not "for us." They predate and will probably outlast humankind. They also function as reminders of the interconnectivity of all living and nonliving things. Chakrabarty discusses personal, literary, and philosophical accounts, where their authors aspire to the planetary by reverently affirming their innermost connection with "stardust," "trees," and, more generally, the

Earth system. But, for him, these planetary connections "remain more poetical than political (in contemporary terms)" (Chakrabarty 118). One of the main challenges of the planetary perspective comes from "the difficulty of bringing these connections within the emancipatory realms of the political" (115) because, from Marxist to right-wing views, "the political" persists as an anthropocentric category of global history. Planetary historians must then navigate two critical questions:

> How do we (re)imagine the human as a form of life connected to other forms of life, and how do we then base our politics on that knowledge? Our political categories are usually imagined not only in profoundly anthropocentric terms but in separation from all these connections. But can we extend them to account for our relationship to nonhuman forms of life or even to the nonliving that we can damage (such as rivers and glaciers)? (126)

The disclosure of planetary history signals an epistemological shift that we are still grappling with, but that should provide the foundation for less anthropocentric political categories.

Although Chakrabarty gestures towards other modes of knowing, he privileges ESS as the main model of planetary knowledge. One of the potential problems with this choice is the traditional scientific framework of ESS, which remains grounded in *Ge-stell* and its reduction of the planet to a mere "standing-reserve."[8] From the perspective of planetary history, the hydroelectric dam is not a "temple" of modernization that glorifies the transformation of the world into a "standing-reserve." Nor is it a monument to the social and ecological disasters that global history has helped uncover. It is a landmark within a wider hydrological landscape where relationships among time scales and rhythms, and between water and electricity, humans and nonhumans, and the living and nonliving, come into play. These relationships call for theories of knowledge that include *Ge-stell* but should not be limited by it.

Otherwise, planetary politics would get reabsorbed into the anthropocentric political categories of global history. And, the disclosure of planetary history would not constitute a significant epistemological shift since the prevalent mode of knowing would remain *Ge-stell* in the form of ESS.

Considering Bachelard's and Heidegger's historical epistemologies, and the role water erosion and hydroelectricity play in their changing landscapes, the disclosure of planetary history could be retold in a way that deemphasizes *Ge-stell* while still raising geological consciousness and decentering the human: knowledge springs from age-old hydroelectric occurrences connecting the living to the nonliving. Primordial cells articulated and enclosed a relationship between water and electricity to survive. This enclosed hydroelectric landscape, from which the Last Universal Common Ancestor (LUCA) emerged around 4 billion years ago, recalls older planetary ones that the wonderstruck human can still intuit when a thunderstorm makes a river flow. Wonder performs an anamnesis that hinges on the common hydroelectric nature of these internal and external landscapes, and that discloses the deep time scale of knowledge formation. What wonder recollects are various modes of knowing like *poiesis* and *Ge-stell*. These epistemologies predate humanity but continue to percolate in landscapes composed of thunderstorms, mountains, rivers, life, and hydroelectric dams. Lakes, ponds, and reservoirs also lend their reflective gaze to deepen the history of knowledge. Their still waters provide a source of reflections on the depth of time as the medium through which wonder remembers the immemorial past and through which imagination induces (in Bachelard's sense) knowledge.

disclosure statement

No potential conflict of interest was reported by the author.

notes

1 The Bachelardian idea of an "epistemological break" was particularly impactful in the development of historical epistemologies through the works of Louis Althusser and Michel Foucault, both of whom adapted it for their own purposes. It also paved the way for Thomas Kuhn's paradigm shift theory.

2 Bachelard's emphasis. Translation (with modifications) from Bachelard, *The Right to Dream*.

3 Claudel's emphasis. The citation is from Claudel 317.

4 Bachelard uses different French expressions to convey the depth of time: "la profondeur du temps," "la nuit des temps," "le temps immémorial."

5 Bachelard also adds wells.

6 My account of Heidegger's style and terminology is particularly indebted to Richard Rojcewicz's critical analysis and translation of the essay in *The Gods and Technology*.

7 See Heidegger, *Hölderlin's Hymns: "The Ister"* 2–4, 135–37, 144–46, 151–53, 162; *Hölderlin's Hymns: "Germania" and "The Rhine"* 29–31, 38, 51–62, 83–84, 90, 120–21, 130, 141–43, 173, 219–21, 232, 260–61.

8 Chakrabarty extolls the "Earth system scientists" for not only bringing the planetary to the fore but also for making it "a category of humanist thought" when, in light of the data on climate change, they began to describe the planetary "as a site of existential concern" (70). He follows this laudatory portrayal of scientists with a dismissal of some of Heidegger's views: "Heidegger's stance against science and his assumption that the nature of human dwelling can be imagined without thinking of the 'astronomical' object, our planet, are positions we cannot support in the time of the Anthropocene" (70–71). As my reading of Heidegger's historical epistemology shows, he was not "against science" but critical of its current dominant version, *Ge-stell*, which he perceived as the driver of a dangerous technocratization.

bibliography

Alunni, Charles. "Relativités et puissances spectrales chez Gaston Bachelard." *Revue de synthèse*, vol. 120, no. 1, 1999, pp. 73–110.

Bachelard, Gaston. *L'air et les songes: essai sur l'imagination du movement.* José Corti, 1943.

Bachelard, Gaston. *Le droit de rêver.* Presses Universitaires de France, 1970.

Bachelard, Gaston. *L'eau et les rêves: essai sur l'imagination de la matière.* José Corti, 1942.

Bachelard, Gaston. *Le nouvel esprit scientifique.* F. Alcan, 1934.

Bachelard, Gaston. *La poétique de la rêverie.* Presses Universitaires de France, 1968.

Bachelard, Gaston. *The Right to Dream.* Translated by J.A. Underwood, Dallas Institute, 1988.

Bachelard, Gaston. "La vocation scientifique et l'âme humaine." *L'Homme devant la science (Rencontre internationale de Genève 1952)*, Les Éditions de la Baconnière, 1952, pp. 11–30.

Bjornerud, Marcia. *Timefulness.* Princeton UP, 2018.

Bontems, Vincent. *Bachelard.* Les Belles lettres, 2010.

Chakrabarty, Dipesh. *The Climate of History in a Planetary Age.* U of Chicago P, 2021.

Claudel, Paul. "L'Oiseau noir dans le soleil levant." *Oeuvres complètes*, vol. 4, Gallimard, 1952, pp. 177–337.

Harris, Paul A. "Stoned Thinking: The Petriverse of Pierre Jardin." *SubStance*, vol. 47, no. 2, 2018, pp. 119–48.

Heidegger, Martin. *Hölderlin's Hymns: "Germania" and "The Rhine."* Translated by William McNeill and Julia Ireland, Indiana UP, 2014.

Heidegger, Martin. *Hölderlin's Hymns: "The Ister."* Translated by William McNeill and Julia Ireland, Indiana UP, 1996.

Heidegger, Martin. *Parmenides.* Translated by André Schuwer and Richard Rojcewicz, Indiana UP, 1992.

Heidegger, Martin. "The Question Concerning Technology." *The Question Concerning Technology and Other Essays*, translated by William Lovitt, Harper Torchbooks, 1977, pp. 3–35.

Murphy, Kieran. *Electromagnetism and the Metonymic Imagination.* Penn State UP, 2020.

Rheinberger, Hans-Jörg. *On Historicizing Epistemology: An Essay.* Stanford UP, 2010.

Rojcewicz, Richard. *The Gods and Technology: A Reading of Heidegger.* SUNY P, 2006.

Serres, Michel. *Darwin, Bonaparte et le Samaritain: une philosophie de l'histoire.* Editions Le Pommier, 2016.

Kieran M. Murphy

Water, water, every where,
Nor any drop to drink.
— *Samuel Taylor Coleridge*

Learning Waters

Gil Anidjar

teach with water. It's nothing very remarkable and I myself do not remember how I settled upon water as a most convenient introduction, an obvious mediation, to pretty much anything I have tried to teach, which is to say, to learn. Did not everything begin (and end too) with water? Thales or the Bible, photosynthesis, the Middle Passage, we ourselves in our mothers' wombs, and more generally, life and its perdurance, its sustenance.[1] Essentialism for the ages. My own beginnings, in any case, would border on the banal, if they did not signify so much about where I live (race and class) and how I teach (tradition, institution, location), the liberties I can responsibly take, or the sheer length to which one might have to go to register and partake of a sense of wonder — and of outrage — on the impossible path toward a collective experience of learning. In this particular installment, learning with water (not quite drinking at the fount of wisdom, nor "reimagining water") is very much about recalling what we know, knowing what we do with the knowledge that we have (the wonder of it, and the outrage) (see Christian and Wong). For, like God, who "made out of water every living thing," water too may be "closer to you than your jugular vein." God is neither water nor blood, of course, yet the Qur'ān may be signaling the nature of an originary, and not unthreatening, *Mitsein*. Being with water, or at least learning with it, means taking the measure of a peculiar and changing distance, a strange, comforting as well as menacing, perhaps divine, intimacy. A learning opportunity, and perhaps a different kind of water. Or indeed *waters*, as the Hebrew language has it, that knows no singular for the "stuff."[2] We are nothing without water, which was there long before us, "delivered," Charles Fishman writes, "4.4 billion years ago" (17).[3] Learning with water would thus entail "speaking of immemorial waters," in Luce Irigaray's powerful phrase, accessing the waters — and the dangers — we ourselves are made of and unmade by (1). In its natural and unnatural history, in other words, and quotidian as it may be, water is, it preserves and also effaces, the stranger in our thirst.[4]

I teach with water. Writing this now, I am beginning to recall how I found my way down

Fig. 1.

this particular water hole, visited and revisited the water learning curve. Like many of us – and prior to that epochal rise in righteous consumption-consciousness that brought *less disposable* (but always already obsolete) water bottles into use – I had finally developed the habit of bringing a bottle of water, of so-called mineral water, to class. A bottle is not a glass, nor is it an oak tree, I don't think, though I too might volunteer that "the water is not special water."[5] That bottle, in any case, or another one just like it, ended up offering itself as an obvious prop and a convenient exemplar. A body of water, which is not one (see Neimanis). This was some years ago, but it had taken me a while to remember water, to learn from my routinely better-hydrated students; to recognize how much of a drain teaching (or indeed, learning) is on the body; how important hydration feels over the course of a two-hour class. Back in graduate school, I had witnessed Jacques Derrida deliver a four-hour lecture without taking a single sip of water. I was awed by the performance and by the absence of water. I thought little of the strain, of the bodily and watery expenditure, his or the audience's. Here and elsewhere, Derrida had gone some impressive length toward elaborating on "le corps enseignant," the teaching body that is at once individual and collective (the French thus designates the teacher's body but also, a plural noun in English as well, "the faculty." And think here of US President Lyndon Johnson's Teacher Corps, for instance). Distinct from "the student body," that collective learning body was, up to that point, seriously lacking in theorization. Not to mention, hydration. Derrida's lecture, incidentally, was partly devoted to a different material, albeit liquid still (see Derrida). Ink. Limited Ink.

I begin (and end) with water. Limited, contained or bound, water. Is there any other kind? But allow me to be more precise. I start the class, almost every first class of any given term, by quietly, if ostensibly, depositing in front of the class, or at the center of the seminar table, a bottle of "spring water," a mug shot (bottle shot?) of which I reproduce, front and back, in Figure 1.[6]

I then invite the students to attend to this classroom instance of the proverbial elephant, although not quite after the desperate manner of the three blind men. I ask them to look (touch and grasp, even listen, if they wish, but not taste) and then describe what they see and perceive. "Canoe-makers along the upper Congo River did not drink water while constructing dugouts, believing that 'otherwise it would leak'" (Dawson 194). There is, I think, wisdom in this parched construction. Such practical, if extreme, exercise in (mostly) *theōria* is in any case meant as an occasion for the students to exert their cognitive, academic attention and consider *what is before them*, and then describe it as exhaustively as they can in their language. "The city child has no opportunities to come in touch with living water," writes Ivan Illich. "Water can no more be observed; it can only be imagined, by reflecting on an occasional drop or a humble puddle" (Illich 76; compare Bachelard's claim that "the same memory flows from all fountains" (8)). Or a plastic bottle.

The exercise, which I attempt to reconstruct below with the accuracy of a court stenographer (we shall see that law does have a hand in water), involves thirst, uncomfortable sitting, and awkward silences, the latter slowly broken by the tentative voices of a few (rarely all) students. The whole thing can be quite tedious, even pointless. It tries everybody's patience, but the slow motion, or perhaps it is the flow motion, does lubricate space and speech. I have feared anger and frustration (I have felt it too, in myself), but there has been no manifest instance of hostility, nor of explicit disagreement. Barring such, it is in any case a very long class, and mostly boring. It unfailingly fails, moreover, to reach an end – exhaustion without exhaustiveness – even if it usually lasts for the entire duration of that meeting, the first class of the term (between 75 and 110 minutes, depending on the format of the course). The explicit premise is that nothing is too obvious. Which is another way of saying that, expertise aside, nothing is either given, or immediate (we keep bumping against Gaston Bachelard's claim that there is "a continuity between the speech of water and the speech of man" (15) – undoubtedly linked for him to the "feminine characteristics" the poetic imagination "nearly always" attributes

to water (14–15)).' Still, as Jacques Rancière would maintain, all of us are *capable* of seeing, or recognizing, an object – matter, water – placed in front of us, particularly an exceedingly familiar object, as is the case here, one that has not suddenly emerged as if from a cloud of unknowing, or another universe (see Rancière).[8] This is no "water walk pedagogy," as it lacks, on the surface at least, those other universes evoked and invoked by Violet Caibaiosai (Christian and Wong 107–12). Nevertheless, even with varying, if limited, degrees of familiarity or experience, and language, we might speak and share what we see with others, whether they are in the room with us, whether they too are seeing – less the forest for the trees, than the waters for the bottle.

In front of us, then, a familiar object. It is a bottle of water not unlike (indeed, plausibly identical to) countless others we have seen and held, perhaps even opened, before. Is this specific bottle really filled with water? Looks can be deceptive and we might be led astray. By a bottle of water? You just wait. Wait and learn. As we are merely looking at the container, for now, we cannot know for certain, yet have no reason to assume otherwise; no reason to distrust that it is, in fact, water. We *recognize* that it is, just like we recognize the object as a whole. A measure of repetition, a measure of confirmation can moreover be secured because the bottle is made of transparent material (surely an important part of our description), and the liquid within it is clear. Clear – though not pure, and certainly not "ultra-pure" – as water.[9] In addition, we can already read the word "Spring" on the green label. A bottle of water then, made of transparent material – plastic – and covered with a label that provides what appears like pertinent information (which will soon require our attention as well). We have seen those before and though we do not know how this particular bottle made it to our pedagogical shores, we know it must have been acquired in some way. Such labeled water containers are oftentimes distributed for free on American campuses and other corporate spaces, but they must still be purchased and paid for. Granted this particular bottle may have been borrowed or stolen (filled with other waters too), but even if it was, that would not be the rule. It was either bought or given, perhaps donated. A transaction is, at any rate, presumed and it was by all accounts necessary for the object to find itself in front of us. The bottle, ostensibly no more than a means to a hydrating end, appeals to our thirsting selves, but it is also, and no less so, a commodity, therefore, one that initially belongs to a commercial register, and this, one might say, *before* it can fulfill its hydrating function. What is more, the commercial offer it constitutes and embodies did not merely respond to a demand. It anticipated it. One might even aver that it hijacked it, offering itself in advance and substituting itself for other waters (wells or water fountains) that might have fulfilled similar hydrating demands. And could still, in fact. Depending on the urgency of our thirst, in any case, this particular quenching implement can justifiably be foregrounded as such in our consciousness, or it can withdraw into a temporal shadow of earlier drinking use (or later, anticipated ones too). What surely forces itself forward, in this instance (in this instant), is less a matter of health or of physiological needs – drinking water – but rather the commercial dimension of the object as commodity. In these two distinct ways, though, the bottle calls on us, it interpellates us, as *consumers*. We buy water; we drink it. We consume water. Within temporal limits, and perhaps simultaneously, albeit differently, the bottle offers itself as an object of our purchasing power and of our drinking needs, an object of consumption. It registers upon two different modes of consumption (bodily, commercial), which it also conflates and collapses.[10]

And yet we have also begun to consider other things, other "earlier" things and, in any case, other modes or layers, facets of appearance, that are no less determining of the bottle we see and seek. The clear plastic, for instance, had registered no less immediately than the water "itself." Within the relative indistinguishability of the two (clarity, transparency),

but away from the consumptions we considered, water and plastic merged in our field of vision, without losing their analytic and perceptual distinctiveness.[11] As an instrument, a container, the bottle certainly appeared, but it never seemed to be made of the water it contains. We knew, we had learned, that it is plastic we are looking at. Aside from its role in holding the water, and independent of its phenomenal or aesthetic value, however vanishing its transparency, the plastic makes and marks the bottle. It shapes and labels it, and the water too; it mediates it. One might even say that it dates it historically and chemically (plastic was not always there and, more generally, did not always exist. It is a recent invention, though not as recent as this particular use, the proliferation of plastic water bottles on the shelves of ubiquitous stores). The bottle is of our time; it is marked as such because we are surrounded as never before by plastic, here available to us in one among a sea of innumerable products (more on the sea, or seas, below). It is of our time because it is the result of the impressive and seemingly endless ingenuity of the petrochemical industry, which managed not so long ago to make plastic out of that other, older historical substance, the decomposed organic remains that slowly and painfully morphed into hydrocarbons now being released onto the surface and atmosphere of the earth. And to a store near you. The bottle is of our time, finally, because it already clogs the future (along with those new electric cars, the batteries of which hold "clean energy," because electricity comes from the air, apparently, and because lithium-iron-phosphate is good for the environment and its future, from mining to disposal). The bottle is made of plastic, and plastic clogs everything now, every body of water and every waterway, each and every living body and more. Including the body of this water. The bottle is made of plastic. It is an object of consumption but it is also a product, the product of chemical ingenuity (and endless financial resources, research and development) in the petroleum industry. The bottle, we could (or should) never forget, but cannot help knowing, is made of oil (itself made more stable for a time by a coating of artificial estrogen, better known as BPA, which many a plastic is now free of – hurray! – just as certain computers were temporarily sold as "arsenic-free," and thus equipped with a new chemistry lesson, a new environmental commitment, in the making of computer screens). The bottle is, equally undeniably, an environmental catastrophe that will linger for centuries, and even millennia, to come (Alaimo 111–41; also see Farelly et al.).

All this is also to say that the bottle is *made*. Is it man-made? Yes and no. The ergonomic quality, the general shape of the bottle, surely indicates a measure of aesthetic intervention and forethought. It was designed to look a certain way, to be held in a convenient, indeed, ergonomic, manner. Yet, for the hand that will hold it, it is unlikely to have been made by hand. Someone may have thought of it, designed it. But it was finally produced mechanically and required no, or very little, direct human handling. Still, humans had a hand in it, who participated in making the bottle a handy contraption, and operated, however remotely, the machinery. It is obvious that there were once workers, skilled and unskilled, that were involved in the making of this bottle, indeed, in the mass production of such bottles in the very many factories where countless units like this one are made. No bottle like this could ever have been produced prior to the industrial age, the post-industrial age, perhaps. It could only have come out of a factory, in any event, there where workers continue to labor, not all of them equally expandable, even if most of them have been replaced by automated machines. Prior to being an object of consumption, prior to its marketing, the bottle is a product of labor, chemical and industrial, and finally social and economic. These temporal priorities have already receded, of course, making the history of the bottle an ever more remote memory. Yet, the bottle still registers and embodies, it stores and manifests that history, the engineering and economic work, along with the further energy and labor that consist

in transporting the bottle to sites of consumption, and finally enable us access, making it possible for us to see the bottle for what it is: a techno-scientific and economic product. A "miracle" of sorts.

We do not really have to exert ourselves to look closer, or more attentively, in order to observe that, intrinsic to the consumptive and productive registers we have begun to attend to (health and nutrition, consumption, engineering and economic production), there is information, which the bottle itself provides by way of its label. Highly visible, the label that surrounds the bottle heightens, announces, and also foregrounds, its aesthetic dimension. We might already mention that such supplement is very much part of its ergonomic design, which appeals to convenience and portability, but also to a particular sensibility. And shapes these too. This bottle is, for instance, ribbed (not all water bottles are), and its middle circumference is narrow – the lightest of suggestion that we might be looking at an hourglass, no more perhaps, than a promise. There is something anthropomorphic, if not outright "feminine" (the lexicon of ad men) in this diminutive version that competes fashionably with the pear-shaped design made popular by other brands. The bottle is, in any case, intentionally molded in a very specific manner, one that is familiar, if not necessarily appealing, but easy enough to recognize, eminently recognizable, in fact, as part of a brand. Here is another level of the economic existence of the bottle as commodity: it has been marketed, formally and informally. It is itself a marketing ploy, appealing to past and future consumption, citing previous iterations and riding on an earlier, older reputation, sedimenting trust. The date on the label – 1845 – signals toward and reminds us of a history that is distinct from the one above. It is history, it is at least a story, one James Salzman tells well, when he recounts that "in 1845, Poland Spring sold its first bottled water in a three-gallon clay jug" (189).

Nothing like a superfluous supplement, the label introduces a distinct liveliness to our field of vision, a different color – literally a splash of color (dark green), no less striking for its singularity and isolation in the midst of transparency and otherwise reflected light and backgrounds – and images as well, surface appearances being, if not everything, certainly inextricable from our perception of the water. In this instance, the image glued onto the bottle is of a rushing river in the thick of a green forest. There are trees and bushes, all realistically pictured and crammed onto the small surface of glossy (plasticized or laminated) paper that surrounds the bottle. They evoke, and are there to evoke, an expansive and pristine setting, a sense of freshness, a natural, untouched environment. *Terra nullius*, perhaps. Unless it is *aqua nullius*, which should already alert us to the making and unmaking of indigenous realms (even liquid ones) by settler logics (Marshall; also on the sea as *res nullius*, see Schmitt 175ff.). Needless to say, this pristine environment does not appear in any way settled, much less sullied, by the bottling factory (much less, factories) that, here advertising itself, depends on the waters presently flowing (no underground extraction appears to be involved); so unaltered, in fact, that the label can further assure us that nothing fills the bottle but "100% Natural Spring Water." The exercise will require still that we read the small print in order to fathom these waters, but for now we can surely register ourselves as addressees, subjects and targets of another discourse, placid spectators of another background view, an aesthetic and marketing perspective, that has made repeated headways onto our consciousness and practices. The image is generic and recognizable at once, recognizable because generic, and carrying the guarantee, at least the assurance and no doubt the promise, that what we see is what we get.

And perhaps it is the case (ignore the plastic, and microplastic), even if another feat of engineering – and of law – is clearly at work, which mediates and makes it possible, under the heading and branding of "Poland Spring," the bottling of waters from no less than *ten or eleven different springs* in the state of Maine. It explicitly says so on the label. This is a bottle of *waters*, which comes from ten *or* eleven springs. That number is, admittedly, hard to read or fathom but it corresponds nonetheless to the label's printed list, which says "Lincoln and/or Ellis Spring, Rumford." Are these two springs (as opposed, presumably, to the other springs in the region) not differentiated? Is the bottling company uncertain of the sources, or extended aquifer, from which it draws? There is room for questioning, which the label incidentally and otherwise encourages as it includes an invitation to ask, to ask about the water (or waters, for it did, after all, differentiate) and about its quality. "For questions or a water quality report call [...]" followed by a phone number and a website.

The label, then, is an invitation. It functions as such as it welcomes readers and consumers to get in touch. It includes, for this purpose, a QR code that not only says "we care," but literally invites us to "scan for water journey." Even without the code, the label shares information, providing us with what we want to know. The label confirms that it brings with it what we want and need. Free of any explicit sign of manufacture, though itself the indisputable and manifest, sedimented result of an entire history of industrial production, and industrial extraction, the label calls on us as we ourselves are: in need of water (and of information). This turns out to be quite a feat of marketing, after all, as we remember again that water is available through other channels, other canals and pipes, equally proximate faucets. There is no need here to rehearse the contested status of tap water and the role of water corporations in its devaluation. The state of water infrastructure, the story of Flint, Michigan and of countless other sites of water emergencies and, more generally, the "global water crisis" (which Jamie Linton compellingly describes as that which "diverts attention from the political and social circumstances that produce such problems and frames their solution in predominantly technical and hydrological terms") – all these contributed more than any marketing strategy could to the proliferation of bottled waters across the planet (Linton 24; further citations below are from the same page). Yet, marketing proceeds apace on billboards, Internet pages, and any number of plastic bottles (with and without QR codes) near you. Like the bottle, like water itself, in Linton's account, the label we are reading "bears the traces of its social relations, conditions, and potential." And the label, no less than the bottle as a whole, tells us that "we are indeed facing a water crisis, and this crisis stems from the fact that we can no longer presume a simple identity for water as well as from the facts of water scarcity and water pollution."

How did it come to this? How did the bottle become a crisis? This is an old story, which the bottle also tells or shows us, and it relates water to law. It is admittedly difficult to read the ® that sits at the end of the word "BRAND" printed vertically on the side of the, well, brand, "Poland Spring." But the © is clearer that inscribes and ensures legal ownership to "NESTLÉ WATERS NORTH AMERICA, INC." – and do note, again, that these are "waters," and no singular "water," that Nestlé North America owns (its headquarters in Stamford, CT, as the label also indicates), thereby partly explaining why we were informed of the distinct sources of water from which the "pure spring water" is drawn or extracted, and finally bottled. The law determines and protects property. Accordingly, and more modestly too, it also establishes the value of the refund one is entitled to receive for the empty bottle in Connecticut, New York, and Maine (5¢). Finally, the New York State Department of Health certificate number is featured on the label (according to the Department's website, 159 facilities are currently certified, among which 17 bear the name Nestlé). There is also a Pennsylvania permit number. Law and health, federal and local, have manifestly been moved to act in concert toward the production and marketing of the bottle in front of us, revealing it for what it is, a legal artifact that sits at the intersection of public health and corporate business interests as well, of course, as customer needs and satisfaction. The label is further enriched with advice (not legal advice, but wise counsel nonetheless) on recycling,

past and present ("made better," and "empty and replace cap"). It includes a warning regarding the danger, specifically the "choking hazard" that the cap – a "small part" – poses "particularly for children." The surrounding green color participates in soothing and comforting us, reminding us that this is a benevolent, albeit potentially dangerous, product, but one generally oriented toward our health and our well-being. Protective provisions with regard to potential side effects or collateral damage (to children, most explicitly, but not to land, air, or indeed, water) are not confined to particularly small print, no more than the legal paraphernalia. They too are mostly lateral, marginal. Nevertheless, they remind us that, whereas Carl Schmitt claimed that *nomos* was always elemental, if primarily of the earth, there is sufficient reason to consider that law (if one may translate with any confidence) has been about water all along, about access to water.[12] Both Arabic and Hebrew, in any case, have preserved some associations between what continues to be commonly referred to as "law" (Islamic, *sharī'a* or Jewish, *halacha*) and water. The Rabbis certainly made explicit their understanding of *Torah* and water. One might say: learning and water. But the association goes, in any event, deeper (see Dellapenna and Gupta). For it is undoubtedly the case that the springs that are listed on the label are now understood as "natural" (they are found in "nature," which used to be the opposite of law, in Greek at least). They are also, for the most part, distinct. Similar to ancient practice (custom or tradition), but having undergone the intensifications of "colonial hydrology" and of capital, law determines the identity of a spring or a well, which includes the right and ability to draw from it, the extension or limitation of its waters to others, the very localization of the waters and their depths or indeed extensions (see Caponera and Nanni; Turner and Neale; the phrase "colonial hydrology" is D'Souza's). In the case of the bottle in front of us, the law determines the source and sources, their location and the property rights, rights of extraction and commercialization. Along with health authorities, the law today (but yesterday too) regulates the water and its quality, indeed, its contents, along with the information given and not given about it. It authorizes the sale of the water in a determined manner (plastic, for instance), and according to distinct jurisdictions, that have themselves legal and political status. The law mediates with authority between water and the polity. At this point in our reading and learning, the law has all but moved into the unavoidable foreground, making the water in front of us a matter of law first and foremost, blessing and transforming the waters into a mere instance of what we might call legal waters, or waters of the law. We will need seas of learning.

learning divisions

The exercise rarely comes to an exhaustive end, although I have tried it in a number of classes with different students, undergraduates and graduates, and in distinct departments (area studies, Religious Studies, Comparative Literature, though students might be engineering majors, or pre-med, or in creative writing). As necessary as it continues to be for me, I am yet to be persuaded the exercise "fits" anywhere. It is an exercise in reading, to be sure (something scholars are still supposed to gain a modicum of command over), an exercise in the collective extension of attention to what is already known, to what can already be known, and is, in any case, what appears within reach of learning. The exercise also raises questions about the divisions of knowledge, such as they make available a given object to what is never a lone reader. For what does it mean to learn some thing? A thing like water, or at least a bottle of water? The recurring interrogations to which disciplines, learning practices or expertise, have been subjected have not fundamentally transformed the classroom as either democratic or interdisciplinary, and certainly not in terms of location within the university and its schools and departments, even if you factor in the digital and the virtual. Nor have these interrogations changed the practical needs (or ingrained habits) to seize upon a

distinct, a framed and fragmented segment of the world at large. Surely, no one can know everything. Not even a large group of people and experts are likely to agree on what they know they know (we all know it is plastic; we do not all know it has been an ongoing catastrophe). So what does it mean to know *some* thing? Different objects, of variable materiality, expanse, and integrity, require different kinds of methods and instruments, different kinds of attentiveness. If you study biology, i.e., living beings, your concern with geology (roughly, the surface of the earth) or engineering (the instruments of observation), for instance, will likely appear secondary and derivative. If you study religion, you might engage with art or with economics in a laudable gesture of interdisciplinarity, but the two (or three) will not be confused, much less substitute for each other. No doubt some objects are granted sufficient solidity to be studied by different sciences, with distinct approaches. Thus, political science may study electoral dynamics all over the globe, whereas the so-called Middle East can serve as the occasional locus of different questions (among which water, of course, and oil too, or again elections, which rarely mix with oil though they obviously should), each receiving a different answer depending on the questioners. Aside from the political scientist, the scholar of law will attend there or elsewhere to different archives and institutions than the historian or, obviously, the engineer. The anthropologist may or may not be interested in religion (say, Islam), or in literature, though she will likely insist that law and gender, for instance, intersect in a fundamental manner, a sufficiently holistic perspective that exceeds matters of interdisciplinarity, and may or may not have to do with understanding culture. There is competition, of course, but the general agreement will be that no discipline, however constructivist, entirely makes up its object (one likely to exceed its "constructedness"), which must have some recognizability in the world. And within the walls of the university. Thus, theology is what one officially studies in this particular corner of the campus. Not God, say. For my part, and with all due respect to Bruno Latour, I have long been struck by, and tried to convey to students, the role language plays (and continues to play) in the division of knowledge. Language and foundational debates. Take the long-standing antagonism between "the social" and "the political." Or the efforts necessary to relate "the economic" to "the religious." Consider that social comes from *socius*, a Latin term, whereas *politeia* is a Greek word that continues to constrict our "political" imagination. Accordingly, *oikonomia* comes from Greek and *religio* from Latin. There is no reason to reduce these terms to their etymological root, but neither is it possible to ignore that they correspond to profound divisions of knowledge and practice that, carried over, might not be fully translatable – and particularly not in the classroom and its constraints, and first of all its temporal constraints (fourteen weeks, at my institution, totaling about thirty hours, which we call, against all conceivable reason, a "semester").

In the classroom and without, it is remarkable to consider that few disciplines have wielded their authority and made a truly universal, one might even say, imperial attempt to claim *everything* as their dominion. More than physics (which could lay claim to every known particle – and its relations – in the universe), it is, judging by the students, economics (today perhaps finance, that most imaginatively creative of disciplines, as one student insisted on telling me) that has made the most forceful claim as the "final instance." Nothing today truly escapes its jurisdiction. Nor can anything dispense with its enabling power (no theoretical physics without a budget). Think "human capital." At the same time, history (a Greek term, again) might be a close competitor. Or should I say, History. The German distinction between *Geschichte* and *Historie* notwithstanding, modern languages have tended to conflate the history that happens and the history told (*Geschichte*, *Historie*, as the Germans have it). Which leaves very little out of the historian's purview. What, after all, is not historical? What object – of whatever kind – could really be said to have no history? What *essentialism*

could exempt itself from change and indeed from history? Until recently – let us date this development to the late twentieth century – not even the most daring anthropologist would have claimed every "race" (or "culture") as a proper destination for fieldwork. No Museum of Natural History ever planned a diorama of an American suburban family (and its water bottles). There are limits to tolerance. And to the universality of mankind.

So there are different claims made by different sciences, with different effects on teaching and learning requirements. Like the proverbial blind men and the elephant, students come to the classroom with different apparatuses, lenses or blinders. Biology does not seek to explain culture (though it is, of course, getting more comfortable with returning to this august heritage). And engineers may need chemistry, but they make no claim to command every substance. I have wondered about the strangely minimal claim to universality made by the study of religion. What other discipline, what other field, could pretend to the entirety of the universe (created or not)? Philosophy and physics, the only alternative contenders, begin to border on the religious once they engage in, say, cosmology. Or the paranormal. Disciplines differ, in any case, with regard to the universality of the claims they make, indeed, with regard to the claim to universality they make, which relates in complicated ways to the nature (or culture) of the object they engage. And then there is the power they exercise, which also depends on institutional arrangements and financial support. Some objects might be contested by different sciences or knowledge practices. Thus, it is obvious to some that "private property," for instance, corresponds to a *legal* conception and understanding that is not universally found. Others might identify it as a *psychological* invariant that only finds its incidental and derivative expression or confirmation in law. To "reduce" religion or race to economic forms of domination may appear as good science or it may be to ignore that religion is, as they say, *sui generis*, allegedly an intrinsic fact of our human, all-too human disposition.

Where does this leave water? And the classroom? What are the contextual limits to which these confine us? What we learned, what we have strived to learn, is not just, as others have pointed out, that water is not reducible to, or even identical with, H_2O, not just that water is a (necessarily impure) medium, that it is, moreover, itself mediated, as Ivan Illich reminded us (with regard to water, we are all engaged in the "provisionization" of Japanese primatologists; the web of relations is too thick, there is no more "wild" water) (Haraway 244–52). There is no understanding, no learning or knowing of water that could be restricted, much less exhausted, by a science of water, nor by a class, not even an advanced seminar (in what discipline?) no matter how sophisticated or specialized, no matter how expansive and interdisciplinary, such hydrology might be. The finitude of science, of any science, means that science (any and all sciences) is akin to the attempt to hold water within cupped hands (it might be enough for a few sips, hardly more). Emanuele Coccia, whose critique of the division of knowledge and organization of sciences might resonate in these last paragraphs, calls for a new "global and universal science," which he proposes to call "astrology" (Coccia 94). Coccia goes on to explain that "biology, geology, and theology are no more than branches of astrology" (94). But the list (which could surely be supplemented) cannot be all-inclusive. There are modes of knowing, and more importantly, modes of being that elude us, and that cannot hold their own promise. They might teach us that to live with water (to die with or without it), to be learning waters cannot stop *at* water; nor will it be helped by Coccia's astrology (which is not to say that such is not to be pursued, of course), nor, for that matter, by Bachelard "poetic chemistry" (Bachelard 46). I do not mean by this, I don't think, that water is a "total being, *un être total*," as Bachelard has it (recalling Marcel Mauss' "total social fact"), who refers with this phrase to "the unity of the element" that water is, along with its "complete poetic reality" (15–16).[13] Bachelard does remind us not to "underestimate the lessons of original matters" (146). For there are more things in heaven and earth, more things *than* heaven and earth, and more waters too, than in any science or philosophy. This, at least, is what we have learned, the students and I, what we have learned from, with – and obviously around, and even against – water.

disclosure statement

No potential conflict of interest was reported by the author.

notes

1

> Let us take seriously this hypothesis, at least for an instant, for the sake of *radicalizing* it: the aim here is to transform what presents itself as a simple empirical finding on the significant and yet contingent connection between *life* and *fluid medium* into a necessary *cosmological* relation. Let us suppose, then, that life has sprung from a fluid physical environment (the content, be it molecules of water or ammonia, doesn't matter) not simply by chance, but because life becomes a possible phenomenon exclusively through fluid environments. (Coccia 30)

On the Middle Passage and the "Waterscapes of the African Diaspora," see Dawson.

2 In his brilliant *H_2O and the Waters of Forgiveness*, Ivan Illich offers the word "stuff" to think about water, or indeed, waters. For more on "waters," see Hamlin.

3 Fishman goes on to explain that

> no water is being created or destroyed on Earth. So every drop of water that's here has seen the inside of a cloud, and the inside of a volcano, the inside of a maple leaf, and the inside of a dinosaur kidney, probably many times.

Soon, the inside of a water bottle too.

4 Alice Outwater titled her fantastic book, *Water: A Natural History*, but beginning as she does with

the "dismantling" of water systems that the fur trade brought about with the extermination of the beaver, the buffalo, and the prairie dog, she is also offering a layered, unnatural history of water.

5 Gotman discusses Michael Craig-Martin's "An Oak Tree," an installation in which "a glass of water sits on a shelf above head level [...] and that glass, now, is an oak tree." In this "act of transformation" – a learning event – the artist "claims the water is not special water" (Gotman 49).

6 I took the pictures, though images of this brand are readily available.

7 Bachelard will go on to wax eloquently about what he calls "the maternity of waters" (118).

8 I found in this book the necessary encouragement to engage in the water exercise since "one could teach what one didn't know" (Rancière 18).

9 Jamie Linton has argued that H_2O is "a modern abstraction" (see also Chakrabarty 75–76, 83–85), which it surely is, but consider that ultra-pure water (UPW), a water that is "10 million times cleaner than regular tap water" (Linton 46) and would come closer to being made exclusively of molecules of oxygen and hydrogen, such water "is found nowhere on Earth because water out in the world is constantly flowing past, over, and through things, from it is absorbing particles" (Fishman 46–47). Incidentally, UPW, a critical solvent in the making of computer microchips is also a deadly poison that, if swallowed, would quickly "leach minerals right out of your body tissues" (48). Most likely, I am told, your cells would simply explode.

10 MacLeod proposes a parallel distinction between two oceans, one "encompasses the movements of capital" and the second, which

emerges in literary figures, religious traditions, mythologies, and everyday language. It is an infinite water in which everything is retained, and where all times mingle together. This is the body of water we refer to whenever we talk about the past as a watery depth. Those who have passed on rise up from its fathomless reaches to speak with us. It is the final outlet of those rivers that so many cultures entrust with the task of receiving and carrying away the dead. (Chen et al. 41)

MacLeod also writes that, for certain objects, among which she counts the water bottle, "the act of assigning exchange value [...] either effaces or instrumentalizes its history [...] the object appears 'new,' like the bottle of water whose origins become unreadable in its seemingly spontaneous genesis by the convenience store refrigerator" (43).

11 "We insist on thinking with *water* – and not, for instance, with air, with plastics, with rare earths, or with any of the other articulable categories of matter that we experience," write the editors of *Thinking with Water* (Chen et al. 5). I do not disagree, but it seems plastic has made the task impossible by now.

12 Schmitt writes, for instance, of "the elemental freedom of the sea" (175).

13 The English translation has "complete being" for "être total." One might contrast Bachelard's phrase with Marcel Mauss' "total social fact." By way of example, nonetheless, Bachelard anticipates on what seems eluded by Coccia's astrology (although science does actively, and surely not entirely unwittingly, pursue it), namely, "the loss of our being in total dissolution [...] Water dissolves more completely [*complètement*]. It helps us to die completely [*totalement*] [...] *Water is the matter of despair*" (91–92).

bibliography

Alaimo, Stacy. *Exposed: Environmental Politics and Pleasures in Posthuman Times*. U of Minnesota P, 2016.

Bachelard, Gaston. *Water and Dreams: An Essay on the Imagination of Matter*. Translated by Edith R. Farrell, Pegasus Foundation, 1983.

Caponera, Dante, and Marcella Nanni. *Principles of Water Law and Administration: National and International*. Routledge, 2019.

Chakrabarty, Dipesh. *Provincializing Europe: Postcolonial Thought and Historical Difference*. Princeton UP, 2000.

Chen, Cecilia, et al., editors. *Thinking with Water*. McGill-Queen's UP, 2013.

Christian, Dorothy, and Rita Wong, editors. *Downstream: Reimagining Water*. Wilfrid Laurier UP, 2017.

Coccia, Emanuele. *The Life of Plants: A Metaphysics of Mixture.* Translated by Dylan J. Montanari, Polity, 2019.

Dawson, Kevin. *Undercurrents of Power: Aquatic Culture in the African Diaspora.* U of Pennsylvania P, 2018.

Dellapenna, Joseph W., and Joyeeta Gupta, editors. *The Evolution of the Law and Politics of Water.* Springer, 2010.

Derrida, Jacques. "Typewriter Ribbon: Limited Ink (2) ('Within Such Limits')." Translated by Peggy Kamuf. *Material Events: Paul de Man and the Afterlife of Theory*, edited by Tom Cohen et al., U of Minnesota P, 2001, pp. 277–360.

D'Souza, Rohan. "Water in British India: The Making of a 'Colonial Hydrology.'" *History Compass*, vol. 4, no. 4, 2006, pp. 621–28.

Farelly, Trisia, et al., editors. *Plastic Legacies: Pollution, Persistence, and Politics.* AU Press, Athabasca University, 2021.

Fishman, Charles. *The Big Thirst: The Secret Life and Turbulent Future of Water.* Free Press, 2011.

Gotman, Kélina. *Essays on Theatre and Change: Towards a Poetics Of.* Routledge, 2018.

Hamlin, Christopher. "'Waters' or 'Water'? Master Narratives in Water History and Their Implications for Contemporary Water Policy." *Water Policy*, vol. 2, 2000, pp. 313–25.

Haraway, Donna. *Primate Visions: Gender, Race, and Nature in the World of Modern Science.* Routledge, 1989.

Illich, Ivan. *H_2O and the Waters of Forgiveness.* Boyars, 1986.

Irigaray, Luce. *Marine Lover: Of Friedrich Nietzsche.* Translated by Gillian C. Gill, Columbia UP, 1991.

Linton, Jamie. *What is Water? The History of a Modern Abstraction.* UBC Press, 2010.

Marshall, Virginia. *Overturning Aqua Nullius: Securing Aboriginal Water Rights.* Aboriginal Studies Press, 2017.

Neimanis, Astrida. *Bodies of Water: Posthuman Feminist Phenomenology.* Bloomsbury Academic, 2017.

Outwater, Alice. *Water: A Natural History.* Basic Books, 1996.

Rancière, Jacques. *The Ignorant Schoolmaster: Five Lessons in Intellectual Emancipation.* Translated by Kristin Ross, Stanford UP, 1991.

Salzman, James. *Drinking Water: A History.* Overlook Duckworth, 2012.

Schmitt, Carl. *The Nomos of the Earth in the International Law of the* Jus Publicum Europaeum. Translated by G.L. Ulmen, Telos Press, 2003.

Turner, Stephen, and Timothy Neale. "First Law and the Force of Water: Law, Water, Entitlement." *Settler Colonial Studies*, 2015, pp. 1–11.

Gil Anidjar

These are complicated waters; much is at stake.

– Derrida and Beardsworth 11

This paper addresses various, sometimes unexpected, rhetorical uses of the figure of water management from the perspective of what Jacques Derrida, affirmatively, saw as the necessity of contamination which is constitutive of "the very possibility of affirmation in the first place" (Derrida and Beardsworth 56). The images of contaminated and contagious waters tackled in this text come from different genres of writing and different times and constitute but a few instances of the fear of contamination. This fear, in turn, puts in motion the figure of water management as a complex rhetorical chart of flows of cultural transmission and control of what Caroline Petronis describes as "contagion's journey out of medicine and into culture" (38). The waters of contagion are "complicated waters," and what I propose in this text is to look at a few examples of how water is, sometimes marginally, used in thinking about contamination and contagion in culture, and of the ways in which thinking in terms of threat, which the two terms educe, has been critiqued through an invitation to a politics of affirmation in posthumanist theorizations of Donna Haraway and Rosi Braidotti, and in the posthumanist poetic perspective of Astrida Neimanis.

Though water, particularly water springs, can be thought about in terms of symbolism of purity and clarity, its association with contaminative threats, which Christopher Hamlin sees as having risen in the first decades of the nineteenth century, are also connected with the transformation of "waters" to "water"

Figurations of Water: On Pathogens, Purity, and Contamination

Agnieszka Pantuchowicz

(321). Hamlin does not answer the question of "why waters ceased to be many and became one (albeit, one with contaminants); and equally why attention shifted from variability to uniformity," and he only underlines a complex interplay of numerous factors in this rise of contaminated water. This rise also includes the discovery of H_2O, "the discovery of water's potential as a disease-transmitting medium [...] the rise of consumer concern about water supply and quality; the importance of water for large industry, and for municipal and domestic cleansing" (321). The concern about water supply and quality also posits the question of cleansing, an activity which – when projected upon the sphere of culture –

makes water management into one of the foundational metaphors we live by and think by. Ideas, like pathogens, can also be contagious though, perhaps paradoxically, they also may fall prey to contagion (which is the case of Plato's fear of mimetic contagion), to distortion, deformation, or misrepresentation. What the idea of contamination inevitably involves is a materialization of purity in which materiality can be seen as pure (or made pure), be it the materiality of the body or the materiality of the world. Purity is a relative term which always carries within itself a trace of an ethical judgement. What seems to be at stake in the case of the idea of uncontaminated water, of pure water, is a complex metaphorization of the material which translates the materiality of water into a nearly spiritual state, and which in fact dematerializes water as a space of potential metaphorical similitude with immateriality. Perhaps the singularization of "premodern waters" about which Hamlin writes in his essay also metaphorically illustrates the modern search for oneness at the cost of the loss of the sense of waters' "infinite variation" (315), of their material diversity. Metaphorically, water management seems to be a way of de-diversifying waters as a carrier of differences seen as contaminators of water's singular ontological purity.

The contemporary popular image of contaminated water is that of sewage gushing into rivers and seas all over the planet incessantly increasing the amount of human pathogens in water. The measure of this threat can be noticed in the quantity of possible illnesses and sicknesses which may possibly attack us:

> The human health effects caused by waterborne transmission vary in severity from mild gastroenteritis to severe and sometimes fatal diarrhoea, dysentery, hepatitis and typhoid fever. Contaminated water can be the source of large outbreaks of disease, including cholera, dysentery and cryptosporidiosis. (World Health Organization 249)

The list of the diseases can be surely extended, and the reader can easily find numerous other, though usually less familiar, names of them by means of any Internet browser. The number of airborne or earthborne diseases is equally electrifying, and what somehow groups air, earth, and water together seems to be the notion of contamination ascribed to their otherwise natural cleanliness.

Though water, perhaps unless distilled, is never clear of other organic and inorganic ingredients, it seems to be the association of its beginnings in the uncontaminated clarity of spring water linked with the spiritual uses of holy springs which translates it into a figure of purity endowed with healing properties. Overtly dissociated from holiness, by the early modern period "mineral waters were clearly part of the domain of capitalism" (Hamlin 320). An uncountable number of mineral water advertisements use various figures to carry its purity to the market. In the 1890s advertisement of "Puralis" mineral water offered by London Pure Water Co., for instance, the purity is associated with an image of a band of angels alongside that of newly born babies. More recently Nestle offers Pure Life water, in Peru one can buy Aqua Vida, while Evian offers Alpine freshness and, spelled backwards, the naivety of the innocence of childhood. Such images of pure purity, both spiritual and bodily, are also a projection of an image of being and remaining uncontaminated, one which also carries a promise of immunity to contamination offered as a bottled commodity void of cryptosporidiosis.

Various springs of truth in philosophy are also watery metaphors which derive from the ideal of uncontaminated existence, with contamination becoming the figure of distortion of an original idea, vision, or intention. The rhetoric of drinking truth, either from *the spring of truth* or *at its very source* also brings in the idea of an uncontaminated river or stream, with pathogens lurking in its lower course. In Plato's philosophical system the access to the pure springs of truth seems to be dependent on exclusive, almost superhuman beings who have overcome the misleading dross of appearances. Unlike in Nietzsche, where the superhuman seems to belong to a different species endowed with a body, in

Plato the superhuman is an ideally bodyless philosopher for whom the metaphor of drinking the purity of truth is as contaminatory as the belief in there being a truth in metaphor. Plato's skepticism concerning mimetic representation and his expulsion of poets from the ideal state as potential carriers of mimetic contagion was also dictated by the fear of contamination of the purity of truth which he found not only in language, but also in all the bodily impediments of our quest for truth: "if we are to have any pure knowledge at all, we must be freed from the body; soul by herself must behold things as they are" (*Phaedo* 11–12). The body, in Plato, is always already contaminated, and what posits a philosopher "beyond all other men" is an autoimmunity of sorts which allows him to release "his soul from communion with the body, so far as he can" (9). Plato's purity can thus be seen as only partly achievable in constant struggle with the contamination by the body, which itself metonymically stands for sickness. The illness of the body is strengthened by its lack of immunity against diseases coming from the outside: "whenever diseases attack it, they hinder us in our pursuit of real being" (11). The material world, including human bodies, is pathogenic in Plato, and the philosophical regulation of life can be seen as an impoundmentary damming of the mind from contamination by the watery material environment which is figured as a muddy water of sorts:

> For everywhere on the earth there are many hollows of every kind of shape and size, into which the water and the mist and the air collect; but the earth itself lies pure in the purity of the heaven, wherein are the stars, and which men who speak of these things commonly call ether. The water and the mist and the air, which collect into the hollows of the earth, are the sediment of it. Now we dwell in these hollows though we think that we are dwelling on the surface of the earth. (64)

The materiality of water is in Plato a hindrance on the way to the purity of the immaterial ether, the pure fifth element which, ideally, directly communicates with the earth which can also be pure, given that there is nothing watery to disturb the communication. Water, like the body, is a material cataractal sediment which clouds the vision of the ethereal, and does so along with mist and air. There seems to be no spring water in Plato, and, as a sediment of ether, water can also be seen as a pathogenic kind of waste. Unlike the materiality of the earth itself, the materiality of water in the company of mist and air is unhealthy; it constitutes a watery and wet environment of our living which is always already polluted, a kind of sewage which constantly attacks the immunity system of philosophers' pursuit of real being. The earth seems to figure in Plato's text as an absolute kind of materiality against which the materiality of water or mist is perceived as its fake and weak species, as dregs or remains which are responsible for the illusory character of what we perceive as our earthly dwelling. From within this fake and contaminated materiality, from the hollows of the earth which seem to be a different rhetorical rendering of the cave, the pure and uncontaminated truth can be revealed only if we free ourselves from it in the same manner we have to free ourselves from our contaminated bodies. The water, the mist, the air, and the body are the soft materials which stand between the absolute hardness of the earth and the absolute softness of the ethereal. Plato's philosopher thus has to live in the state of chronic vulnerability, immunizing himself with the certainty of the hard, earthly foundation of the purity of the ether. Water, in Plato, is never epistemologically pure, and it demands a constant kind of purification through the hard resistance of those "beyond other men," of the supermanly men of knowledge.

overflowing

Though the fatherhood of the philosophical idea of superman, or overman, is usually ascribed to Friedrich Nietzsche, Plato's philosophers ruling as kings from *The Republic* may well be seen as prototype versions of this figure (see Plato, *The Republic* 153). Nietzsche's *Übermensch*, however, does not occupy the position of power. Rather, it figures as a soft and watery overflow of the borders of the human which protects us from pitying, like Plato, our own vulnerability. Before his descent from the mountains Zarathustra blesses "the cup that wants to flow over, such that water flows golden from it" and carries the reflection of bliss (Nietzsche, *Thus Spoke Zarathustra* 3), the watery overflow being the sign of his self-overcoming. The crucial aspect of Nietzsche's overcoming of the human is the renunciation of egotism and care for the other which, however, do not involve pity or compassion. As Eva Cybulska notes,

> in compassion one regards another's suffering as one's own (*Mitleid*, like "compassion," derives from "suffer with"), by wanting to relieve the suffering of the other one wants to relieve one's own. Hence, in Nietzsche's view, even compassion is ultimately egoistic. (6–7)

Nietzsche celebrates the body as a singular-plural kind of being whose vulnerability should also be celebrated rather than escaped, and the truly sovereign individual, writes Sharli Paphitis,

> does not seek to escape the misery and pain that comes along with being vulnerable to all the chance and necessity that the world holds in store for us, but seeks to actively affirm it, live through and with it. (134)

It is perhaps for this reason that Zarathustra is a water bringer and a water drinker, something unacceptable for the otherworldly soothsayer who desires and demands wine as a means of bringing back health. Fed up with being fed with watery speeches, the soothsayer says:

> And even though I hear water splashing here, like the speeches of wisdom, namely abundantly and tirelessly, I want – wine! Not everyone is a born water drinker, like Zarathustra. Nor is water fit for the weary and the wilted: we deserve wine – only it provides sudden convalescence and instant health! (Nietzsche, *Thus Spoke Zarathustra* 230)

Water drinking is not a way of imbibing pure truth for Zarathustra, but rather a way of honest living with the body. Also his teaching – seen, or heard, as water splashing – does not posit him as a bringer of truth, but as a bringer of affirmation, of a "yes, yes" which Jacques Derrida associates with Nietzsche's commitment to the idea of eternal return:

> Thus, you cannot think the name or names of Friedrich Nietzsche, you cannot *hear* them before the reaffirmation of the hymen, before the alliance or wedding ring of the eternal return. You will not understand anything of his life, nor of his life and works, until you hear the thought of the "yes, yes" given to this shadowless gift at the ripening high noon, beneath that division whose borders are inundated by sunlight: the overflowing cup of the sun. (Derrida, *Otobiographies* 13)

The metaphor of the overflowing cup of the sun translates light into liquid, perhaps into the flow of water whose affirmation is the affirmation of the inevitability of inundation of borders and limits, also of the limits of beginnings and ends of life which blur and merge in the incessant processes of begetting the will of life rather than constitute a thinkable kind life. For Zarathustra, thinkability of life is posited by the unwise as an object before which they kneel, the object of worship resulting in uncreative passivity and observance. Human values, or valuations, have been placed in a skiff, which "the people" observe from the perspective of their being a river whose task is to securely carry them along. The values are safely "seated in the skiff, solemn and cloaked," endowed with "pomp and proud names" by the dominating will of the wisest (Nietzsche, *Thus Spoke Zarathustra* 88). The skiff, perhaps also Noah's Ark, carries life, the Life whose task is immortality, the eternal life of religions. From this perspective the river appears as a threat against which "the wise" struggle so as to carry on their domination. Zarathustra's response to this is a paradoxical kind of obeying oneself as a way of overcoming domination and command: "the one who cannot obey himself is commanded. Such is the nature of the living" (89). This kind of obeyance consists of following one's will of life which figures in *Thus Spoke Zarathustra* as the flow of the river which, incessantly begetting its own beginning, returns to the beginnings of life:

> Now the river carries your skiff along: it has to carry it. It matters little whether the breaking wave foams and angrily opposes the keel! The river is not your danger and the end of your good and evil, you wisest ones; but this will itself, the will to power – the unexhausted begetting will of life. (88)

The will of life is reflected in the flow of the river whose water, unlike in Plato, does not stand as a sediment of ether, as a waste of sorts which contaminates the purity of philosophical visions. Neither is the will of life a promise of immortality, but that of a constant survival, of the Derridean way of living-on without having to live, without an imperative to live which translates life into a command (see Derrida, "Living On" 79). Living on is, for Derrida, a way of autobiographing which, like any kind of writing, does not have a stable kind of beginning, one established once and for all. If we want to approach [*aborder*] a text, also to approach the text of "Living On," "it must have a *board*, an edge" (81). This edge, however, may always turn out to be a mobile one. Derrida formulates this possibility in an interrogative spirit:

> What if you started reading it after the first sentence (another upper edge), which functions as its first reading head, but which in turn folds its outer edges back over onto inner edges whose mobility – multilayered, quotational, displaced from meaning to meaning – prohibits you from making a shoreline? (81)

What Derrida states in a declarative spirit in the next sentence is a metaphorical allusion to water, to flood, to the impossibility of there being a life of a text without the possibility of being submerged: "There is a regular submerging of the shore" (81).

This rhetorical movement from the materiality of writing to the materiality of water seems to be a gesture which accompanied Derrida's critiques of metaphysics where the present has always been read as uncertain, as delayed, as watery and indeterminate. Figurations of waters seem to be frequent guests in his writings, and as Rebekah Sinclair notes in her article on aqua-biographies,

> [w]ater, canals, channels, troughs, springs, floods, geysers, streams, dams, rains, weather, pools, tides, wells, oceans, seas, shores, tears, and rivers meander through Derrida's texts, precipitating an affirmation of difference, fluidity, absence, and movement. (354)

If Plato's water lives a contaminatory, and thus also a parasitic, kind of life, Derrida, far from associating it with purity, sees in its submerging of the shore the work of deconstructing the seemingly simple and obvious separation of the inside from the outside, of the stability of land from the waving of the sea. The sea proves the materiality of his philosophy, and deconstruction is thus brought down from the institutional academic confinement to the shores of seas and banks of rivers where it, quite simply, happens. It is thus not only a problematization of foundations, but also an attempt at bringing the fluidity of borders and edges to perception and experience, also of the experience of the allegedly unproblematic experience of reading a book.

To flow rather than to be is not a secure kind of ontological position. Rather, it can be viewed as a confession of fragility, a confession of vulnerability which Nietzsche described in the introduction to *Human, All Too Human* as taking sides against himself, against the idols and ideals which he managed to un-cherish:

> Lonely now and miserably self-distrustful, I took sides, not without resentment, against myself and for everything that hurt me and was hard to me. Thus I once more found the way to that courageous pessimism that is the antithesis of all romantic fraud, and as it seems to me today, the way to "myself," to my task. (9)

If one is bound to be incessantly flooded, if the water, also the water within our physical bodies, this continual deluge destabilizes the manly hardness of the universal permanence of identity on all possible levels of thinking the human. This may seem to be a pessimistic position, but via the courage of facing our frail constitution and vulnerability, via Nietzsche's courageous pessimism, we may see the ways this vulnerability can be abused by those who kneel before the stability and greatness of human nature, its superior position in the Anthropocenic uses and abuses of its alleged strength. Water, along with all its pathogens, does contaminate the epistemological and the ontological security of human position with aquatic fluidity, but this does not exclude an affirmatory attitude to it, something that Roberto Esposito sees as "affirmative biopolitics that has yet to come" (10). The projection of pathogenic contamination upon the epistemological and political sphere of identity translates political states into semi-biological bodies for which securitization of purity and health is the main task.

immuning

The mechanisms responsible for the rise of Aryan racism in the 1930s resulted exactly from the immunitary politics of purity. The eugenic idea of improving the race

> is always accompanied by a negative eugenics, one designed to impede the diffusion of dysgenic exemplars. And yet, where would the space for increasing the best exemplars be found if not in the space produced by the elimination of the worst? (Esposito 128)

The perspective of the elimination of contamination, however impossible, creates an imaginary space empty of any pathogenic elements and thus not needing any negative eugenics, a utopian kind of stabilized purity for which no improvement is needed. This inevitably futuristic perspective complicates the space of the functioning of power and inscribes expansion of purity as a crucial aspect of securitization. Esposito finds the relationship between

preservation and development in Nietzsche's problematic:

> Development presupposes duration, but duration can delay or impede development. Preservation implies expansion, but expansion compromises and places preservation at risk. Here already the indissolubly tragic character of the Nietzschean perspective comes into view, not only because the effects are not directly referred back to their apparent cause, but because the wrinkle of a real autonomy opens between the one and the others: the survival of a force opposes the project of strengthening it. Limiting itself to survival, it weakens itself, flows back, and, to use the key word in Nietzschean semantics, *degenerates*, which is to say moves in the direction opposite its own generation. (Esposito 94)

Nietzsche's will of life, however, seems to be degenerating only when purified of the contamination with death, and its duration does not ensue in the linear time of progression. Degeneration is linked in Nietzsche with idiosyncrasy, with singularity and uniqueness of an identity which disaffirms everything that is not "me." As an alternative to "idiosyncrasy of degenerates" whose main moral ground is condemning, he proposes affirmative immoralists who

> have opened our hearts wide to every form of understanding, comprehending, approving. We do not easily negate, we seek our honor in being those who affirm. Our eyes have been opened more and more to that economy that needs and knows how to use all that the holy craziness of the priest, the sick reason in the priest, rejects – that economy in the law of life that draws its advantage even from the repulsive species of the sanctimonious, the priest, the virtuous. – What advantage? – But we ourselves, we immoralists, are the answer here. (Nietzsche, *Twilight* 29)

What is thus also suspended is the law of self-preservation which Esposito finds to be "coextensive with the entire history of civilization" (54). Modernity did not invent the question of self-preservation but, as Esposito notes, it is self-preservation that "invents modernity as a historical and categorical apparatus able to cope with it" (55). This apparatus, equipped with medical knowledge and rhetoric, constitutes an organized body which is hostile to all thinkable kinds of contamination:

> Born from the struggle of cells against infectious bacteria, life is now defended by the state against every possible contamination. Racial hygiene is the immunitary therapy that aims at preventing or extirpating the pathological agents that jeopardize the biological quality of future generations. (128)

Plato's impure water which, as we have seen, parallels the impurity of the body, is to be overcome by philosophers rather than by the community of the republic. An immunitary therapy is hidden in the practice of philosophizing of those who rule the state and in the works of guardians who manage the otherwise contaminated state without decontaminating it. According to Esposito, Plato is "sensitive to the demand for keeping pure the *genos* of the guardians and more generally of the governors of the polis," and does not move "in an immunitary direction, one that is oriented to the preservation of the individual" (Esposito 54). Modernity's biocratic dream of medicalizing politics is not fully present in the premodern culture, it "stops short of politicizing medicine" (54).

However, another group of people who should be "tended" in Plato are slaves, whose threat to the social order makes it necessary to keep them in constant check and, like pathological agents, in separation from the free. Ideally, they should be absolutely individuated, not speaking the same language: "in this way they will more easily be held in subjection: secondly, we should tend them carefully, not only out of regard to them, but yet more out of respect to ourselves" (Plato, *Laws*, n. pag.). Holding in subjection for the sake of the respectful health of the state is a way of immunization of the state, and of assuring the smoothness of the functioning of its system. Good management improves economy by way of securing its safety, and though its slave

agents are not literally extirpated, they are deprived of rights and thus moved to the sphere which Aristotle's idea of a natural slave offered to man-footed creatures (*andrapodon*), depriving them of the possibility of participation in political life (see Fiskesjö 163).

The practices of extirpating allegedly pathological agents are also strongly linked with the notions of progress and improvement, as contamination can be always seen as gradable. The possibility of reducing human life to bare life (*vita nuda*), which Giorgio Agamben ascribes to the political potency of sovereignty (see 93), is an act which may serve the purpose of cleansing the social space via selection and segregation. What is involved in such reductionism is, as Nietzsche sees it, the idea of improvement which frequently consists in taming and breeding:

> People have always wanted to "improve" human beings: this, above all, was called morality. But hidden under this same word is a completely different tendency. Both the *taming* of the human beast and the *breeding* of a particular human species have been called "improvement": only this zoological terminology can express the realities – naturally, realities of which the typical "improver," the priest, knows nothing and wants to know nothing. (*Twilight* 38)

What he provides as an example of such an improvement are The Laws of Manu, "this absolutely Arian achievement," an organized frightening "with the nonbred human being, the mishmash human being, the chandala" (40). This code "sets the task of breeding no fewer than four races at once," one of the races being that of outcastes or untouchables. "This law," writes Nietzsche,

> forbids that they be brought grain or seed-bearing fruits, or that they be given water or fire. The same edict declares that the water they need may be taken neither from rivers nor springs nor ponds, but only from the entries to swamps and from hollows made by animals' hooves. Furthermore, the chandalas are forbidden to wash their clothes or to wash themselves, for the

water which is provided to them as a favor may be used only to quench their thirst. (40)

The chandala are offered only the kind of water which, for Plato, obstructs the access to the philosophical truth. The muddy waters which the chandala are offered to survive stand in opposition to the waters which opulently flow in *Matsya Purana*, with Manu "making a libation of water" (*The Sacred Books of the Hindus* 16) before the flood from which life was saved by Vishnu avatarized as a fish.

In Plato it is light rather than water whose management is offered in his allegory of the cave – the prisoners are denied the purity of sunlight while the philosophers as it were bathe in the brightness of truth. Water in the allegory is located between the shadows of reality and the sunlight of the truth as a kind of mirror which only reflects light and is classified among alien places. In order not to be blinded by the sun, one who is released from the shadowy world of illusions should try to go out of the cave-like dwelling gradually:

> "Then I suppose he'd have to get accustomed, if he were going to see what's up above. At first he'd most easily make out the shadows; and after that the phantoms of the human beings and the other things in water; and, later, the things themselves. And from there he could turn to beholding the things in heaven and heaven itself, more easily at night – looking at the light of the stars and the moon – than by day – looking at the sun and sunlight."
>
> "Of course."
>
> "Then finally I suppose he would be able to make out the sun – not its appearances in water or some alien place, but the sun itself by itself in its own region – and see what it's like." (Plato, *The Republic* 195)

There seems to be no chance of being released in the case of the chandala who are bound to drink water from swamps and hollows, with water management left in the hands of the priestly readers of the Vedas, the dam builders controlling access to the source of life and knowledge. However impure the Ganges may now be, it is the separation from any pure waters which establishes the chandala as an impure race which functions as a constitutive outside to the alleged purity of other social races. The chandala are projected as impure both within and without, inside and outside, a living kind of contamination brought about through drinking nothing but pathogenic waters thus giving rise and support to Nietzsche's "Aryan humanity" in which purity of blood parallels the innocuous nature of pure water (*Twilight* 41). Though philosophy in Plato seems to be bloodless, those who do not philosophize are also in a way drinkers of deadly waters who have, however symbolically, crossed the five rivers of death and reached the dominion of Hades. As Allan Bloom notes in his "Interpretive Essay" on *The Republic*, for Plato,

> [t]he activity of philosophy – the soul's contemplation of the principles of all things – brings with it a pleasure of a purity and intensity that causes all other pleasures to pale. For the philosopher, living as most men do is equivalent to living in Hades as conceived by most men. (*The Republic* 357)

managing

Water management is inextricably linked with various ways and contexts of managing purity and health. If the water allowed to be used by the chandala in Nietzsche may be called "untreated wastewater," then mammoth parts of the twenty-first-century world have to use it in irrigation, thus also contaminating food chains and triggering a number of diseases mentioned at the beginning of this text. Since water treatment systems are usually very costly, their efficiency varies throughout the world, and the figures provided by research in the field of water management may make one fear that the resources of pure waters can be found mostly in reservations of nature or only in some periods of time: "Earth contains approximately 1351 million km^3 of water, of which only 3% is available freshwater resources suitable for drinking and irrigation" (Ungureanu et al. 1). This is worsened by the fact that "wastewater is generated continuously and equally throughout the year, but the demand for irrigation is cyclic" (9). The phrase which is used with reference to the use of wastewater is "wastewater reuse" (11), which quietly connotes the possibility that what we use as water has always already been used. In the European Parliament regulation the phrase appears as "water reuse," rather than "wastewater reuse" (*Regulation EU 2020/741 of the European Parliament and of the Council, on Minimum Requirements for Water Reuse*).

Perhaps we could say, paraphrasing Jean Baudrillard, that we are all chandalas, though such as deceived by the promise of a return of our access to clear waters. Though this deception seems to be a serious philosophical question, its social and political strength speaks through various seemingly less sophisticated considerations of contamination in broadly understood "popular culture." Frank Zappa, for instance, was not a philosopher, and yet his ironic critique of environmental practices can be seen as a kind of "dystopianism" in which the pastoral back-to-nature ideal of man and nature is revealed as a political and ideological manipulation (see Ingram 139). Environmental laws, as Zappa put it, "were not passed to protect our air and water," but "to get votes" ("The Central Scrutinizer"). Water management promises purification which nostalgically refers to times from before industrialization and mechanization, while its actual results are reminiscent of what Zappa, slightly jokingly, saw in his posthumously released album *Civilization Phase III* as dark water:

Monica:	D-a-a-a-a-r-r-r-k W-a-a-a-t-e-r-r-r
Spider:	Yeah, it's trying to say something ...
Monica:	D-a-a-a-a-r-r-r-k-k-k W-a-a-a-t-e-r-r-r
Spider:	I know ... It's not trying to say something to us at all ... It's trying to say something to the pig
John:	Dark water ...
Spider:	I forget ... It's ...
John:	Dark water on top of the muck ("Dark Water")

Zappa's dark water on top of the muck announces its presence as a kind of inevitable contamination of the world in which the circulation of the excremental cannot be simply prevented.

A monumental exposition of an attempt at such prevention can be seen in Rome's Cloaca Maxima, a part of the Roman sewerage system and an invention which kept the Romans' excrements in invisibility. However, the Cloaca Maxima was originally designed for different purposes "as a monumental, open-air, fresh-water canal," and only later transformed into "a massive drain flushing away Rome's unappealing waste" (Hopkins 1). Praised by Pliny for its durability, one of "Rome's most solid but dubious glories" became in the 1880s a tourist attraction which still figures as such in the 2017 list of favorite places in the city (Gowers 24):

> If you cross the Palatino Bridge, look down to your left to see a double archway right down next to the water. The inner archway (made of marble and sometimes COVERED in graffiti) is the Cloaca Maxima – an original Roman sewer, and one of the oldest sewers in the world. It might not be as impressive as the colosseum, but this ancient drainage system made Rome possible. Gross stuff has been coming out of this drain for almost three thousand years! (Lorenz, n. pag.)

The affirmative attitudes toward the sewer may be an example of the *qua negata grata* principle. This attitude seems to be carrying a trace of the pleasure which Freud read into children's expulsion of feces and their enjoyment in playing with them. The graffiti on the walls of the Cloaca Maxima may well be seen as a kind of affirmation of its space as public rather than hidden, as a space handy for expressing one's complex emotions by "writing on the stall," regardless of one's gender. According to James Green, "toilet graffiti is a unique window into the relationship between gender, language, and social context" (282). The *latrinalia* on the walls of the Cloaca Maxima also point to the possibility that contact with pathogens may be in some sense attractive. It is in fact inevitable, and constitutes, like contamination in Derrida, a kind of fate which is carried by the very idea of contact. Prevention of contact lies, as we have seen, at the very heart of the Manu logic of untouchability which, in Nietzsche, constituted a negative outside of the otherwise clean society and a tool of its improvement. For Derrida,

> [c]ontact would be a priori contaminating. Graver yet, the risk of contamination would surface before there is contact, in the simple necessity of tying together interruptions as such, in the very seriality of traces and the insistence of the ruptures. And even if this unheard-of chain does not retie threads but hiatuses. Contamination then is no longer a risk but a fate that must be assumed. ("At This Very Moment" 167)

This assumption is also an affirmation, and admission, of contact with the material and the real which no regulation can prevent. Water management is also an attempt at water regulation in which contaminated water and the threat of drowning in a flood overlap. Derrida's epidemiological and immunological tropes of contamination which Peta Mitchell (see Mitchell 77) traces in his writings do not literally address the issue of water pathogens, yet the triad of contamination, contact, contagion read through the contaminating nature of clarity through metaphoricity may well be, also metaphorically, translated into water management as a management of contacts and flows in relation to broadly understood otherness.

flowing

Water can be rhetorically posited as a threatening other both as an unstable and fluid element dangerous to the security of the sedentary life of humans on the solid land, and as a carrier of deadly pathogens. Rebekah Sinclair addresses the first of the pair of threats, following Derrida, as "ontopological solidity" (Sinclair 361), which is rhetorically expressed in the construction of various types of walls,

dams, and locks, controlling all kinds of flows, including flows of people. Dams and sluices are also built as mechanisms that stop the linguistic flow of difference: "The lock which controls the flow of water into the canal, the tongue which controls the flow of difference and alterity into the language, is always precarious" (358). The flow of differences is correspondingly the issue of alien infiltration into one's own domestic and familiar linguistic space. Unless hospitably affirmed, the uncertainty of otherness may be expressed through the rhetoric of contamination. Writing which contaminates the purity of speech is the idea which Derrida critiques and rewords in his own opulent amount of writing. Related to it is the question of migrants and refugees weakening and contaminating the ontopological purity of identity which Derrida raises in, among others, *Monolingualism of the Other*. This book, writes Sinclair, "is filled with attention to fluids: seas, shores, floods, canals, waves, rivers, and tsunamis" which "all meander through and soak its pages" (353). Regulation of flows of difference and its association with water can be seen in various discourses of migration policies in which land borders appear as dams or water locks protecting the land from being flooded not only by water, but by a sick kind of water whose image is carried by its pathogen-carrier associations. This double threat of water threatens a double kind of space – the territory, and the interiors of what Peter Sloterdijk calls apartment individualism confining us to the architectural spaces of our homes and of ourselves as insulating from the outside:

> The apartment is developed into an ignorance machine or into an integral defense mechanism. It provides architectural support to the basic right not to pay attention to one's environment [...] It materializes the basic fact that human openness to the world is always complemented by avoidance of the world. (540; I quote after Bergthaller 167)

The threat of a death by water is a kind of anamnesis of the environment, perhaps the voice of

Zappa's dark water whose image haunts the cleanliness of human civilization, and whose measure Freud famously saw in the use of soap, the absolute disregard of its contaminatory properties:

> Dirt of any kind seems to us incompatible with civilization; we extend our demands for cleanliness to the human body also, and are amazed to hear what an objectionable odour emanated from the person of the Roi Soleil; we shake our heads when we are shown the tiny washbasin on the Isola Bella which Napoleon used for his daily ablutions. Indeed, we are not surprised if anyone employs the use of soap as a direct measure of civilization. (55)

The use of water metaphors with reference to migrants and refugees does not only render them as "beings out of place and time, without the solidity of coherent memory, language, autobiography," as Sinclair writes, but also projects upon them various kinds of impurities connected with dirt and diseases (366). For Donald Trump, for instance, Mexicans "flowing" across the border were not only held responsible for spreading drug addiction in America, but also for transforming America into a dumping ground and for flooding it with diseases:

> The largest suppliers of heroin, cocaine and other illicit drugs are Mexican cartels that arrange to have Mexican immigrants trying to cross the borders and smuggle in the drugs. The border patrol knows this. Likewise, tremendous infectious disease is pouring across the border. The United States has become a dumping ground for Mexico and, in fact, for many other parts of the world. (Neate and Tuckman, n. pag.)

The leader of the Polish political party now in power expressed the fear of immigrants following almost the same pattern of argumentation, though leaving some space for the possibility of examining and checking the unwanted arrivants:

> After all, there are already symptoms of very dangerous diseases that have not been seen in Europe for a long time. Cholera on the Greek islands, dysentery in Vienna. Various types of parasites, protozoa, which are not dangerous in the organisms of these people, and can be dangerous here. This does not mean discriminating against someone, but you must check. (wPolityce.pl, n. pag.; trans. A.P.)

Examples of this kind of discursive constructions of pathogenic floods spreading diseases can be, needless to say, multiplied, and their task is to increase the immunological vulnerability of "hosts" as opposed to the immunological strength of the carriers. Like water, to which sickness is hardly ever ascribed, immigrants, without any kind of affective doubt insensibly flow and kill, the killing being in the case of immigrants from Islamic countries a fulfillment of their mission. In the case of Poland, where I happen to live, it is the very association with Islam which is associated with the threat of dechristianization. Even in seemingly objective publications on the issue, the Islamic flood is posited as an attempt at a cultural conquest:

> On the other hand, little knowledge of Islam on the part of Europeans leads to theories about an alleged plan of conquest of the modern world by Islam. These are fundamentally impossible to fulfill and, for the most part, false. However, it cannot be denied that some Muslims in Europe are engaging in constant anti-Western propaganda, and socially and culturally Islam is beginning to flood the West. (Guź 241; trans. A.P.)

The political rhetoric of water management translates states into islands for which water, perhaps paradoxically, can also be seen as a protective moat, a watery barrier against hostile inflows. It is not only Trump's wall which is supposed to stop migrants and refugees flooding across the US border from the south. Another kind of strategy used on the Mexican border is the channeling of flows of migrants

> to the most precarious, dangerous places to cross the Rio Grande and the deserts beyond. It is no accident that so many

refugees die in the rushing waters of the Rio Grande or the inhospitable deserts beyond, as the state weaponizes those geographies precisely to drown flows of migrants, or else turn them to dust. (Sinclair 361)

Such a homeopathic use of water against its rhetorical double is also a standard procedure in the domestic policies of keeping order. Armored cannon water trucks sending powerful streams of water against protesting crowds are a peculiar example of water management proving that the softness of water is only one of its images. Harnessing of the power of water is also a means of controlling its flows which, if unharnessed, not only flood the land, but also change its surface. Water left to itself is in a way ahead of man as in the image of the flood of the river overtaking Achilles in *The Iliad*:

> he [Achilles] tried to run clear, away from the advancing water, but the river streamed on in pursuit, crashing loud behind him. As when a man channels water from a dark-welling spring and directs its flow among his plants and garden-plots, knocking the dams from its trench with a mattock in his hand: as the water starts to flow it clears all the pebbles from its path, then gathers speed and runs gurgling down over the sloping ground, outstripping the man who guides it. So the river's rolling wave was always overtaking Achilles, however fast he ran. (Homer 21.255–64)

The greatest of the Greek warriors loses his race with water. However, he survives the flood, perhaps thanks to his having been impregnated against death in the river Styx. His immersion in water in the race described by Homer does not necessarily render water victorious, but may be read as a reminder of human belonging in nature from which there is no escape to safely insulated apartments. As Felix Mauch notes,

> the belief that it is possible to develop a reliable safety measure is just as deceptive as the hope that water crises and disasters are merely an exception to the norm. On the contrary, danger is a constant, essentially

inherent component of the human water relationship. (69)

storying

Water need not be imagined as an element external to our bodies, and immersion in water may be also an initiation to what Astrida Neimanis proposes as reimagining embodiment which she links with reimagining water: "Put otherwise, changing how we think about bodies means changing how we think about water" (19). This is not an easy change, and given the depth of the furrows of anthropocentric disaffirmation of man's others it may be seen as strongly unwelcome. Though we are all watery creatures, the water within us is kept in conceptual invisibility so as to protect the solidity of our minds and bodies. This solidity also entails productivity and immersion in the capitalist property principle through which John Locke initiated the conflation of being with having. Neimanis's proposal addresses Rosi Braidotti's taking a neo-materialist position of "zoe-geo-centrism" which anagrammatically codes "ego" only as a part of our earthly belonging among transversal subjectivities:

> A neo-materialist vital position offers a robust rebuttal of the accelerationist and profit-minded knowledge practices of bio-mediated, cognitive capitalism. Taking "living matter" as a *zoe*-geo-centred process that interacts in complex ways with the techno-social, psychic and natural environments and resists the over-coding by the capitalist profit principle (and the structural inequalities it entails), I end up on an affirmative plane of composition of transversal subjectivities. Subjectivity can then be re-defined as an expanded self, whose relational capacity is not confined within the human species, but includes non-anthropomorphic elements. *Zoe*, the non-human, vital force of life, is the transversal entity that allows us to think across previously segregated species. (Braidotti 42)

Neimanis liquidizes the living matter of the non-human, simultaneously liquidizing the border on which "embodiment meets water" and posits this fluid encounter as a question of the survival of the world which is threatened by various managements of water which inevitably turn out to be catastrophic:

We live at the site of exponential material meaning where embodiment meets water. Given the various interconnected and anthropogenically exacerbated water crises that our planet currently faces – from drought and freshwater shortage to wild weather, floods, and chronic contamination – this meaningful mattering of our bodies is also an urgent question of worldly survival. (1)

Capitalocenic (see Haraway) water management takes some care of water mostly in order to keep up the means of production, to keep the working power healthy and some people wealthy. Any other imagining of water seems to be so far an academic postulate which does not make it through the stereotypes encouraged by school education and media. This seems to be the case with *Open Schools Journal for Open Science*, for example, a peer-reviewed publisher of "papers by school age students from Primary to Secondary schools across Europe under the mentoring of their Teachers" where in an article titled "Water Purity" the task of water management is seen exactly as a means to the improvement of productivity:

When water comes from improved and more accessible sources, people spend less time and effort on their natural collection, which means they can be productive in other ways. This can also lead to greater personal safety by reducing the need for long or dangerous routes to collect water. Better water sources also entail lower health costs, as people are less likely to get sick and suffer medical costs and are better off staying productive. (Bousiou et al., n. pag.)

To reimagine water and imagine our watery embodiment otherwise than in terms of water's use and reuse is an uncertain project, and Neimanis considers its possibilities with caution: "We may start to wonder about the possibilities for reimagining water, when imaginaries and figurations are as vulnerable to redirection as the flows of the river themselves," and the "imaginaries hold no guarantees" (182). Traces of such imaginaries, however, have been marked, sometimes implicitly, in numerous writings and stories of the world; in Homer and Nietzsche, in Derrida and Frank Zappa. But reimagining the watery world is also a matter of rereading it. Donna Haraway names this world "the Chthulucene – past, present, and to come" (160), having no doubt that its existence is something to be found and experienced rather than invented. Haraway's "kinning" of the world is an experience which, importantly, can be read, and it does not demand that we all jump into the sea which, as is well known, may also be a water of trouble. For Haraway this experience is a kind of narrative, and "[i]t matters which stories tell stories, which concepts think concepts. Mathematically, visually, and narratively, it matters which figures figure figures, which systems systematize systems" (160). Neimanis's reimagining of water is also a story, though one which problematizes the telling of the story which may be the story told by water, and from water, perhaps in the way Alice Oswald makes the river Dart tell us its/her story in the poem titled *Dart*.

One of the figures which appear in the poem is that of a sewage worker whose identification with the dirty water in which and with which he works and the idea that he might be also a participant in the process of producing "stinkmass of loopaper" seems to be unthinkable:

sewage worker
It's a rush, a splosh of sewage, twenty thousand cubic metres being pumped in, stirred and settled out and wasted off, looped back, macerated, digested, clarified and returned to the river. I'm used to the idea. I fork the screenings out – a stinkmass of loopaper and whathaveyou, rags cottonbuds, you name it. I measure the intake through a flume and if there's too much, I waste it off down the stormflow, it's not my problem. (Oswald, *Dart* 30)

The sewage worker, however, also belongs to Oswald's river, works within its materiality, making the management of water into a part of the narration of the river, which, perhaps similarly to Frank Zappa's dark water, is also a complaint of water made sick. Oswald's river, writes Janne Stigen Drangsholt, "constructs, and unceasingly alters, its being in encounters with the other" (177). All the "I"s in the poem, including the "I" of the poet, speak the river, give voice to "a mob of waters" (Oswald, *Dart* 10) which do not claim any individual sovereignty. "All voices should be read as the river's mutterings," writes Oswald in the preface (5), the muttering offering us a polyphonic text, the voice of the open river, whose voice is also the polyphonic voice of water, the voice of fish and fishermen, experts on the river and canoeists, one of whom drowns in its currents with a folk song on his lips. The river in *Dart* is the melodious noise of human activity which it shapes and by which it is shaped. The narrative is an aquatic history that liquefies facts and events, absorbs them, and rewrites them in a translation into a language through which the original can only be intuited both by the readers and by the human inhabitants of *Dart*. This original itself is not a simple text because what is attempted to be translated is the experience of materiality. Both the readers and the humans within the poem are constructed, or perhaps deconstructed, around what John Parham sees as "material relation to the river," thus intuiting "the ecological basis of human nature, even while remaining, for the most part, aware of the contingent, provisional, forever shifting ground that characterises that relationship" (125).

Alice Oswald dedicated her later book, *The Thunder Mutters: 101 Poems for the Planet* (2005), to a rake. This movement from water to a tool may seem surprising, but at the very beginning she mixes nature, art, and technology through bringing in a watery musical instrument – a "dew's harp":

A dew's harp is a rake (in old Devon dialect). This book is dedicated to the rake, which I see as a rhythmical but predictable instrument that connects earth to our hands.

Raking, like any outdoor work, is a more mobile, more many-sided way of knowing a place than looking. When you rake leaves for a couple of hours, you can hear right into the non-human world, it's as if you and the trees had found a meeting point in the sound of the rake. (Oswald, *The Thunder Matters* ix)

Thus positing her own penchant for gardening as an aesthetic kind of labor, she also translates rake into a tool-like instrument whose music is owed to its contact with dew, another embodiment of water. The work of raking her garden is a kind of listening to various sounds and voices of the non-human, of the world to which her belonging longs, and which can be traced to an old language for which music, work, and dew were inseparable experiences of the world. The work of the rake contaminates the dew, but it simultaneously enlivens other voices, and the task of the raking is not simply to clear some space for growing tomatoes, for example, but rather to intuit the sources of this complex music, however atonal it may be. Whether one calls this a posthumanist perspective or a realist one seems to be irrelevant, as the very "category" of posthumanism may be easily used and catachrestically abused for various ways of protecting humanism and humanity as categories as untouchable as Nietzsche's drinkers of sick water. Perhaps water is sick, and has been such not only since the construction of the Cloaca Maxima, but this sickness unto death is also what all of us happen to be. This Kierkegaardian formula is not confined to "us" as humans, but to us as Haraway's "critters" whose kinship relations cannot be documented, as critters *sans papier*, who migrate in the watery world of Neimanis, and into it, regardless of the degree of water's sickness. Let me finish this text with yet another reference to watery imagery in a more recent "popular culture" text than Frank Zappa's "Dark Water":

Sick river
Where are my brothers?
No fish swimming
Where is my home?

We came here to feel everything
I want to bathe in the river
Flow through me
River my sister
(Ooh) I'll care for you
(Ooh) I'll care for you (Moonsign, n. pag.)

Water can be sick, also suffer, and this suffering may be a perspective from which Oswald's sewage worker may begin to care. Perhaps caring, mutually, rather than managing, can be a lesson of water, a story which is telling a sometimes whimpering story, rather than one that has been told, finished, and ended with a bang.

disclosure statement

No potential conflict of interest was reported by the author.

bibliography

Agamben, Giorgio. *Homo Sacer: Sovereign Power and Bare Life*. Translated by Daniel Heller-Roazen, Stanford UP, 1998.

Bergthaller, Hannes. "Living in Bubbles: Peter Sloterdijk's Spherology and the Environmental Humanities." *Spaces In-between: Cultural and Political Perspectives on Environmental Discourse*, edited by Mark Luccarelli and Sigurd Bergmann, Brill, 2015, pp. 163–74.

Bousiou, C., et al. "Water Purity." *Open Schools Journal for Open Science*, vol. 3, no. 3, 2020, https://doi.org/10.12681/osj.23364.

Braidotti, Rosi. "A Theoretical Framework for the Critical Posthumanities." *Theory, Culture, & Society*, vol. 36, no. 6, 2018, pp. 31–61.

Cybulska, Eva. "Nietzsche's Übermensch: A Glance Behind the Mask of Hardness." *Indo-Pacific Journal of Phenomenology*, vol. 15, no. 1, 2015, pp. 1–13.

Derrida, Jacques. "At This Very Moment in This Work Here I Am." *Psyche: Inventions of the Other*, vol. I, edited by Peggy Kamuf and Elizabeth Rottenberg, Stanford UP, 2007, pp. 143–90.

Derrida, Jacques. "Living On." Translated by James Hulbert. *Deconstruction and Criticism*, edited by Harold Bloom et al., Seabury Press, 1979, pp. 75–176.

Derrida, Jacques. *Monolingualism of the Other OR Prosthesis of Origin*. Translated by Patrick Mensah, Stanford UP, 1988.

Derrida, Jacques. *Otobiographies*. Translated by Avital Ronell, Shocken Books, 1985.

Derrida, Jacques, and Richard Beardsworth. "Nietzsche and the Machine." *Journal of Nietzsche Studies*, no. 7, 1994, pp. 7–66.

Drangsholt, Janne Stigen. "Sounding the Landscape: Dis-placement in the Poetry of Alice Oswald." *Crisis and Contemporary Poetry*, edited by Anne Karhio et al., Palgrave Macmillan, 2011, pp. 167–79.

Esposito, Roberto. *Bíos: Biopolitics and Philosophy*. Translated by T. Campbell, U of Minnesota P, 2008.

Fiskesjö, Magnus. "Outlaws, Barbarians, Slaves. Critical Reflections on Agamben's *Homo Sacer*." *HAU: Journal of Ethnographic Theory*, vol. 2, no. 1, 2012, pp. 161–80.

Freud, Sigmund. *Civilization and Its Discontents*. Translated by Joan Riviere et al., Hogarth Press, 1930.

Gowers, Emily. "The Anatomy of Rome from Capitol to Cloaca." *The Journal of Roman Studies*, vol. 85, 1995, pp. 23–32, www.jstor.org/stable/301055. Accessed 25 May 2020.

Green, James A. "The Writing on the Stall: Gender and Graffiti." *Journal of Language and Social Psychology*, vol. 22, no. 3, 2003, pp. 282–96.

Guź, Jerzy. "Muzułmanie i neofici muzułmańscy – zagrożenie dla Europy Zachodniej czy szansa na pokojowe współżycie? Wprowadzenie do zagadnienia." *Acta Erasmiana*, vol. 6, 2014, pp. 235–66.

Hamlin, Christopher. "'Waters' or 'Water'? – Master Narratives in Water History and their Implications for Contemporary Water Policy." *Water Policy*, vol. 2, 2000, pp. 313–25.

Haraway, Donna. "Anthropocene, Capitalocene, Plantationocene, Chthulucene: Making Kin." *Environmental Humanities*, vol. 6, 2015, pp. 159–65.

Homer. *The Iliad*. Translated by Martin Hammond, Penguin Classics, 1987.

Hopkins, John. "The Cloaca Maxima and the Monumental Manipulation of Water in Archaic Rome." *The Waters of Rome*, no. 4, 2007, pp. 1–15.

Ingram, David. *The Jukebox in the Garden: Ecocriticism and American Popular Music Since 1960*. Rodopi, 2010.

Lorenz, Marie. "Favorite Places in Rome." 2017, jsis.washington.edu/wordpress/wp-content/uploads/2019/01/Favorite-Places-in-Rome.pdf. Accessed 14 Mar. 2022.

Mauch, Felix. "The Perils of Water: Floods, Droughts, and Pollution as Natural Hazards and Cultural Challenges." *On Water: Perceptions, Politics, Perils*, edited by Agnes Kneitz and Marc Landry, *RCC Perspectives*, no. 2, 2012, pp. 63–70, www.environmentandsociety.org/sites/default/files/seiten_aus_1202_water_web_color-7_0.pdf. Accessed 11 Feb. 2022.

Mitchell, Peta. "Contagion, Virology, Autoimmunity: Derrida's Rhetoric of Contamination." *Parallax*, vol. 23, no. 1, 2017, pp. 77–93.

Moonsign. "Sick River." *Okay You First*, 1919.

Neate, Rupert, and Jo Tuckman. "Donald Trump: Mexican Migrants Bring 'Tremendous Infectious Disease' to US." *The Guardian*, Monday 6 July 2015, www.theguardian.com/us-news/2015/jul/06/donald-trump-mexican-immigrants-tremendous-infectious-disease. Accessed 12 Dec. 2021.

Neimanis, Astrida. *Bodies of Water: Posthuman Feminist Phenomenology*. Bloomsbury, 2017.

Nietzsche, Friedrich. *Human, All Too Human*. Translated by P.V. Cohn, Macmillan, 1913.

Nietzsche, Friedrich. *Thus Spoke Zarathustra*. Translated by Adrian Del Caro, Cambridge UP, 2006.

Nietzsche, Friedrich. *Twilight of the Idols; Or, How to Philosophize with the Hammer*. Translated by Richard Polt, Hackett, 1997.

Oswald, Alice. *Dart*. Faber and Faber, 2002.

Oswald, Alice. *The Thunder Matters: 101 Poems for the Planet*. Faber and Faber, 2005.

Paphitis, Sharli. "Vulnerability and the Sovereign Individual: Nussbaum and Nietzsche on the Role of Agency and Vulnerability in Personhood." *South African Journal of Philosophy*, vol. 32, no. 2, 2013, pp. 123–36.

Parham, John. "'Two-Ply': Discordant Nature and English Landscape in Alice Oswald's Dart." *Revista Canaria de Estudios Ingleses*, vol. 64, 2012, pp. 111–29.

Petronis, Caroline. *Blurring Contagion in the Information Age: How COVID-19 Troubles the Boundaries of the Biomedical and Socioinformatic*. Duke UP, 2021, dukespace.lib.duke.edu/dspace/handle/10161/22645. Accessed 12 May 2022.

Plato. *Laws*. Translated by Benjamin Jowett, *The Project Gutenberg*, 2013, www.gutenberg.org/files/1750/1750-h/1750-h.htm. Accessed 14 Dec. 2021.

Plato. *Phaedo*. Translated by F.J. Church, The Liberal Arts Press, 1951.

Plato. *The Republic of Plato*. Translated by Allan Bloom, Basic Books, 1991.

The Sacred Books of the Hindus. Translated by various Sanskrit Scholars, Apurva Krishna Boss, Indian Press, 1916, archive.org/details/in.ernet.-dli.2015.45856/page/n3/mode/2up?q = water. Accessed 12 Feb. 2022.

Sinclair, Rebekah. "Agua-Biographies: Derrida on Water, Ontopology, and Refugees." *The Journal of Speculative Philosophy*, vol. 34, no. 3, 2020, pp. 353–66.

Sloterdijk, Peter. *Sphären III: Schäume*. Suhrkamp, 2004.

Ungureanu, Nicoleta, et al. "Water Scarcity and Wastewater Reuse in Crop Irrigation." *Sustainability*, vol. 12, 2020, pp. 1–18, https://doi.org/10.3390/su12219055.

World Health Organization. *Guidelines for Drinking-Water Quality: Fourth Edition Incorporating the First and Second Addenda*, 2022, apps.who.int/iris/rest/bitstreams/1414381/retrieve.

wPolityce.pl. "Kto przesadził? Kaczyński: Imigranci mogą przynieść nieznane choroby. Celiński: To język nazizmu! Mówiło się, że Żydki mają tyfus." *W polityce*, 13 Oct. 2015, wpolityce.pl/polityka/268356-kto-przesadzil-kaczynski-imigranci-moga-przyniesc-nieznane-choroby-celinski-to-jezyknazizmu-mowilo-sie-ze-zydki-maja-tyfus. Accessed 11 Jan. 2022.

Zappa, Frank. "The Central Scrutinizer." *Joe's Garage*, Village Records "B," 1979.

Zappa, Frank. "Dark Water." *Civilization Phase III*, Universal Music Group, 1994.

Agnieszka Pantuchowicz

OPEN ACCESS

Now, my feeling is that today, when of course ontology is all the rage again – the word, and the concept, and the project of ontology are back in many forms and on many sides, as though there were something very desirable about ontology, as though it were an object of philosophical desire to formulate an ontology, as though the very word "ontology" were irresistibly seductive – my feeling is that those attempts have not registered the force of Derrida's arguments […]
– *Geoffrey Bennington (Moreiras 41)*

What does it mean for feminist thought to think of life on Earth according to a discourse of material maternality where the latter is conceived of in terms of facilitative connective filiation? And why should we consider Astrida Neimanis's volume, *Bodies of Water*, a significant contribution to feminist theory worthy of critical engagement? *Bodies of Water* presents a compelling feminist phenomenological elaboration on a vast textual reservoir of liquid water to construe life's connection to water as maternal in its materiality. Neimanis's aim is to urge us to acknowledge that a common (watery) way of being alive is shared in their embodiment by all forms of life in the hope that this would lead us to think and act more responsibly. Relying on the work of Luce Irigaray informed by Deleuze and Merleau-Ponty, Neimanis develops a lexicon of maternal water in terms of "amniotics," "hydrocommons," "planetary breastmilk" and "posthuman gestationality." Also termed as the "onto-logic of amniotics,"

Mère Métaphore: The Maternal Materiality of Water in Astrida Neimanis's *Bodies of Water*

Eszter Timár (iD)

gestationality is represented in the figure of the amnion, "the innermost membrane that encloses the embryo of a mammal, bird, or reptile" in the safe environment of water (Neimanis 95). Generalized as a basic ontological unit of life not limited to amniotes but including any cell as an enclosed body of water, this generalized maternality will be constitutive of life itself:

My proposition is that specific bodily waters – breast milk here, or amniotic waters […] – are material metonyms of a planetary watery milieu that interpermeates and connects

This is an Open Access article distributed under the terms of the Creative Commons Attribution-NonCommercial-NoDerivatives License (http://creativecommons.org/licenses/by-nc-nd/4.0/), which permits non-commercial re-use, distribution, and reproduction in any medium, provided the original work is properly cited, and is not altered, transformed, or built upon in any way.

bodies, and bathes new kinds of plural life into being. (39)

While the phrase "planetary gestationality" does not itself appear in the text (separately, however, both terms feature quite frequently), it condenses well the overall project: published in the *Environmental Cultures* series at Bloomsbury, planetariness is as significant a term for the text's understanding of endangered life on our planet as the sense of gestationality is associated with the waters that provide the means of life on Earth.

My point of departure for this article is that this figuration of water's maternal materiality seems to be conceived in accordance with what Geoffrey Bennington calls the desire for ontology in my opening epigraph. Without aiming to argue for a general "registry" of the force of deconstruction, I am interested in this article in engagements with sexual difference, materiality and maternality relying on the resources of deconstruction and psychoanalysis. I do this to suggest that the construction of the discourse of maternal connectedness (including a resulting incitement of gratitude) in the name of affirming life is in fact haunted by figures of separation, loss and anxiety concerning the idea of maternality and materiality. While my argument will rely on in part by revisiting relevant scholarly discussions that might be considered "old," or "outdated," I suggest we consider the kind of interpretive and critical practices we see in deconstruction or psychoanalysis as approaches interested in the rhetorical and affective reading of texts. When I think of the compelling force of *Bodies of Water*, it is Kant's dynamic sublime that first comes to my mind in part because of their resonances of imagery and also, and this will be my first act of revisitation, because of Paul de Man's reading of it in his discussions of the aesthetic ideology of materiality. Simply put, this is important because Kant, in his attempt at placing the sublime as the connective bridge of all his critical work preceding the *Critique of Judgment*, discusses a way of seeing nature that concerns the very

meaning of materiality. In several of his late texts, Paul de Man provided readings of the relevant passages in Kant in order to unpack this discourse of materiality. Let me here indicate the resonances by recalling that Kant's notion of the dynamic sublime deploys the Western idea of figuring nature as a veiled mother citing the inscription of the Temple of Isis:

> Perhaps nothing more sublime has ever been said, or any thought more sublimely expressed, than in the inscription over the temple of Isis (Mother Nature): "I am all that is, that was, and that will be, and my veil no mortal has removed." (194)

Planetary gestationality is a version of this Mother Nature, a figural construction which greatly helps orchestrate the discussion on materiality in the dynamic sublime for Kant. Paul de Man's discussion of materiality in relation to the dynamic sublime will not just show that Neimanis's work is an elaboration of the terms of the Kantian text on the sublime, it will also provide the opportunity to catch a glimpse of what I consider these haunting figures of loss. Another such act of revisitation concerns Neimanis's reading of Irigaray. When we read *Bodies of Water* bearing in mind the question "How does this text refer to materiality as a kind of uncontestable foundational term?," we find a continuous pulsing discourse of braiding the terms "discourse" and "matter." On the one hand, the text often assures us that materiality and discourse are inseparable, that discourse is part of materiality; it is implicated within it. On the other hand, though, the text also employs a distinction between metaphor and metonymy that posits them as very different in terms of their relationship to matter. While metonymy has free access to materiality whose oneness with discourse is secured by metonymy's maternal coursing through matter, metaphor seems to be trapped in language with no access to materiality. To discuss Neimanis's use of these terms, I will rely on Diana Fuss's appreciative deconstruction of Irigaray's own discourse on metaphor and metonymy to suggest that Neimanis takes on from Irigaray both the gendered construction of these tropes and the particular way this gendered construction breaks down. In my final section I will turn to Elissa Marder's more recent work on what she calls the maternal function. Here, unlike in Neimanis's figure of contained connection, the maternal is discussed in terms of a radical separation and an associated anxiety in which figures of birth and death both mark the idea of maternality. My reading will focus on showing ways in which the Kantian dynamic sublime and Neimanis's discernment of metonymy can be considered as featuring tropes of death within the discourse of nature as facilitative mother.

With one chapter devoted to the imagery of breast milk, another to amnionic waters, this maternality (while acknowledged to be also abyssal) is primarily facilitative. Embodiment is always facilitated by water: bodies beget other bodies by some sort of watery arrangement.[1] Neimanis illustrates this by referring to a wide range of texts relevant for this sense of wateriness: scientific texts on pharmaceuticals influencing the hormones of frogs and fish along with highly contested theories of so-called pseudo-science such as Masaru Emeto's experiments with water or speculative theories of human pre-history such as the aquatic ape hypothesis. Interested in what these texts perform (and not whether they can in fact be considered verified), Neimanis reads these all as belonging to a common reservoir of the imaginary of wateriness and our human belonging to it.

What makes the volume so deserving of a careful reading is that she combines this textual reservoir of water with an important intervention in feminist theory. In order to infuse feminist new materialism with feminist phenomenology, Neimanis carefully cites all major feminist theorists usually associated with new materialism (see, for instance, page 6) while also tracing the legacy of some of the great inspirational figures of poststructuralist feminist theory (e.g., Cixous's *écriture féminine*), weaving the voices of these different domains into its own text it presents a complex feminist chorus, in the wake of which planetary

gestationality may be thought.[2] The link to new materialism is important because of the specific significance of materiality in *Bodies of Water*: water's maternality is inseparable from its materiality.[3] This material aspect of posthumanist lived embodiment is connected to the way the volume is conceived as a proposal for a radical inflection of ontology:

> The importance of water for the gestation, maintenance, and proliferation of bodily life is hardly news to anyone with a rudimentary understanding of the life sciences. But water's biological workings also reverberate in an important philosophical proposition – in an onto-logic – that helps us rethink dominant Western ontologies that privilege a static and separated way of bodily being. An onto-logic is a common way of being that is expressed across a difference of beings. As opposed to the way in which "ontology" might be traditionally understood, an onto-logic does not propose to solve the question of "Being," nor does it purport to reveal or describe all of being's facets or potential expressions. An onto-logic can rather gather or highlight something that helps us understand *a common how, where, when, and thanks to whom that certain seemingly disparate beings share.* (Neimanis 96; italics mine)

As this quote suggests, this mission takes place in the general idea of ontology: onto-logy seems to be part of the answer to the ethical and ontological obligations mentioned above in proposing a shared commonality that reverberates through difference. Water here is posited as a material guarantee of a commonality that invites, if not prescribes, a sense of gratitude. The referent of this "thanks to whom," the "who," is the personified figure of this maternal and material water. What is ontologized in Neimanis's volume through the idea of water in its liquid state is a combination of figures of the feminine side of sexual difference as they appear in the work of Luce Irigaray. Irigaray is being read here as a thinker of materiality; Neimanis leaves Irigaray's discussions of the patriarchal discourse of Western thought including engagements with Lacanian psychoanalysis unconsidered. It is as if these discourse-oriented aspects of Irigaray's work were simply issued by her specific onto-logy. I suggest that this decision of reading Irigaray without an attention to language or psychoanalysis is aiding Neimanis in her desire to ontologize the figures of maternal embodiment (the amniotic sac and the lactating breast) in order to construe her idea(l) of hydro-commons as a way of being connected. The sense of this commonality infused with gratitude is also affirmed by the gesture of presenting the cited material from feminist theory as overall complementary where theoretical differences are insignificant in light of a more profound agreement. Since water here is something like the mother of life (that which life needs to be possible) and all live bodies are alive because they contain water as it traverses through them, the offspring (life or lived bodies) is never quite separated from the mother.

Given this silence on language and psychoanalysis in Irigaray's work (while implicitly relying on it) makes the task of reading the rhetorical construction of maternal materiality with the help of deconstruction and psychoanalysis all the more promising. The combined effect of this reading will show, I hope on the one hand, that the construction of maternal materiality as something more serious than a mere rhetorical construct is itself constructed via rhetorical means. On the other hand, it will suggest that this rhetorical construction reveals necessarily menacing aspects of maternality at the heart of planetary gestationality. This is all the more important since it is unclear how such a discourse conceiving the essence of the materiality of life in terms of a filial connection infused with gratitude may provide space for the possibility of radical dissent and debate when it comes to our feminist responses to the eco-crisis we have been living in.

the kantian sublime and maternal materiality

Neimanis takes the term "planetary" from Gayatri Spivak who introduces it to resist the sense of unification or political homogenization of "global" (Neimanis 144–45). "Planetary" in this sense stands for a sense of unlimitable multiplicity of difference. Applied to the terms of gestationality, it denotes the sense that this maternal connection is shared across such multiplicities of embodiment. However, the combination of the concern for life on Earth and the imagery of "amniotics" (as a sense of shared bathing) also evokes the ideas of planet or planets in the term "planetary," and this association is fortified by Neimanis's consistent reliance on the lexicon of "materiality" in terms of the imagery of the watery amnion. The singular and the plural of "planet" might signify considerably different ideas. The singular form includes the iconic image of our "blue planet" representing life as the rare miracle confined to our home (only possible to imagine as a whole from a viewpoint out in space), whereas the plural always refers to at least one other planet, drawing our imagination in the direction of celestial bodies in the sky. The idea of planetariness thus invokes both the figure of our home as a milieu of nature harboring life as well as the idea of what lies outside of this planet, itself made to appear like a precious amnion itself. Gestationality based on the maternally-metonymically conceived idea of water as a medium of life, on the other hand, especially the idea of all water on Earth, invokes vastness and is as such very close to the figure of the ocean: our convention of referring to Earth as the blue planet combines the idea of water with the image of Earth viewed from space.[4] This linking of ocean and outer space connects planetary gestationality to the Kantian notion of the dynamic sublime (associated with nature). As is well known, the sublime for Kant is a certain mixed affective state of pleasure developing out of unpleasure and emerging as a result of experiencing a sense of vastness represented to us by nature. Kant's discussion of the sublime plays a crucial part in his third *Critique* meant to serve as the bridge between the first two critiques. In doing so, he works an old Western discourse on the sublime into an affect that represents a radical freedom only open to man. Importantly, his discussion on the dynamic sublime contains two elements also at work in Neimanis: figuring nature as a mother and understanding the dynamic sublime as guided by a discussion of phenomenal materiality. The combination of ocean and sky appears precisely at the moment when, in his reading of Kant, Paul de Man introduces the idea of "material" vision to juxtapose it with the idea of phenomenal materiality. The most important quote from Kant on the sublime selected by de Man is the following:

> If, then, we call the sight of the starry heavens *sublime*, we must not place at the foundation of judgment concepts of worlds inhabited by rational beings and regard the bright points, with which we see the space above us filled, as their suns moving in circles purposively fixed with reference to them; but we must regard it, just as we see it [...] as a distant, all-embracing vault [...] Only under such a representation can we range the sublimity that a pure aesthetic judgment ascribes to this object. And in the same way, if we are to call the sight of the ocean sublime, we must not think of it as we ordinarily do [...] For example, we sometimes think of the ocean as a vast kingdom of aquatic creatures, or as the great source of those vapors that fill the air with clouds for the benefit of the land, or again as an element that, though dividing continents from each other, yet promotes the greatest communication between them; all these produce merely teleological judgments. To find the ocean nevertheless sublime we must regard it as poets do [...], merely by what the eye reveals [...] – if it is at rest, as a clear mirror of water only bounded by the heavens; if it is stormy, as an abyss threatening to overwhelm everything. (Kant's *Critique of Judgment*, italics original, qtd in de Man 80)

Writing on phenomenality and reference in Paul de Man's work, Andrzej Warminski connects de Man's texts on the Kantian sublime to a quote from the earlier "Resistance to Theory": "What we call ideology is precisely the confusion of linguistic with natural reality, of reference with phenomenalism" (Warminski 14). In Warminski's interpretation, de Man here argues that it is in fact tropes that "accomplish the phenomenalization of reference" (Warminski 14), rendering reference a function of language, and ideology the effect of this phenomenalization.[5] If Kant, in the quote above, develops a "vision that is purely material, devoid of any reflexive or intellectual complication [...] of any semantic depth and reducible to the formal mathematization or geometricization of pure optics" (de Man 83). In other words, the appearance of this peculiar vision introduces a tension between materiality and phenomenology and Paul de Man argues that Kant ends up performing a gesture of disarticulation: what is meant to bridge the previous critiques ends up showing a conflictual heterogeneity (de Man 83). This reading of Kant suggests that the posthuman phenomenology Neimanis develops in the figurations of water would qualify as a gesture of ideological production of maternal materiality.[6] I will look at the way this phenomenalization is carried out rhetorically by Neimanis in the next section. Equally important for me is that the images associated with this material vision, the sky as a vault, the ocean as either a mirror or as a threatening storm, can be considered as marked by figures of death, loss and anxiety.[7] I will return to this question in my final section on the maternal function.

the tropes of maternal materiality

For the gesture of the discursive infusion of the maternal into the material, Neimanis relies on the work of Luce Irigaray on sexual difference, in particular her work on Nietzsche, *Marine Lover of Friedrich Nietzsche*, in which Irigaray exploits the phonetic isomorphism and gendered agreement of the French words for "sea" and "mother," *mer* and *mère*. Neimanis's explicit aim is to braid together this Irigarayan legacy with the thought of Deleuze and Merleau-Ponty. Her text also consistently builds on Irigaray's work on metaphor and metonymy. These terms are strategically used throughout the volume: across its chapters, "metaphor" signals a kind of linguistic limitedness in sharp distinction to a non-metaphorical reality of sorts. Let me provide a series of snippets featuring metaphor: "imaginative 'interventions' [are] never conceptual fantasy or metaphor" (Neimanis 5); "the wateriness of bodies is always more than metaphorical" (7); "rethinking water demands a position that is never 'just' metaphorical" (22); "watery embodiment is neither an abstract concept nor mere metaphor" (49); "the sea is not simply a metaphor for the female mother or the womb" (84). Metonymy, however, seems to be on the side of ontology: we "are the watery world – metonymically, temporarily, partially, and particularly" (27); "PET bottles [...] are the metonyms of Anthropocene water" (177). The basis for this distinction, according to which the essence of metonymy locates its origin in matter rather than language (whereas metaphor is securely lodged in language without the capacity to permeate matter) is provided by a contrasting analogy to continuity or contiguity, and it is only in these terms that Neimanis relies on Irigaray's work on these tropes without explicitly citing it.

Consider the following snippets in which the distinction between metaphor and metonymy provides a guarantee of ontology through the idea of contiguity: "always more than metaphorical, we can trace in Irigaray's work a contiguity or continuity (rather than analogy) with the elemental" (Neimanis 77); "maternal origins are rather *contiguous* with deeper and wider seas" (84). The underlying, tacit suggestion here seems to be that maternal materiality is materially metonymical. In other words, metonymy's figurative, discursive force is in continuity with what Neimanis calls the "onto-logics" of life. In this schema of the metonymical maternal materiality of planetary life, then, metonymy is tasked with securing the ontological status of wateriness based on contiguity.

In her chapter on Irigaray in *Essentially Speaking*, Diana Fuss examined closely Irigaray's engagement with sexual difference, psychoanalysis and analogical figures of speech. Carefully reviewing scholarship engaging with this question, including several works suggesting that it is wrong to try to simply expose a defining essentialism in the texts, Fuss here argues that our reading of Irigaray should not be limited to settling the question whether she essentializes sexual difference. Instead, she wants to examine this oeuvre as an intervention into the intertextual realm of philosophy and psychoanalysis. This includes the reading of Irigaray's combined deployment of sexual difference, femininity, a rhetoric of fluidity, and the relationship between metaphor and metonymy.

Fuss connects Irigaray's preference for liquids over solids as part of her critical engagement with the discourse of the phallus. "According to Irigaray," Fuss tells us citing *This Sex Which is Not One*, "Western culture privileges a mechanics of solids over a mechanics of fluids because man's sexual imaginary is isomorphic: 'production, property [...], order, form, unity, visibility, erection'" (58–59). And femininity will be associated with a language of liquids, represented by the series "continuous, compressible, dilatable, viscous, conductible, diffusable" (Irigaray in Fuss 59). A similar tendency to counter her interpretation of the Lacanian phallus in order to carve out discursive space, in Fuss's reading, where the feminine subject can speak her pleasure (articulated around her well-known figure of the "two lips"), concerns her critique of Lacan's use of metaphor and metonymy. Here Fuss gives a helpful account of the way Lacan adopted Roman Jakobson's conceptualization of metaphor and metonymy as the two rhetorical poles constitutive of language as system of signs: metaphor as substitution by similarity is seen as the selective aspect of signification, while metonymy, substitution by proximity or contiguity, is seen as the sequential order of linguistic meaning-making. Lacan adopts this theory to psychoanalysis in accordance with general theories of language such that metaphor "dominates" over metonymy, and the phallus, for Lacan is a metaphor that gives meaning to sexual difference in general (Fuss 64–65). The important point for my purposes here is that, as Fuss quickly shows, "the relation between the penis and the phallus is as much one of association or metonymy as similarity or metaphor" (65). This deconstruction of the distinction between metaphor and metonymy also holds for Irigaray privileging metonymy. As Fuss puts it:

> Irigaray has this to say about a woman's historical relation to metaphoricity: a woman is "stifled beneath all those eulogistic or denigratory metaphors" (*Speculum*, 142–43); she is "hemmed in, cathected by tropes" (*Speculum*, 143) and "rolled up in metaphors" (*Speculum*, 144). One wonders to what extent it is truly possible to think of the "two lips" as something other than a metaphor. I would argue that, despite Irigaray's protestations to the contrary, the figure of the "two lips" never stops functioning metaphorically. Her insistence that the two lips escape metaphoricity provides us with a particularly clear example of what Paul de Man identifies as the inevitability of "centering a system of tropes at the very moment we claim to escape from it" (1984, 72). But, what is important about Irigaray's conception of this particular figure is that the "two lips" operate as a metaphor for metonymy; through this collapse of boundaries, Irigaray gestures toward the deconstruction of the classic metaphor/metonymy binarism. In fact, her work persistently attempts to effect a historical displacement of metaphor's dominance over metonymy; she "impugns the privilege granted to metaphor (a quasi solid) over metonymy (which is much more closely allied to fluids)" (*This Sex*, 110). (66)

In other words, Irigaray's deployment of the metaphor of metonymy is part of a feminist project of superimposing the distinctions between liquid and solid, metonymy and metaphor on the distinction between femininity and masculinity in order to not simply "impugn the privilege granted to metaphor," but also to grant the privilege she jerked out of phallocentrism to the metonymy of liquid femininity. However, as Fuss shows, the deconstruction of the distinction between metaphor and metonymy frustrates Irigaray's aim to fasten metonymy to femininity as much as Lacan's aim to fasten metaphor to masculinity. Importantly for the implications for Neimanis's use of these tropes, Fuss shows that at the moment when Irigaray thinks she escapes metaphoricity, she in fact introduces in the sexuated and embodied image a metaphor for metonymy. Embodied materiality does not escape metaphoricity but is brought into relief thanks to it.

In *Bodies of Water*, the tension between metaphor and metonymy is linked to the idea of materiality in a double gesture. Metonymy is freely and organically flowing from matter through discourse, while metaphor is confined to language. This confinement guarantees a clear boundary between matter and discourse, which in turn allows for valuing the former as originary and present in its maternality. Conceding Fuss's point that Irigaray's two lips is a metaphor of metonymy, we may consider Neimanis's discursive figure of planetary gestationality as a variation of the Irigarayan legacy of associating metonymy and femininity: a metaphorical representation of maternal materiality. The explicitly avowed imagery of maternal materiality as profoundly nourishing rests in part on tying this gendered discourse of metaphor and metonymy to the idea of access to materiality. As a result, the feminine metonymical has access to materiality whereas metaphor whose agency is too limited to access materiality is confined to mere language thereby appearing as secondary and deprived of its phallocratic privileges.[8] In the metaphor of maternal materiality (where materiality includes language and discourse), metaphor's confinement to language appears like a figure of containment not unlike an amniotic sac. In my final section, I will show that the undecidability between this imagery of containment – facilitative amnion or etiolation through confinement – will correspond to a similar undecidability between birth and death in the imagery of the maternal function.

mère métaphore: planetary gestationality and the maternal function

In *The Mother in the Age of Mechanical Reproduction*, Elissa Marder argues that the figure of the mother is always marked by a constitutive, traumatic anxiety of having been born without "being present" at one's birth (at least as a subject) and this profound loss of missing one's birth figures in the imagery of mourning (including the distinctions of mourning and melancholia or introjection vs. incorporation). Instead of considering it as a paralyzing force arresting life, this anxiety is consistently interpreted as a source that propels us to the future: it is a force of life by being a force in part always marked by death. Clearly then, for Marder the maternal is associated more with separation than with connection or containment. Marder distills three specific figures in which this anxiety of the maternal appears and I suggest that these figures all inform the figural construction of planetary gestationality.

One of these is the "womb-tomb." Psychoanalytic theory posits failed mourning as the psychic incorporation of the lost other into an internal object that refuses to be given up. Marder's main source here is Abraham and Torok's contribution on the crypt (including Derrida's reading of it). The crypt is a figure of a contained preservation of the lost object. The figure of the womb-tomb connects Neimanis's amniotic maternality to the haunting imagery of the crypt in metaphor's containment in language. In light of Fuss's deconstruction of Irigaray, we may recall that the amnion is also a metaphor, the metaphor of maternal metonymy. In the end we have a series of figures that, far from separating maternality from metaphor, in fact ensure that this distinction is set up through an interplay of maternality and metaphor in both the image of the amnion and the gesture of enclosing metaphor. In one instance we have the amnion and life, in the other we have the enshrined "mummy." We could think of this figure as *Mère Métaphore*: if the wateriness coursing through planetary gestationality produces a composite image of material amnionics enshrining "mere" metaphor, it is because it itself is a metaphor of a maternality that is no more sustaining than threatening.

Another figure of the maternal function is the "photographic" memory of the primal scene. Based on a close reading of Freud's texts on birth and anxiety, in her account of the trauma of the primal scene Marder emphasizes that the unconscious memory of witnessing copulating parents is recorded at such an early time that the mental apparatus capturing the event lacks any frame of interpretive reference. It is like a snapshot, "the *mechanical reproduction* of an impossible image" (Marder 170; original emphasis). According to Marder, the primal scene is templated on the maternal function, that is, the anxiety of birth. This shifts Freud's emphasis on Oedipal threats of castration to the maternal function, a gesture that seems somewhat similar but is also affectively significantly different from Irigaray's "impugnation." This image of the presubjective snapshot precipitated by the maternal function corresponds to what de Man identifies as Kant's disarticulation of phenomenal materiality and material vision. What Kant designated as teleological ways of conceiving of these appearances of nature (the various kinds of phenomenalization of materiality) tend to suggest a sense of admiration or gratitude because of a certain facilitative appraisal of the sky and the ocean: as spaces and means of life. The way poets see the sky and the ocean, on the other hand, creates a view of these natural phenomena as if it could strip them of the conventional conceptual ways of making sense of them, thus letting go of this rhetoric of facilitative maternality. What remains in Kant's text is a series of figures: the starry sky as an "all-embracing vault," the placid ocean as a perfectly still surface with no depth, mirroring air and finally the stormy ocean as murderous. All three images have a strong chilling effect. If Marder's snapshot resonates with the Kantian sublime, it is not only because of the conceptual resonance between the crucial significance of the lack of interpretative mediation for Kant's sublime and for the maternal function organizing the primal scene in Marder via Freud, it is also because conceiving nature as maternal seems to entail figures of loss, anxiety and death.

I would like to end on a note about the sense of obligatory gratitude I heard in the quote on onto-logy in my introduction. As I mentioned, instilling a sense of gratitude for Neimanis motivates a renewed posthuman responsibility towards our fellows in the hydrocommons (Neimanis 16–17). In closing, let me recall what Marder calls the maternal prosthetic, the third figure of the maternal function in discussing the question of collectivity and demands of responsibility. Just like in our readings of the Kantian sublime and of Irigaray, we will find Irigaray's imagery of the ever-connected facilitation of life complemented by the figure of maternality as distantly and hauntingly menacing. Here Marder relies on Avital Ronell's *Telephone Book* to argue that our conventional imagery of Western technology is a manifestation of the maternal function by manifesting the wish to be connected to the ghost haunting from presubjective life. Taking her cue from Ronell's remark that "[t]here is always a remnant of the persecuting, accusatory mother in the telephone system" (Ronell 144), Marder writes:

> And, because there can be no telephone without another telephone, the telephonic matrix binds all its units together through a techno-maternal network in which each individual number loses its singularity by becoming answerable to a symbolic collectivity. This collectivity, furthermore, reproduces itself by transmitting voices that dictate orders into the ear. The first such order of the telephone is the demand to answer its call. The call from the other that comes to us through the telephone retains something of the voice of the (undead) mother who returns, with a vengeance, to issue imperatives and regulate compliance. (118)

This image of technicity may appear as the exact opposite of Neimanis's Irigarayan vitalist-organicist marine mother. Since so far maternal figures have tended to duplicate themselves according to organicity, facilitation and life on the one hand, technicity, death and anxiety on the other, the quote above sounds almost as if the horrifying image of the compulsion to pick up the phone to listen to the persecuting voice of the "mummified mummy" (Marder 119) were a negative flipside of an image of *Bodies of Water* in which feminist posthuman phenomenology picks up a conch to listen to the oceanic chorus of feminist theory on live embodiment. Reading Neimanis with the help of Kant, de Man, Fuss and Marder suggests that figuring the maternal as exclusively nurturing and life-affirming cannot fail to be haunted by figures of some foundational anxiety over life and death. Marder's work is rooted in figures of loss and mourning while at the same time conceiving of anxiety as what propels us into futurity. In combination with de Man's difficult work on language, reference and materiality, it may open us to the task of coming to terms with the idea of life and materiality as always marked by separation, anxiety and death. This would perhaps enable us to respond differently to our feminist desire for ontology and to render our responsibility concerning the current manmade waning of Holocenic bliss less bound by the looming figure of an ever-present ancestral material maternality.

disclosure statement

No potential conflict of interest was reported by the author.

notes

1 The abyssal aspect of this maternality is emphasized as what renders it radically unknowable by a generalized masculinist gaze. Masculinity, in turn, is rendered into images of solids, as if antithetical to water figured as essentially fluid. For instance, bitumen is considered masculine (Neimanis 27). At the same time, nonliquid states of water are not really considered and when they appear, they are associated with masculinity. Consider semen: "semen is not female mucus [...] masculine waters tend to freeze, harden, and evaporate" (89).

2 The volume presents an intervention in several domains of feminist theory: phenomenology, posthumanism and new materialism. As for the first two, the focus on the wateriness of lived embodiment, "an ontological and ethical imperative" (Neimanis 42), provides an opportunity to forge

a posthuman, "different kind of phenomenology – one that can divest itself from some of its implied and explicit humanist commitment" (31). This posthuman phenomenology then aids feminist new materialism in having its language of agency "tempered" by "attunement, listening, and observation" (42).

3 Since much of the theoretical gist is provided by the Deleuzean reading of Irigaray, the project will resonate especially well with parts of new materialism that also share this Deleuzean orientation (considered as vitalist by Gamble et al.). It is because of this resonance that I consider my deconstruction-motivated argument to be joining the work also discussing the ontological projects in new materialism which rely on deconstruction (see Basile, and especially Mercier for his discussion on the relationship between the material turn and the linguistic turn).

4 On imaging Earth from space, see the first chapter of Kelly Oliver's *Earth and World*.

5 Importantly, Warminski offers his interpretation while warning against a typical misreading of the quote that would still posit a knowable and clear separation between natural reality and language based on an assumed knowledge of what language indeed is (9–10).

6 After all, any organicist reading of Kant, according to de Man, pledges allegiance to a "Schillerization" of Kant (de Man 131), a legacy of interpretation that considers phenomenality as reference and thereby adding force of ontologizing interpretations (of nature).

7 Relatedly, for an interpretation of Paul de Man's oeuvre on rhetoric as a work of mourning, see Siebers.

8 Something strange happens to synecdoche such that it finds itself more closely related to metaphor than metonymy when Neimanis says that the "passage from body of water to body of water (always *as* body of water) is never synecdochal or metaphoric; it is radically material" (86). I call this strange not because the conceptualization of synecdoche is erroneous since it has traditionally been always classified as a kind of metonymy. This idea would affirm a sense that we should always be able to apply a rhetorical taxonomy based on the idea of the "proper" meaning of terms such as metaphor or synecdoche. It is crucial for my purposes in this article to recall that deconstruction, in discussions on metaphoricity, has cast a critical light on such a policing of proper meanings (see Derrida and Moore as well as Gasché 307–18). However, synecdoche's ambivalent placement is significant for understanding the construction of materiality as maternal in Neimanis's work. For in a passage on political and ethical action drawing on Haraway, Neimanis asserts the following: "These actions [...] are never in themselves a perfect metonym of an imaginary (i.e. a part that faithfully and felicitously condenses the whole) because this would imply that the imaginary comes first, before the work required to enact it" (176). Here, unlike above, "perfect metonymy" is understood in terms of synecdoche (since conventionally, synecdoche is understood as a figure showing either part for the whole or whole for the part). These quotes show that while the text wants to rely on the properly differentiated meanings of these figures in order to posit a clear distinction between matter and language, these tropes can't be securely bounded off; they flow and seep through one another.

bibliography

Basile, Jonathan. "The New Novelty: Corralation as Quarantine in Speculative Realism and New Materialism." *Derrida Today*, vol. 11, no. 2, 2018, pp. 211–29.

De Man, Paul. *Aesthetic Ideology*. U of Minnesota P, 1996.

Derrida, Jacques, and F.C.T. Moore. "White Mythology: Metaphor in the Text of Philosophy." *New Literary History*, vol. 6, no. 1, 1974, pp. 5–74.

Fuss, Diana. *Essentially Speaking: Feminism, Nature & Difference*. Routledge, 1989.

Gamble, Christopher N., et al. "What Is New Materialism?" *Angelaki*, vol. 24, no. 6, 2019, pp. 111–34.

Gasché, Rodolphe. *The Tain of the Mirror: Derrida and the Philosophy of Reflection*. Harvard UP, 1986.

Kant, Immanuel. *Critique of the Power of Judgment*. Translated by Paul Guyer and Eric Matthews, Cambridge UP, 2000.

Marder, Elissa. *The Mother in the Age of Mechanical Reproduction: Psychoanalysis, Photography, Deconstruction.* Fordham UP, 2013.

Mercier, Thomas Clement. "Old and New Matters." *Síntesis. Revista de Filosofía*, vol. 4, no. 2, 2021, pp. 1–18.

Moreiras, Alberto. "On Scatter, the Trace Structure, and the Opening of Politics: An Interview with Geoffrey Bennington." *Diacritics*, vol. 45, no. 2, 2017, pp. 34–51.

Neimanis, Astrida. *Bodies of Water: Posthuman Feminist Phenomenology.* Bloomsbury, 2017.

Oliver, Kelly. *Earth and World: Philosophy After the Apollo Missions.* Columbia UP, 2015.

Ronell, Avital. *The Telephone Book: Technology, Schizophrenia, Electric Speech.* U of Nebraska P, 1989.

Siebers, Tobin. "Mourning Becomes Paul de Man." *Cold War Criticism and the Politics of Skepticism.* Oxford UP, 1993, pp. 89–110.

Warminski, Andrzej. "Allegories of Reference: An Introduction to Aesthetic Ideology." *Ideology, Rhetoric, Aesthetics: For de Man.* Edinburgh UP, 2013, pp. 3–37.

Eszter Timár

You: Is this inside or out? I mean, is this thing part of my skin? It's like a dome, bloating outwards, liquid inwards, its roots clutching into my pores. If I move my hand, it moves with it. I can probably shake it off completely, throw it away, never to find its way back. I think. But I also have the feeling that if I stay put, this thing will get absorbed into my body. A spill sucked in a kitchen towel. My body will swallow it. Or it will swallow me. Is this thing in or out?

Me: We had a pact, remember? No, you don't, I can tell. Are you getting bored? We had a pact. Never to be away from each other. We really meant it then. Not just different countries or cities. Rooms. Beds. Corners. Minutes. Never to be away from each other meant sharing a waking time, a sleeping time, our mad insomniac time. Sharing even the moment of involuntary blinking. Initially you were faster than me. My eyes would flutter shut at the same time as yours, but yours would always open up earlier, my need for retinal liquidity more deeply entrenched, turn inside for longer, an eye shut to the world and open to a fear or a desire within perhaps. Anyway, I learned to catch up and eventually I would let my desire flow outwards, opening my eyes even earlier than you, no hesitation no introspection, however involuntary. Just togetherness. So we might have been looking outside, say away from each other, a Netflix show or a passing group of people; but our movements were determined by that space inside. Not my or your space, not our body features of cute individual personality, not our skins that form me and you, ha! nothing like that, we are well beyond that, you and I. No, it was the space between us that had become

The Other Water

Andreas Philippopoulos-Mihalopoulos

our true inside space, a manic collectivity (one is a crowd, two is the world), manic not obsessive, manic not desperate, whatever you might be thinking now, we never were any of that. We were always in the process of becoming what we thought we could become, with ups and downs of course, lots of them; sometimes it worked better than others, you would get upset when I would not, or I would feel morose when you would, moods and mania, not neatly distributed pros and cons of course; but on the whole, the inside space worked well enough, like a little bouncy bubble squeezed between us, tight just before bursting, your breathing in by necessity paired with my breathing out, no room for two chests expanding at the same time, that bubble should not burst, that water was precious. Still is.

You: I try. I really do.

Let me pretend that your actions affect me. Let me pretend I can feel what you are doing. Let me pretend I can speak. Let me pretend that you annoy me. Let me pretend you can understand me. And let me vent. Because I am annoyed. It's as if you do it on purpose. Especially that obsession of yours to enclose me, channel me, control me, put me in narrow waterways or large deposits, trap me in reservoirs, frame me behind long dams or in tiny tubes. No, you don't understand – you don't hurt me, you cannot hurt me when you do these things. It is your attitude that irritates me, that bossy pitiable macho egomania with which you think you can control me, and your faux-rational tendency to measure me, weight, speed, density, frequency. It is such a bore when you try to impose your sense of rhythm on me: ebb and flow, streams and currents, waves and tsunamis. You study my comings and goings and jot them down in order to catch them next time, or to not be caught unawares by me. You use me to relax or stimulate yourselves, you count waves to sleep, you count oceans as if they were human syncopated breaths.

You: I want to scratch but I am not sure I should. It looks solid but I think there is a membrane keeping it together. Skin-like, my skin-like, but not quite my skin. Very clever, all this transparency. Nothing to distinguish membrane from inside, or whatever that thing is that looks like being on the inside. It's not itchy really. Just inviting. It's grown again since last night, I am sure. But it tends to grow smaller during the day or at least some days. I need to understand this better. I think it has to do with the moon. I think I want to touch it. I have kept my distance so far, as much as I could anyway, but now I want to touch it. Should I? Look, the right part of my body is turning, I am folding inside, I am about to, the bubble is perfectly positioned on the middle finger of my left hand, pulsating, unleaking moist containment, I want to be

touched it says. Made to be touched even – can I say that? Look, I am touching it.

Me: May I touch too?

You: In a minute.

Human rhythms are so shallow I can barely hear them. They ride a different temporality than I do, a temporality of day and night, forgettably short seasons, unregistrable geological epochs. You even talk about my history and my composition in ways that make sense to you, and yeah fine, carry on, see if I care. You want me to obey the rhythm that you impose on me – see how you can never see beyond your little selves? – a breath of rising and falling, a living regularity because life is regular and water is life, right? Ok. But you really ought to know, – well you do not need to, I do not even think you can know, but it is good sometimes to show you that you cannot know – anyway, you really should try to understand that my breath is not of your life, or of any life. My breath is time. My breath is of a universe that hosts me in globular suspension between planets, in vast clouds of a rain that will never fall, in fathomless oceans suspended in space and floating about unsupported: my breath is there, rounded up in a water that you will never drink. My breath is polarised, spread across aeons, breathing in when nothing was impossible and breathing out when the possibilities will have shut forever.

But ok, you cannot conceive this. Let's focus on your planet, that hydrospheric apparition on stilts in the great hall of cosmic gossip. Even then, you think of me as percentages, oh wow so much of the surface of the earth, no really, so much of a human body, eye-rolling stuff. But just shut up and listen for a moment and you might just about understand that my breath is deeper and more cavernous than your deepest history. My breath is caught in the rattle of a dying sun, hidden under strata of a geology that ignores you, deep in the centre of what you call your planet and with whose body you will never manage to sleep. My breath is liquidity in waiting, tangled with chunks of eternity.

You: Don't. We still are in the same space.

Me: When did things change? It was that evening. As usual, you forgot to lock the front door. Always the same story. I could never tell whether you were actually forgetting or you were trying to make a point about safety or openness or something. Big sore point between us this.

My reasons for wanting to lock were quite specific: not so much to keep the world out but to keep our water in, to stop it from running out and mixing with the water outside. We had become rather possessive of our water – our very own water. We still entertained the idea, however tenuous, that our water was special, more limpid, a brighter emerald than any other water. We had the illusion that our water knew us, that it was part of us. We liked to think that our whole love affair was lovingly mediated by this gentle, domesticated water of ours.

You stuff so much in me that sometimes an itch gathers in my armpit and then planets get swallowed up. No, not really. I mean, I do scratch and planets do get swallowed up but not because of what you stuff into me. It would be interesting if causality worked like that: someone thinks of placing a monster, a terrifying kraken shaking the seas, or a sluicing sea serpent coiling up storms, and boom, storms are cooked, seas are bloated and planets are doomed. If only! Even your crazy plastic excreta poured out of your civilised stomata that reek of self-importance are not enough to pull my causal strings. These desperate games of yours, beasts of control and apparitions of governance, are less than stick toys for me. What if your Poseidon shakes his trident and your Hydra screams with all her heads? What if your Ran sucks in everyone found adrift on my navel, your Tipua roars from the depths of my stomach, your Tiamat copulates with stinky Abzu to create a cluster of rheostating gods controlling your very own bodies? Looming Leviathans nestling in me, but in reality, gorily imagined by you and against you, palisades of torture – and what really irritates me is that you are using me as your excuse for the stupidity of your species. Well, you can keep your Ras and Aquariuses, your Scyllas and even your Aphrodites, 'cause I am gobbing them out now, one by one, splatting them on your faces, tears for the end of creation.

Yet, some evenings, when we were indulging sweet nothings, like sofa time with a good bottle of wine, I'm sure that we were both sharing the same lurking doubt that perhaps our water wasn't that special after all. We never talked about this. In fact, I cannot know that it is not just me, but I really could swear that, at those moments, when our feet were idly plodding on the surface, toes flirting with each other's or with the legs of the sofa and the moss-like carpet saturated by our familiar, domesticated water, your eyes would open up to a different world, a world outside where saints and demons might have mixed differently and your presence would have been like a red round hot collateral ready to shriek away in pleasure.

But I never asked you and now it's too late.

What would the point be anyway? I often imagined, no I actually knew, not that I'd seen it but it was as good as that, I certainly heard it happening, anyway it haunted my dreams sometimes, when stress from work and the constant screaming of life became unbearable and my skin crawled away from all other skins, human and planetary: those nights I heard, in my dreams but with this piercingly real sound, as if the alarm clock got morphed into the crackling sound of my dream at the time, I heard the slurping sound of emptying water, waves rushing out from underneath our door, locked or unlocked it didn't matter after all, a domestic kenosis, a horizontal waterfall moving from within our flat and out towards the world, ships draining their waterload, useless as it is and imported from other seas, now ready to be filled with noxious oil, slow and heavy as my dreams, mixing with other waters from other cities; and then, large swathes of water, ours or others' or no-one's, waves sliding on top of other waves but in the opposite direction, this time entering our home and slowly filling what the previous water had left behind, the muddy floors and the wet newspapers we left floating on the floor the previous night, even the bottom shelves of the bookcases with their books bloated and sticky.

You: But we are still in the same space, aren't we.

You know I don't speak, don't you?

You know you are just hearing your own voice, booming vicariously through what you think is me. You are borrowing again from my munificence. It's fun to know that you can never win. It's fun to know that there is only one way, and that it is my way.

Can you feel the strings puppeteering you through the paragraphs? And to think I do not even have arms.

You: I don't feel like speaking.

Me: Listen to me.

You: I can't hear a thing.

Me: You must dive in. Then you will.

You: I don't think so. I can try but.

Me: May I touch it now?

You: OK. Gently though.

Me: I don't think I can feel anything – am I touching it?

You: Raise your arms a bit more, yeah like this. Maybe stand on your toes? Wait, don't, not so much, you might break it.

Me: I still cannot feel anything – it's like touching nothing, air, not even a breeze. Have I reached the membrane?

You: I am not sure. I think you have. It should be just above you. What can you see?

You judge me by what you see. Always bound by your presence, yet miraculously always missing out on the present – how on earth do you manage that! Anyway, you just judge me by what you see: big waves, oh angry, threatening, vengeful, whatever. Lapping wavelets, ah so welcoming, peaceful, meditative. But if you were to propel yourselves a little out of your orbit to see time for what time is, if you were able even for a flash to rush through aeons and stellar deaths as I do, you might see me carving the Grand Canyon in an instance of capillary boredom, or falling on your planet's desire for centuries, continuously, relentlessly, a cataclysm to drown all cataclysms, that made you just a

few minutes later wake up and smell the coffee. Your "findings" are so stuffy, you make me weep! You put them in little books and claim the moral importance of its truth: you have been a bad boy, have some flooding to sort you out.

You: You always talk about the future. I can't.

Me: I am sorry. It's because I am afraid.

You: I cannot promise much.

Me: When did things change? It was that afternoon. You were swimming in that lake we discovered after we walked up the mountain for hours. It wasn't even on Google maps. It was supposed to be a dried-up basin. Yet that afternoon it was so filled with grey metal water that it seemed an extension of the sky. I was on the shore, looking out for you, still deep in our pact but trying to adjust to new things, other futures, distant presents. Your swimming was slicing the water in two, your body was drawing the distinction between water and clouds. You were my horizon.

You: Nothing has changed.

Me: May I try again? I think it heard us. I can try and touch it again.

You: Try. Why do you think it heard us?

Me: Because we are it.

I am not simply passing, you say. I have a purpose, you say. Look at the beauty generated in these little stories we make up, you say. Look at the art and the literature. Look at the little everyday and the pleasure of seeing a child play in a garden. Look at our loving, our growing old together, our orgasms and our longing.

Not that I want to disappoint unduly but the deadline for all this is coming sooner than you think. In a few cosmic battings of eyelids, I will be gone from earth, evaporated in trellises of interplanetary frivolity, off to play somewhere else with things neither better nor worse than you.

Me: When did things change? It was that morning. You wrote a word in the air, I could not read it but I liked the way your fingers moved. You looked at me meaningfully but I could not reciprocate. I was on the other side of your word. A mirror reader. I had to start reading from the end. I think it ended in a flourish, a long line trailing the lower part of an E or perhaps an L. That's all I could get, no matter how many times you repeated the gesture looking at me expectantly. I could only see the end.

Then a screen between us, like a shower cubicle, your breath misting it over, your finger tracing the word across the tiny globules that your body was emitting. Finally you said. It is final, I said.

You: But you managed to read it, didn't you?

Me: No, that was not the point.

You: Our distance became water.

Me: No, we failed. We needed a screen between us to understand each other. So sad.

You: But we needed to control it. How else? We needed to attract its attention, project it on the screen, make it visible. How else? That was the only way we had.

Me: I always hoped we could do it without dams.

I have conjured you up, or rather lend you an end of my amoeba-like existence for a while. But not for free. The price is fair: you are giving me a helping hand to carry on with my games. Perhaps you have not realised, and you probably cannot realise that either, but I'll say it once more: at some point, we will merge again. And you will become me – not the other way around.

You: Are we in or out?

disclosure statement

No potential conflict of interest was reported by the author.

Andreas Philippopoulos-Mihalopoulos

Index

Agamben, Giorgio 115
Ahmed, Sara 34
Alaimo, Stacy 3
aletheia 91, 92
Amin, Kadji 36
Amsterdam canals 51
Anand, Nikhil 2
Anidjar, Gil 2, 4
anthropocentric settler sovereignty 29–31
aqua nullius 102
aquapolitical regimes 21, 28
Armored cannon water trucks 120
Aryan humanity 116
Atlantic modernity 9
autogestión 81
autopoiesis 20

Bachelard, Gaston 2, 4
Bakker, Karen 4
Barad, Karen 15
Beemster Land Reclamation Project 57
biopower 8, 11
Bloom, Allan 116
Boast, Hannah 2
body enfleshed 22
Border Patrol 29
Bowker, Geoffrey C. 14
Brody, Jennifer DeVere 36

Cajete, Gregory 21, 22
Carson, Rachel 12
Casarino, Cesare 9
Chakrabarty, Dipesh 4, 92–4
chemical process 13
Chen, Cecilia 1, 2
chlorinated water 36
Chow, Jeremy 3
Clark, Nigel 11, 12
The Clipper Queerz party 42, 43
Cochabamba water war 4, 71–81; ownership and social property 75–8; social–historical context 73–5; social property and the politics of presence 78–81
colonial hierarchies 9

conquest of maritime imagination 53–6
correcto ejercicio de la democracia 80
cosmology 21
critics 2
Cybulska, Eva 112
cycles of conquest 23

Dart 122
deep time theory of knowledge 4
DeGeneres, Ellen 35
Deleuze, Gilles 2
De rebus Indicis 54
Derrida, Jacques 4, 98, 109, 113, 118
De Wolff, Kim 2
Dutch people 58

Earth system science (ESS) 93, 94
ecosexuality 39
electromagnetic induction 86–9
epistemological break 86
Erickson, Bruce 35
Estes, Nick 20, 28

Fanon, Frantz 13
feminist review 2
field theory 87
Finding Nemo (film) 35
flesh 13, 21
Foucault, Michel 11

Garduski, Anne 13
geologic corporeality 8
geopower 8, 11, 12, 15
Ge-stell 92, 94
Gilio-Whitaker, Dina 26
Gilroy, Paul 9, 10
Glissant, Édouard 26
global water crisis 102
the globe capturable 4
Gómez-Barris, Macarena 42, 43
Grosz, Elizabeth 8, 11, 12
Grotius, Hugo 54–63
Guattari, Felix 2
Gunkel, Henriette 13

INDEX

Halberstam, Jack 35
Hameed, Ayesha 14
Hamlin, Christopher 109
Haraway, Donna 14, 120
Hawkins, Gay 2
Heidegger, Martin 4, 89–92
Helmreich, Stefan 2
H₂O and the Waters of Forgetfulness (Illich) 2
hydrocommons of wet relations 3
hydroelectricity: electromagnetic induction 86–9; river poiesis, erosion, and fluctuation 89–92
Hydrohumanities: Water Discourse and Environmental Futures offers the term hydrohumanities (De Wolff) 2
hydrological turn 1
hydropoetics 34; queerness 34
hydropower: from bios to geos 11–13; borderscapes 9–11; concept 11; hydroelectric power production 9; limitations of embodiment 9; obliteration 8; resistant residuality 13–15

Illich, Ivan 2
imagination 87–8
imperial ecocide 53
improvement 115
infrahumanity 9
intercorporeity: animated water 23–5; flesh of the world 21–2; Sonoran Desert 23
International Border and Water Commission (IBWC) 30
intimacy 53
intracorporeality: indigenous contestations 26–8; settler colonial aquapolitics on border 28–9; transitive movement 25

Jordahl, Laiken 27
Juliet Milagros Palante 37, 42
Juliet Takes a Breath (novel) 37, 45

Kasserman, Bonnie 28
Klaver, Irene J. 3

LaDuke, Winona 22
Lagrangian fluid dynamics 9
Land-taking projects 52, 56–8
learning with water 97–106; bottles 98; clean energy 100; ergonomic quality 101; ultra-pure 99
lines of force 87
Linton, Jamie 2, 4
Lorde, Audre. 44
Lovelock, James 24

magnetic field 87
Mare Liberum 54, 55, 60
Margulis, Lynn 24
mass-scale water development 85
materiality 111

maternal materiality 126–34; the kantian sublime and 129–30; planetary gestationality 132–4; the tropes of 130–2
Mauch, Felix 120
Mawani, Renisa 53–5, 59–61
Maynard, Robyn 55
Mediterranean functions 7
Mentz, Steve 2
Merleau-Ponty, Maurice 20–2, 24, 25, 29
metal sheets 51
migrant crisis 7
migratory necropolitics 12
Mississippi River 30
modernization 4
morality 115
Morrison, Toni 30
Murphy, Kieran 4

native greenery 52
natural electricity 4
necropolitics 12
Neimanis, Astrida 2, 3, 5, 12, 13, 120, 126
Netherlands 52–3
Nietzsche, Friedrich 111–12, 115
Noys, Benjamin 5

oceanic space 9
onto-logic of amniotics 126
Oswald, Alice 122
ownership 75–8

Pantuchowicz, Agnieszka 5
Peters, Kimberley 9
Philippopoulos-Mihalopoulos, Andreas 3
philosophical discourses 2
physical matter 13
planetary gestationality 127, 132–4
planetary history 92–4
Plumwood, Val 27
poiesis 92, 94
pools 34; alliterative allure 35; articulates 35; multifaceted materiality of 36; parties and politics 42–6; smell of 36
Povinelli, Elizabeth A 10, 15
"pre-/transindividual" framework 12
Protevi, John 2
Pugliese, Joseph 3

queer hydropoetics 34
queer pooling 46–7
Quitobaquito Springs 26

Ranciére, Jacques 99
REAL ID Act (2005) 26
reclaimed land 51
reclamation 52
res nullius 59–63
Rivera, Gabby 42
Rosello, Mireille 53, 56, 64

sacrifice zone 8, 15
Sagan, Dorian 20
Sakowin, Oceti 21
Salzman, James 101
Sandilands-Mortimer, Catriona 35
San Pedro River 29–30
Satgar, Vishwas 53
Saved! (film) 36, 37; diving in, coming out 37–9
Serres, Michel 2
Sharpe, Christina 13, 14
Shipwreck Modernity 10
Simondon, Gilbert 12
Sinclair, Rebekah 113
Social Power and the Urbanization of Water (Swyngedouw) 2
social property 75–81
Spicer, Edward 23
Sprinkle, Annie 39–41
Star, Susan Leigh 14
Steinberg, Philip 9
Stelder, Mikki 4
Stephens, Beth 39–40
sublime 129, 130
Sundberg, Juanita 28, 29
Sutton, Elizabeth 57
swimmer poetics 35
Swyngedouw, Erik 2, 4
symbolic potency 1
Szymborska,Wislawa 1, 2

Talbayev, Edwige Tamalet 3
Timár, Eszter 5
tinajas-catch basins 25, 30
Todd, Zoe 21
Tohono O'odham people 20, 21, 25
Tomba, Massimiliano 4

untreated wastewater 116
Urcaregui, Maite 3

van Ittersum, Martine Julia 58
Vernadsky, Vladimir I. 22, 24

Warminski, Andrzej 130
Water Makes Us Wet: An Ecosexual Adventure (document) 36, 39–41
water management 116–18
Western phenomenological tradition 21
What is Water? The History of a Modern Abstraction (Linton) 2
white innocence 57
Wolff, W. J. 52

Yates, Julian 2
Yazzie, Robert 22
Yusoff, Kathryn 10, 12, 15

Zarathustra 112
zoe-geo-centrism 120